Also by Samuel G. Freedman

Letters to a Young Journalist

Who She Was: My Search for My Mother's Life

Jew vs. Jew: The Struggle for the Soul of American Jewry

The Inheritance: How Three Families and America Moved from Roosevelt to Reagan and Beyond

Upon This Rock: The Miracles of a Black Church

Small Victories: The Real World of a Teacher, Her Students, and Their High School

BREAKING

10▶

*The Season in Black College Football
That Transformed the Sport and
Changed the Course of Civil Rights*

THE LINE

SAMUEL G. FREEDMAN

Simon & Schuster

New York London Toronto Sydney New Delhi

Simon & Schuster
1230 Avenue of the Americas
New York, NY 10020

First Simon & Schuster hardcover edition August 2013

SIMON & SCHUSTER and colophon are registered trademarks of Simon & Schuster, Inc.

For information about special discounts for bulk purchases, please contact Simon & Schuster Special Sales at 1-866-506-1949 or business@simonandschuster.com.

The Simon & Schuster Speakers Bureau can bring authors to your live event. For more information or to book an event contact the Simon & Schuster Speakers Bureau at 1-866-248-3049 or visit our website at www.simonspeakers.com.

Designed by Aline C. Pace

Manufactured in the United States of America

10   9   8   7   6   5   4   3   2   1

Library of Congress Cataloging-in-Publication Data

Freedman, Samuel G.
Breaking the line : the season in black college football that transformed the sport and changed the course of civil rights / Samuel G. Freedman.
p. cm
1. Football—United States—History. 2. College sports—United States—History. 3. African-American football players—Biography. 4. Discrimination in sports—United States—History. I. Title.
GV950.F74 2013
796.332—dc23   2012042465

ISBN 978-1-4391-8977-1
ISBN 978-1-4391-8979-5 (ebook)

Dedicated to
Christia Chana Blomquist
Ahava Gdola
אהבה גדולה
From Forever to Forever

*

In Memory of
David Freedman
1921–2010
Who Taught Me about Football and Civil Rights

Freedom is heavy. You got to put your shoulder to freedom. Put your shoulder to it and hope your back hold up. And if you around here looking for justice, you got a long wait.

—August Wilson, *Two Trains Running*

Contents ▶

BREAKING THE LINE

BEHIND GOD'S BACK

In the tumultuous moments after the 2007 Super Bowl ended, the two contending coaches met at midfield. Standing only inches apart, the bills of their hats nearly touching, they exchanged words of congratulation and respect. Then they embraced. Tony Dungy of the Indianapolis Colts and Lovie Smith of the Chicago Bears had been colleagues for five earlier years on the staff of the Tampa Bay Buccaneers. They were friends who spoke by phone almost weekly. They shared a fervent Christian faith. And what ultimately bound them together on this rainy February night was the force of history itself.

Dungy and Smith were the first African-American coaches ever to lead a team into the Super Bowl, the most watched game in the nation's most popular sport, virtually a civic holiday for tens of millions of Americans. While there were necessarily a winner and a loser in the game—Dungy's Colts had beaten Smith's Bears 29–17—the adversaries were allies in the urgent and ongoing endeavor of bringing racial equality to sports and through sports to American society.

The road to their landmark achievement, however, was one little known in white America and shrouded by the passage of time even to many blacks. It started in 1837, when a group of Quakers founded a school in Philadelphia called the Institute of Colored Youth, which was subsequently expanded into a college and renamed Cheyney University. Over the succeeding decades, more than one hundred other colleges and universities for black students arose in the United States, with the vast majority of those institutions springing up in the South after the Civil War. Some of them were founded by white philanthropists or liberal religious denominations with an idealistic commitment to educating and elevating a formerly enslaved people. Many others, however, were created by governors and legislatures in the South as a means of preserving the iron rule of segregation and inequality in public schools.

Despite that cynical design, these black colleges subverted the Jim Crow regime. They served as the agency of black achievement and the epicenter of black pride, a kind of secular equivalent to the African-American church. Decades before a hip-hop entrepreneur titled a clothing line FUBU—meaning "For Us, By Us"—those words could have been the slogan for black colleges. On their campuses, black PhDs taught black students, black presidents and black provosts and black deans held sway. For more than a century, these colleges turned out the vast majority of America's black doctors, lawyers, pharmacists, ministers, teachers, musicians, librarians, and accountants; to this day, the black colleges and universities that form 3 percent of America's total number enroll 16 percent of African Americans in higher education. Black campuses gave birth to the marching bands, step shows, and fraternities and sororities that were and still are cherished expressions of African-American culture.

The civil rights movement depended on the racial pride, leadership skills, and academic prowess developed by black colleges and universities. As one of their most illustrious alumni, W.E.B. Du Bois, wrote in the NAACP's magazine, *The Crisis:* "It is the race-conscious black man cooperating together with his own institutions and movements who will eventually emancipate the colored race." Black colleges produced such civil rights leaders as Thurgood Marshall, Martin Luther King Jr., John Lewis, Andrew Young, Diane Nash, Ella Baker, and Jesse Jackson. Black colleges groomed the young vanguard of the Freedom Rides and lunch-counter sit-ins. In their commitment to self-determination, to uplifting the race, to not waiting for the white man to do it for them, only asking the white man not to stand in the way, black colleges manifested a strain of African-American life that was at once traditional and radical. It is the strain of Booker T. Washington and Zora Neale Hurston, of Malcolm X and August Wilson.

The road to Tony Dungy, Lovie Smith, and the 2007 Super Bowl ran through the market town of Salisbury, North Carolina, on the afternoon of Tuesday, December 27, 1892. Twenty-three years after Rutgers and Princeton had played the first college football game in American history, Livingstone College and Biddle University became the first black colleges to take up the sport. Far from being the sort of well-born gentlemen whom Rutgers and Princeton educated, the players on Livingstone had to fashion their own cleats from work shoes and patch and pad their old clothes for uniforms.

Yet when Biddle bested Livingstone by the unlikely score of 4–0, because a touchdown was accorded four points, a heritage was born. As both college and pro football remained almost entirely segregated for decades, as they integrated only fitfully in the years after World War II, as the conventionally prejudiced opinion of the time held that blacks were not intelligent enough to be coaches or quarterbacks, a parallel universe of black excellence in football flourished in the black colleges strewn across the border states and the South. That universe had its own black sportswriters and black publicists and black all-America teams and black bowl games.

All of it went virtually unnoticed by white America. In the heyday of radio, stations almost exclusively broadcast the games of white colleges.

From the mid-1950s through the late 1960s, peak years of civil rights activity, the National Collegiate Athletic Association and the major networks colluded to tightly limit the number of televised games, which invariably featured teams that were mostly, if not entirely, white. Even after the US Supreme Court declared public school segregation unconstitutional in the *Brown v. Board of Education* case in 1954, even after state universities in the South admitted a handful of black students under the protection of federal troops, football powerhouses such as Alabama, Georgia, Texas, and Louisiana State pointedly preserved all-white football teams. In a part of the country where college football functioned almost as a religion, the success of those teams was eagerly construed by segregationists as proof of white supremacy.

The most gifted black players and coaches were both nurtured and trapped within their separate domain. With a mixture of bravado and bitterness, they called the all-black athletic conferences "the chitlin' circuit," a term borrowed from the string of ghetto theaters plied by black musicians and comedians. Ignored most of the time, slighted the rest, the men of black football tempered their skills and forged their reputations, as one college coach put it, "behind God's back." Until the mid-1960s, not even colleges in the North would hire a black coach, and when they finally did so, it was only as an assistant. The modern NFL did not draft a black player until 1949, have a black assistant coach until 1957, appoint a black head coach until 1989. Blacks who played quarterback in college, if they were selected at all by pro teams, were routinely switched to other positions. A white quarterback who could run with force or evasiveness, like Bobby Layne or Fran Tarkenton, was valued for such skills; with a black quarterback, those same talents became the rationale for being involuntarily moved to wide receiver or defensive back. Sometimes those reassignments came suspiciously soon after that black quarterback had shown promise at his original position.

The road that started in Philadelphia in 1837 and passed through Salisbury in 1892 made its way during 1967 to the campuses of Grambling College in northern Louisiana and Florida A&M in Tallahassee and finally to the Orange Bowl stadium in Miami on the night of December 2. Then and there, the Grambling Tigers and the Florida A&M Rattlers met in the Orange Blossom Classic, the black college championship game, and for many years the largest annual gathering of any kind of black Americans.

Grambling and Florida A&M were the most storied teams in all of black college football. Their respective head coaches, Eddie Robinson and Jake Gaither, were legendary within their world. Their quarterbacks, James Harris and Ken Riley, were the best ever to have played the position at each school. All around the coaches and players, in that eventful year, swirled the crosswinds of civil rights activism, black nationalism, white backlash, growing integration, slum insurrection, soaring hopes, and dashed expectations.

Competitive athletics are inextricably part of America's national culture. Sports are an arena in which our values and mores, and too often our biases and bigotry, are literally played out. For most of their careers, Robinson and Gaither had held themselves at a cautious remove from the freedom movement. In private, they had supported it; in public, they had watched their words, lest they endanger the tenuous acceptance, the provisional status, that the Jim Crow South had granted them for their gridiron success. For a long time, they trusted that the sheer quality of their teams would speak for itself and provide their most persuasive argument for racial equality.

Over the course of four months in the summer and fall of 1967, as their teams headed for a showdown in black football's title game, a game played in the same city as that groundbreaking Super Bowl some forty years later, Eddie Robinson and Jake Gaither stepped off the political sideline and took a stand. In the tradition of Paul Robeson, Joe Louis, Jesse Owens, and Jackie Robinson, they put their sporting achievements in the service of social change. What happened when they did is an essential chapter of sports history and black history and, most of all, American history.

1

DRAW WATER WHERE YOU CAN

Jake Gaither and Eddie Robinson
in Their Time, 1937–1966

L ate in the summer of 1937, Jake Gaither drove south toward Tallahassee, Florida. In all his life, some thirty-four years, he had rarely if ever ventured so deeply into the former Confederacy. He was heading toward the best coaching job he had ever received, and he was heading, too, into a city lately inflamed by a lynching.

Gaither had grown up in mining hamlets and county seats along the Appalachian ridge, knotty places that even below the Mason-Dixon Line had small black populations and little history of large-scale slaveholding. More so, as the son of a pastor and a teacher, young Jake formed part of the Negro elite. His parents could afford to send him at sixteen to a combined high school and college in Tennessee that had been founded by the abolitionist wing of the Presbyterian Church. There, at Knoxville

College, he was taught and coached by white men enlightened for their time, and there he met the classmate, Sadie Robinson, whom he married four years after graduation.

Sadie sat next to him now in their car, leaving behind Virginia, where they had resigned their jobs teaching and coaching, respectively, so Jake could assume the position of assistant football coach at Florida Agricultural and Mechanical College. The first day's drive brought the couple to Atlanta, and the next morning, they set off on Highway 19 for the final leg, to Tallahassee, the source of the job and the trepidation.

Along the highway, the land spread out flat and fertile, nothing like the hollows and crags of Jake's youth. The region was known as "Plantation Trace." Its fields supported the cotton and peaches and pecans that once depended on slaves and now on sharecroppers; its woods sheltered the quail that the masters of antebellum mansions hunted for sport. Through Albany and Moultrie, past the remnants of the prison camp for Union soldiers at Andersonville, down into Thomasville, where a spur off the main highway led straight to Tallahassee, the Gaithers drove and worried.

Just past the Florida border, the couple felt so thirsty they decided to risk pulling up at a country store. Jake walked apprehensively through a clutch of white men out front and toward the tall one sitting imperiously behind the counter. "Could I have two Coca-Colas?" he asked. Without moving, without getting up, the man pointed to a shelf and said, "There it is."

Cokes shakily in hand, unharmed yet unnerved, Jake got back into the car. When he had first signed his contract with Florida A&M earlier in the summer, the decision had seemed simple enough. Even as an assistant, a position there meant a raise in both salary and prestige from his previous job, at St. Paul Junior College, a Negro school. He had been recruited to Florida A&M by its new head coach, Bill Bell, whom Jake had met while both were earning their master's degrees at Ohio State. The segregation laws that forbade blacks from attending the South's state universities also made money available to pay their tuition for advanced degrees on integrated campuses in the North. So there in Columbus, formerly a station on the Underground Railroad, now a refuge from Jim Crow, Gaither and Bell had taken classes together, had lived in the same black boardinghouse, and had talked enough football over the dinner table for the A&M coach to make his offer.

In the weeks between accepting the job and moving to Tallahassee, however, Jake Gaither had read some disturbing news about his prospective home. The story appeared in all the leading black papers—the *Pittsburgh Courier, Chicago Defender, Baltimore Afro-American*—as well as the major big-city dailies in the Northeast. Early on the morning of July 20, four white men wearing masks had forced a night guard to unlock cells at the Leon County jail. The men yanked out two black teenagers, Richard Ponder and Ernest Hawkins, who had been arrested the previous day for breaking into a downtown store and slashing a police officer. Holding Ponder and Hawkins at gunpoint, the vigilantes drove about three miles outside the city and ordered the boys to run for their lives. As they did, the white men fired off more than twenty rounds. "This is your last warning, negros," read one of the handwritten signs the killers left beside the corpses, "remember you might be next."

Gaither, for one, got the warning loud and clear. He called Coach Bell and the college president, J.R.E. Lee, to ask if he and his wife would be safe in Tallahassee. The higher-ups offered enough reassurance to keep Gaither from withdrawing, but not enough to keep a Coca-Cola stop from renewing his distress. If anything, the weeks since the double killings only offered more evidence of Tallahassee's hostility. Florida's governor, Fred P. Cone, persisted in describing the crime as an ordinary murder rather than a lynching. The *Daily Democrat,* Tallahassee's newspaper of record, referred to it merely as "an unfortunate incident." The editorial went on to approvingly observe, "As lynchings go, last night's was about as free from the usual unsavory angles as any we have heard about. The method adopted was quiet, orderly."

At the end of two days and 850 miles, the Gaithers reached Tallahassee. For the city's whites, life was proceeding without particular upset. The annual livestock market set its tents and pens and auction blocks on the outskirts of town. Farmers drove their wagons downtown for Saturday shopping. The Ritz theater offered escapist antidotes to the Depression with Shirley Temple in *Wee Willie Winkie*, followed by Clark Gable and Jean Harlow in *Saratoga*.

Here in the Panhandle, a part of Florida more akin to the Deep South than the Atlantic Coast, the social order rested on laws and customs that confined Tallahassee's blacks, 40 percent of the city's thirteen thousand residents, immovably on the bottom. Segregation governed restaurants, theaters, schools, parks; certain churches still had their slave pews intact. The political and commercial aristocracy, known locally as the "golddusters," reigned over the strata of small businessmen, civil servants, redneck laborers, and, finally, Negroes. Living in Smokey Hollow and Frenchtown, most of them avoided going downtown whenever possible. "Blacks in Tallahassee," one historian later put it, "never ceased to fear violence and with justification."

Descending from the State Capitol and crossing the railroad tracks, the Gaithers climbed the last hill in town. At its crest, they took in their first view of Florida A&M. Jake saw a set of five or six wooden army barracks, unpainted and badly weathered, which constituted the male dorms. "This Building Will Be Replaced," read a sign, "When Funds Are Available For A New One." Until recently, the road into the campus hadn't even been paved. Most of the classroom and administrative buildings were wood frame. Patches of sugarcane grew wild. Only as Jake continued did he spot the Carnegie Library with its stone portico, the redbrick Colonial Revival administration building, the quadrangle and band shell.

The people of A&M liked to claim that their hill was the highest in Tallahassee. The assertion was just one of many ways they had of defying the minimal expectations and miserly funds Florida's all-white government begrudgingly provided. In exactly a half century, Florida A&M had scraped its way from being the Normal College for Colored Students, tasked with producing tradesmen, farmers, and teachers, to a nationally accredited, four-year academic institution. Gaither's new boss, President Lee, had been born into slavery, trained by Booker T. Washington at Tuskegee, and imbued with the civil rights ethos by the National Urban League. He insisted on a college that taught liberal arts alongside the practical skills of animal husbandry and carpentry, that offered Shakespeare productions in addition to a working dairy, that created courses in Negro history and literature.

The achievement required a contortionist's talent. For all his erudition and savvy, Lee had to extract money from the autocrats of the State Capitol, and doing so required him periodically to play the "Yes, massa" role. He annually hosted legislators for a day of entertainment on campus, with students demonstrating their skill at brickmaking and performing the Confederate anthem of "Dixie." Politicians told "darkie" jokes from A&M's lectern. When Lee once asked the legislature for a raise in salary to $4,000, Governor Cone declared during a cabinet meeting, "There's not a nigger in the state of Florida worth four thousand dollars a year."

So Jake and Sadie Gaither felt scared for good reason. During the next ten days, until football practice began, it took all their courage just to buy furniture from white stores for their empty apartment. With the first whistle on the gridiron, though, Jake's fears fell away, displaced by challenges. The A&M football team had gone 2-4-1 the previous season and was only one game above .500 for the decade. Many of the players weighed in the 150s, even 140s. They practiced in a cow pasture, and played home games on a bumpy plane of scrub grass carved into a hillside, without shade, bathrooms, or permanent seats for whoever the spectators might be.

By his own description, Gaither had been an ordinary college player who "never missed a game but never knocked their socks off." He still cut a handsome figure with his pencil mustache, center-parted hair, firm chin, and tapered physique, but at 5-11 and 170 hardly a physically intimidating one. Coaching had been an unintended career choice. He had grown up watching lawyers argue cases in the county courthouse and as a student he had set their profession as his goal. Modeling himself on his articulate, impassioned hero Clarence Darrow, Gaither had been almost unbeatable as a college debater. It took his father's death, while Jake was in college, to redirect him into the more reliable direction of education.

In the first coaching job of his life, at a high school in North Carolina, Gaither's team went scoreless in losing every game. The indignity focused his sense of vocation, and it instilled an appetite for knowledge that sustained him through every obstacle. While in his first coaching job, Gaither heard that the defensive coach for Amos Alonzo Stagg's celebrated teams at the University of Chicago would be speaking to a clinic at Duke University. Gaither wrote to Duke's head coach, Wallace Wade, to ask permission: "I know that the laws of the state won't permit Negroes to go to Duke University or to attend the clinic . . . I would like to come to be the janitor . . . and sweep the floors just so I could hear the lectures." Wade never even wrote back. Inwardly furious, Gaither traveled to clinics in Chicago and Minnesota, where his color was tolerated.

He learned techniques and strategies, and he discovered that football had a place for the eloquence and intelligence and competitive streak he had once hoped to use in the courthouse. But for a Negro who aspired to college coaching, the North offered no more prospects than the South. In fact, it offered fewer, because the preponderance of black colleges were in the South. So south Gaither went, south as far as Tallahassee, south as far as Florida A&M's hilltop, a sanctuary of black dignity and self-determination amid a landscape of hatred and degradation. There, on land that had once been a governor's plantation, Gaither set to prove his own worth and his people's. As John Hope, the president of Morehouse College, had put it early in the century, "The same instincts that make a man love dangerous sports make him dare to do noble deeds."

In Jake Gaither's first season, Florida A&M went 6-1-1, winning its conference. That record was an augury of things to come.

+ + +

One day in June 1941, a thirdhand message reached a young man named Eddie Robinson at the feed mill where he worked in Baton Rouge, Louisiana. A tiny black college two hundred miles upstate, the Louisiana Negro Normal and Industrial Institute, was looking to hire a football coach. The offer had made its way from Robinson's wife, Doris, who was attending a training course there for teachers, to her mother in Baton Rouge, one of the few black people in town with a home telephone, and finally on foot to the mill. Even if Negro Normal Institute was just a flyspeck of a place, commonly known as Grambling for the hamlet in the piney woods where it was set, this opportunity to coach football reached Eddie Robinson as a godsend.

For nearly his entire life, he had aspired to no other occupation. Robinson was the sole child of a third-generation sharecropper and a maid who earned a dollar a day. He had spent his first six years in the farming town of Jackson, sleeping on the floor of a shotgun shack without heat, water, or electricity, connected by a plank walkway to an outhouse. When his parents' marriage broke up, he moved to Baton Rouge, where his father had found a job at the Standard Oil refinery. Soon after, as the elder Robinson moved through a series of homes and women, Eddie started his own working life. He shined shoes, hawked papers, hauled ice, cut hair, bused tables, bagged shrimp, sold strawberries, delivered sandwiches. He learned to box and walked the streets with the gloves tied to dangle over his shoulders, practicing his punches, advertising another form of self-reliance.

Robinson's neighborhood embodied the same trait. Wedged between two hubs of white power, the Louisiana State University campus and the downtown district around the capitol building, the black section known as South Baton Rouge in certain ways thrived under segregation. The district contained the full spectrum of Negro life—from gambling spots and backyard chicken coops to churches and shops by the dozens, restaurants and nightclubs, a newspaper called the *Sepia Socialite,* a baseball field known as Ethiopian Park. Migrants from the countryside such as Robinson's father lived there, doing unskilled labor or household service, but so did pharmacists, doctors, insurance agents, tradesmen, professors. No matter that they were modest shotguns and bungalows, 80 percent of the neighborhood's homes were owned.

Jim Crow had ruled Baton Rouge since the overthrow of Reconstruction, and the doctrine not only segregated institutions but also permeated the most incidental encounters. Black women in Baton Rouge were not allowed to try on a dress or hat in a downtown store. Any Negro was required to step off the sidewalk to make room for any passing white. When the city installed sewers, the pipes ended just before South Baton Rouge. Meanwhile, a brothel in the black section that catered to white customers was allowed to operate with impunity.

As a boy, Eddie had his own instructive encounters with white supremacy. Once, he was picked up by the police for supposedly stealing a customer's watch while making ice deliveries. As the cops drove him to the station, Eddie recalled the stories he'd heard of jailhouse beatings and false confessions. Fortunately for him, the missing watch turned up before he was booked. Another time, Eddie sneaked into Tiger Stadium for an LSU football game, not realizing that Negroes were forbidden. Kicked out and sent home, Eddie then took a beating from his father's belt for having crossed, however innocently, a treacherous racial boundary. He later found an acceptable way back into the stadium by joining the all-black maintenance crew that worked on game days.

Segregation felt permanent to Eddie Robinson, immutable, unchangeable. "We had come up with segregation all our lives," he would later recall, "and nobody had ever told us it was wrong. We accepted it and you just grew up with the thing." What the Negro could try to control and preserve was his sense of self-worth. Sports became Eddie's chosen means of expressing that sovereignty.

He listened to all of Joe Louis's fights on the radio his mother had bought for that specific purpose. During the broadcast of the Brown Bomber's rematch against Max Schmeling, the German champion embraced by the Nazi regime, Eddie heard something astonishing: a Negro being referred to as an American. Much closer to home, Eddie saw a model of pride and purpose in the form of Julius Kraft—chemistry teacher, shopkeeper, amateur-theater director, and, most important, football coach at all-black McKinley High School. Every Monday and Wednesday during the autumns of Eddie's childhood, Kraft would bring his team in full uniform through the black stores and gathering spots to sell tickets for the weekend game. Those players, Eddie noticed, called their coach "sir."

Still in elementary school, Eddie practiced football in his street clothes and organized games on vacant lots. He sketched out plays in his school notebooks till his exasperated teachers snatched them away. By the time Eddie was a junior at McKinley, he was starting at quarterback, and he proceeded to lead the team to two straight unbeaten seasons and be elected class president for good measure. He went on to play quarterback at Leland College, a black Baptist school just outside Baton Rouge, and to be groomed for a future of coaching by his coach there, a northern-trained theologian named Ruben Turner. When Turner took along Eddie on recruiting trips around the state, and even more so when he brought him to a coaching clinic in Chicago, he was showing as much of the outside world as Eddie Robinson had ever seen.

In a state where fewer than 10 percent of Negro teenagers attended high school, McKinley High and Leland College served strivers who embraced their role as the vanguard. "We were infected with the idea of getting ahead," recalled Gardner C. Taylor, a product of both institutions who later became a prominent minister and civil rights activist. "We thought of education as sacred."

Along the way, Eddie courted a classmate named Doris Mott, and even young love contained an element of self-improvement. Doris was the daughter of the Negro middle class—her father a brakeman on the Illinois Central, her mother and aunts all teachers—who even attended boarding school for a time. With the money from his odd jobs, Eddie treated her to movies, and later the jazz bands that played the Temple

Roof Gardens, atop the five-story building that was the tallest in South Baton Rouge. He always said that he knew he'd won her when she danced with him to "Stardust."

Yet by the summer of 1941, at the age of just twenty-two, Robinson saw his dream of coaching already imperiled, swamped by the exigencies of daily life, circumscribed by the realities of segregation. He had eloped with Doris two months earlier, shortly after graduating together as English majors from Leland College. By midsummer she was pregnant, and Robinson was working two jobs, nights on an ice truck and days at the feed mill, lugging 150-pound sacks for twenty-five cents an hour as boll weevils infested his skin. Plenty of lives in South Baton Rouge went no further. So when that message about the coaching job arrived, Robinson said yes to Grambling—sight unseen, salary undetermined, risks unknown or ignored.

In the racial geography of Louisiana, Baton Rouge's hostility was mitigated by Catholic and Creole influences as well as by Huey Long's stint as governor, when he carved the political divide along the line of class rather than color. Grambling, by comparison, was a black pinprick in the state's Protestant, redneck north. Long, who had grown up fifty miles from Grambling in Winnfield, was the exception that proved the rule: the surest way to defuse anger at the wealthy caste of planters and businessmen was to grant poor whites official superiority over blacks along with the extralegal latitude to wield it. In the early decades of the century, three parishes (counties) in northern Louisiana recorded the most lynchings of any county in the nation.

Ruston, the closest town to Grambling, had a particularly gruesome reputation. During the early fall of 1938, fewer than three years before Robinson's trip, two white men had been beaten, one of them fatally, and a white woman sexually attacked. While a state laboratory was analyzing the fingerprints of a suspect, a black teenager from Ruston named W. C. Williams, a mob hunted him down. Williams was whipped with the belt from a cotton gin and raped with a heated metal poker until he "confessed." Then, as several hundred spectators approvingly watched, the mob lynched him and riddled his body with bullets. No one was ever arrested for Williams's murder. As the episode was reported nationally in the Negro press, it imparted palpable, lasting fear five miles away, in Grambling.

The racial hierarchy applied even to enemies of the United States. Early in World War II, the government built an internment camp outside Ruston for German prisoners, many of them officers who were Nazi Party members. Grambling's blacks cooked their food and washed their clothes while the Germans were provided with recreation, a canteen, and a camp newspaper. Some, barely supervised, took outside work as loggers. Then, when the war ended, the POW barracks were sent to Grambling to be used for faculty housing.

The private high school that evolved into a junior college and ultimately Grambling had been founded in 1901 by a group of black farmers who pooled enough money to buy land and hire a young protégé of Booker T. Washington's as principal. For nearly forty years, the school-cum-college had no electricity, running water, indoor plumbing, or brick buildings. At one point in the late 1920s, the Negro Normal Institute raised money to continue functioning by ordering musical instruments from Sears on credit and sending around a student band to entertain wealthy whites with minstrel shows.

Even after some modern utilities and a few permanent buildings arrived in 1939 under the New Deal, the Negro Normal Institute continued to hold the most pragmatic goals. The school trained teachers for black elementary and secondary schools that, in many cases, operated only three months a year. It taught students how to farm and fix and build. In a program called the "College of Common Sense," instructors traveled to the black settlements of northern Louisiana, installing toilets, assembling front steps, making beds out of orange crates. On Grambling's own land, agriculture professors sent coeds in their saddle shoes out to dig sweet potatoes. The village's primary link to the outside world was a mail train that passed through twice daily. Often, in the absence of any other diversions, the townspeople lined the tracks to watch.

As for football, Robinson was taking over a failing, almost moribund program. Negro Normal Institute had played only nineteen games since taking up the sport in 1928, winning exactly four times. During three seasons, it hadn't even been able to field a team. Only 40 of its 175 students were male. Then again, it took a desperate school to make such a risky hire—a twenty-two-year-old whose only coaching experience had been on Baton Rouge sandlots.

But the school's new president, Ralph Waldo Emerson Jones, had seen enough of the wider world to want Grambling to become part of it. He had grown up as the son of a dean at Southern University in Baton Rouge, and earned a master's degree in mathematics at Columbia University in New York. Hired by Negro Normal Institute as a professor in 1926, he was the first faculty member there to hold an advanced degree. As president he wrung approval from the state for a full four-year curriculum in 1940. And perhaps because he remembered how much the Southern and McKinley High football games had meant to blacks in Baton Rouge, Jones decided to put some of his meager budget into resuscitating football at Negro Normal Institute. Football could be one way, perhaps the only way, for an obscure little school up in the piney woods to get noticed.

Eddie Robinson signed on for $63.25 a month and moved into a rooming house. City people until now, he and Doris got sick from bugs in the well water, and fell asleep to the foraging sounds of possums and raccoons. "It was," she said years later of Grambling circa 1941, "just nowhere." Eddie Robinson's penchant for self-reliance proved to be a necessity as much as a choice in his new job. Without any assistants save the school's night watchman, Robinson not only coached football and basketball but also lined the field, drove the team bus, trained the drill team for halftime shows, made sandwiches for the players on road trips, taped up sprained ankles and knees, and called in game stories to local newspapers.

The news was not so good that first season. Grambling went 3-5, and Robinson returned home in a fury after each loss, tearing his hat off, getting so worked up Doris worried he'd have a heart attack. "Maybe we better go back to Baton Rouge," she told him, "and you get a job at Standard Oil."

In Robinson's second season, 1942, Grambling was unbeaten and unscored upon. With so many young men mobilized for World War II, the college canceled its football seasons in 1943 and 1944, leaving Robinson to conscript coeds to test the single-wing plays he was devising. In spite of isolation, lynching, illness, and anything else, he had made up his mind to stay in Grambling, and he expressed the conviction in words that consciously echoed some of Booker T. Washington's most famous. "You have to put down your bucket somewhere," he put it, "and draw water where you can."

In the summer of 1945, with the world war nearly over and the football season soon to begin, Eddie Robinson drove Grambling's station wagon to Baton Rouge and New Orleans. He was recruiting black veterans who had played high school ball and now could attend college on the GI Bill. He went from house to house, wearing a coat and tie to impress the parents, and telling their grown sons, "I'm starting a program here, and for a good program, I need good people."

It took no small amount of persuasion to coax city folks to move to a campus one recruit recalled as "just a little old shanty-looking thing." It took no small amount of will to convince men who had already been through war to take orders from a coach only twenty-six years old who had been safely Stateside. Those players called Robinson "Mule" because he worked them as hard as pack animals. After one particular loss, he confiscated their meal books for weeks, until they beat Grambling's archrival, Southern, in a season-ending game.

But after taking commands from white officers in the military, those veterans appreciated having a black man in charge. And this black man, they soon discovered, was not above any task. When a player was going to miss a game because his father needed help with the cotton harvest, Robinson went into the fields with them. Besides, winning bred faith, and Grambling went 40-16-2 for the rest of the decade.

Bible in hand, like a circuit-riding preacher, Robinson traveled through the countryside, entering the shacks of sharecroppers and pulp-wood cutters, assuring parents who hadn't gone past elementary school, "Your boy will graduate college and your boy will go to church on Sunday." To those boys, Robinson offered a gospel grounded in his own experience. "Football teaches the lesson of life," he put it some years later. "It cultivates in the athlete the ability to pay the price. No struggle, no strength. No fight, no fortitude. No crisis, no courage. No suffering, no sympathy. No pain, no patience."

As word spread about what Robinson was doing at Grambling, young players wrote him to beg for a chance. They sent letters listing their report-card marks and their times in the hundred-yard dash; they sent letters composed in capital letters on lined paper. One hopeful apologized for the web of creases on a page, explaining, "Sorry my neace [*sic*] got to the letter when I was in the bathroom sorry!!!" Another told Robinson, "You have been reading the letters of a young man who has never had a taste of honey." A third closed by stating, "Coach this may sound funny but you are the man for my future. Please help."

For these young men, Robinson presented himself as a role model. Besides football and class and church, he showed them what it meant to be a husband and father, the kind of consistent and reliable man absent from his own childhood and those of so many of his Grambling players. "Miss Doris," as most of Grambling called his wife, taught English at the black high school in Ruston and sang as a soloist with the college choir. Eddie made a point of walking through campus holding hands with her, still sweethearts. He ate lunch with her at home on any day she wasn't teaching. And when Grambling players stopped by the coach's home in the evening, as they were permitted, they would often get a plate of dinner from Miss Doris and a glimpse of her and Eddie listening to their favorite Ellington and Sinatra records.

In the midst of pervasive race hate, Robinson showed how to wear stoic dignity as psychic armor. He endured when Grambling's team bus broke down and a white mechanic said, "Don't bring that nigger bus in here." He endured when the police kicked his team off a practice field in

Montgomery, Alabama, leaving it to drill in a parking lot. He endured when a white coach told a clinic how stupid a particular Negro player was to have returned a punt from the end zone. He endured when local newspapers, in the wake of the *Brown* decision, printed letters calling blacks "monkeys" and quoted state legislators describing integration as a "Grand Canyon of socialism."

On the field and off, Robinson implemented his own version of separate but equal. In it, a black had to be better than a white merely to have an equal chance—better in the classroom, better on the field, better in his character. For Robinson, there was no point in railing against the unfairness of the world; resentment would devour you from the inside out. There was only the perpetual effort to improve the self and uplift the race. "When you get your opportunities," Robinson often told his team, "make the most of them." Football happened to offer an especially concrete way of proving what blacks could accomplish. Football had the same rules for either race, the same field, the same penalties and points. Excellence in the end had to be recognized. "If they throwing and catching, if they blocking and tackling," Robinson said of white schools, "that's what we doing, too."

Being a "race man," paradoxically, made Robinson a patriot. Instead of being embittered by what blacks were denied in America, he was heartened by what blacks achieved in America. "This is a great country," he said much more than once. "If you are willing to pay the price, you can be anything you want here, even if it comes slow sometimes." On another occasion he put it this way: "If you've never been a minority, it's hard to understand the feeling that you are not quite an American. You find peace with yourself on that day when you decide 'I'm as much an American as anyone else.'"

+ + +

Early in the football season of 1953, Jake Gaither composed a letter to a former player named Bradley Mitchell. After starting for several years at split end for Florida A&M, Mitchell had graduated with a degree in industrial education and taken a job teaching and coaching in West Palm Beach. "Here is what I want you to do," Gaither wrote. "Send me the drop on your best boys. I don't want any whom you are in doubt about. I only want your exceptional boys." Mindful of the recent armistice ending the Korean War, Gaither added, "Include any boys who might be coming back from the service." And then, in an apparent reference to divisive internal politics at Mitchell's high school, the coach offered some advice: "Take care of yourself. Be tactful in every respect. Keep your mouth shut. Do your work. Keep out of trouble."

That letter served as a kind of Rosetta Stone, a decoding ring, for the man Jake Gaither was becoming in midcentury at Florida A&M. Appointed head coach in 1945, he went 9-1 in his opening season, beginning the Rattlers' six-year reign as conference champions. His FAMU team was the black college cochampion in both 1950 and 1952. More than establishing excellence—indeed, dominance—on the field, Gaither efficiently set himself at the hub of a wheel that extended the length and breadth of Florida. The Gaither network reached 750 miles from Pensacola to Jacksonville to Miami, wherever black people lived, worked, went to church, attended school, and, most important, coached or played football.

Within a decade of becoming head coach, Gaither had built a staff composed of former players. He had sent out other alumni, such as Bradley Mitchell, to become coaches at Florida's black high schools. His trust in those protégés, and their trust in him, allowed Gaither to recruit the most talented black ballplayers in the entire state by typewriter and telephone. When Gaither left Tallahassee, it was less often to entice a football prospect than to deliver a speech about history or religion; he delivered dozens in a year, to a high school's commencement or a fraternity's Founders Day, to a conference of black YMCAs or Women's Day at the Bethel A.M.E. Church. (Sadie Gaither once called him "the talkingest man I've ever seen.") As his letter to Bradley Mitchell revealed, Gaither took the position of being a paragon seriously.

Gaither called his ideal player "the hungry boy." He was the son of a mother who cleaned white folks' houses, wiped white babies' behinds. He was the son of a father who picked oranges, mined phosphate, tapped pine trees for turpentine. He was orphaned or abandoned and being raised by his grands. He was the first in his family to go to college, and he was away from home for the first time in his life. He came into Tallahassee in the back rows of a Greyhound or the Colored car of the Gulf Wind train, and he lugged his footlocker up the hill to campus.

"I don't mean hungry for food in his stomach and clothes on his back," Gaither once said of such boys, "but hungry for recognition, hungry for the satisfaction of ego, hungry to be recognized as 'I'm somebody.' I love to deal with the hungry boy. I don't know that I could coach the rich man's son."

To them, Jake Gaither was coach, teacher, preacher, father. He bought them shoes when they had none, paid for the dentist when they couldn't afford it, sprang for boxes of candy when they angered a girlfriend, covered their registration fees until they could reimburse him. He laid down just three rules in return, three inviolable rules: "Get your lesson. Stay out of trouble. And give me all you've got." And the coach, too, got something out of the contract. He got some of life's holes filled. As a child, Jake had lost the twin brother who died at age one. He had seen his parents adopt two castaway children, one the son of a local prostitute, the other a boy born to a white woman's illicit affair with a black elevator operator. Despite all those incentives to make a family, Jake and Sadie had never been able to have children. His players were the closest thing to a family he would ever have.

A man who had once aspired to the minister's pulpit or the attorney's office, a man who had earned a master's degree at Ohio State and done additional study at Yale, Gaither transformed head coaching into something more prestigious and encompassing. In a time and a place that would never permit a black man to become an executive, Gaither made himself a CEO in all but official title. He and Sadie built a brick home in the neighborhood of College Terrace, where the Florida A&M professors and administrators lived. He coached the football team and chaired the physical education department, while she taught English at the university. Their social crowd was composed of historians and sociologists, ministers and musicians, and the most elite handful of them, including Gaither, had been inducted into Sigma Pi Phi, a fraternal organization centered on black men in the professions. Founded in 1904 and commonly known as the Boulé, after the council of aristocrats in ancient Greece, Sigma Pi Phi counted among its earliest members W.E.B. Du Bois. Indeed, Gaither and his Tallahassee peers epitomized the "Talented Tenth" of whom Du Bois had written and from whom so much was expected.

Tucked between the pages of the Gaither family Bible was a compelling clue to his racial sensibility. It was a yellowed clipping, evidently from a Negro newspaper published around America's entry into World War I. Gaither had first read it as a teenager and preserved it for a half century. The article espoused a philosophy and strategy that later, in World War II, would be called "Double Victory." It linked black patriotism in wartime to the black right to equality at home:

> [W]e go to make the world safe for Democracy. We are going in spite of discrimination and prejudice, we are going in spite of mob violence, we are going in spite of Jim Crowism, we have no bitterness, no hate is surging in our breasts, even though these injustices cry out to high heaven, our faith is steadfast, our hearts beat true. It is our hope that out of this awful struggle a true Democracy will rear its altar, giving out shining hope and promise to the black man in America, a real Democracy that knows no creed nor color . . . a Democracy which shall fold its protecting mantle about the shoulders of all men.

When Gaither spoke to black audiences over the years, he repeatedly invoked the same thesis. Implicit in it was his unshakable faith that black sacrifice would inevitably be recognized and rewarded. Gaither believed in his imperfect nation's better angels. As he put it in a 1952 speech for the black workforce of a wood-pulp company:

> I want to talk to you not as Negroes but as American citizens who have a glorious past and a rich and fertile future in the development of this great country. This is your land. The country that you helped build and develop. The country that you must live and die to protect. You are somebody. You are an American. I love to think of my people fighting in the war of the Revolution—giving birth to the greatest democracy the world has ever known. I like to think of my people following Teddy Roosevelt in the Battle of San Juan Hill. I like to think of the part my people played in the War to Save the Union. I like to think of how valiantly my people fought in the Argonne Forest of the First World War. I like to think of the courageous stand of my people in the Battle of the Bulge. I like to think of the glorious history the Negro has.

On the football field, too, winning was about more than winning for Jake Gaither. It was about proving black equality, black capacity, black excellence. Years ago, the white man hadn't let Gaither attend that coaching clinic at Duke, so here at A&M, starting in the mid-1950s, Gaither had created his own. He invited both black coaches and white ones. Some of the best in the nation—Ben Schwartzwalder of Syracuse, Frank Howard of Clemson, Woody Hayes of Ohio State —sat in wooden tablet chairs under the Spanish moss as Gaither led his outdoor lessons and, not coincidentally, stealthily integrated Tallahassee. Ultimately, Gaither attracted even Bear Bryant, whose all-white teams at Alabama embodied the same dogma of racial supremacy that the state's governor, George Wallace, espoused. When Bryant scoffed at Gaither's offensive scheme, saying it could never work at a big-time school, Gaither shot back, "I'll tell you what. I'll take my players and beat yours with it, and take your players and beat mine with it."

With his dare, Gaither was asking for the impossible. Well into the 1960s, a decade after the US Supreme Court had struck down public school segregation, the color line remained nearly impregnable in football. A white team would never play a black team. A black man would never be allowed to coach white players. In the Southeastern and Southwest Conferences, only perpetual doormats such as Kentucky and Southern Methodist had been desperate enough to recruit one or two blacks. Victories for racial equality, at least on the football field, could take place only by Gaither's kind of inference and indirection.

"For a black boy, this is not just a game of football," he put it. "He is carrying a cross of fifteen million blacks on his shoulders. . . . This has to be the dominating factor in the life of any black. There is no place in our life for mediocrity." For Gaither, the bromide about losing being good for building character was worse than a cliché. It was a rationalization of slavery and segregation. "A man beaten, humiliated, lying flat on his back with opponents walking up and down his back is in no mood to talk character building," he told a black audience during a speech in the 1950s. "We have been losing all of our lives. We need to feel the exhilaration of winning. We were losing in the days of slavery—under the lash of the slave driver's whip."

2

THE LABORATORY FOR MANHOOD

Florida A&M, August 31, 1967

On the last morning of August and the first morning of football practice, Jake Gaither sent the team's trainers into the male dorms, each emissary with a whistle at his lips. They strode down the hallways, blistering the air with their alarm. Some of the veteran players had already jolted awake several times during the night, their vigilant nerves jumping to a car horn or passing train. Others, having slept in their jockstraps and jerseys, quickly opened their doors now to prove they were up. For the rest, the trainers stood at each portal and screeched and screeched and screeched some more until even the deepest sleeper surrendered.

It was five o'clock in the morning, more than two hours before sunrise and more than two weeks before the start of classes. The only students on the entire campus were the football team and the marching band, each unit assembled for the brutal rigor of preseason drills. With the sky still dark and the air thick with moisture and gnats, the players headed for the practice fields and the six o'clock start. There would not be breakfast, not even water, until the session ended three hours later.

Gaither stood at the gate to the fields. By now, at age sixty-four, he had gray in his mustache, furrows on his face, thickness in his middle. He walked with a rolling, slightly unsteady gait, and the skin twitched at the corner of his mouth, letting out a soft hissing sound; both weaknesses were the consequence of a brain tumor decades earlier that had nearly taken his life. A streak of gray indicated the place where a surgeon had cut through the skull. And though some players believed Gaither had a metal plate in the spot, nothing but hair and skin were covering his brain there.

Regardless of age and infirmity, after twenty-two seasons as head coach, Gaither was a certifiable legend. His teams had won 179 games and lost just 31; they had been named black college champions seven times. He had sent his young men into pro stardom—Willie Galimore for the Chicago Bears, Bob Hayes for the Dallas Cowboys. He was on a first-name basis with NFL coaches and was privately consulted by Florida governors who had little use for other black leaders.

The campus itself had grown more formidable over Gaither's years. Florida A&M was a university now, known by the acronym FAMU. It had its own hospital and law school, a growing complement of graduate programs. Amid the oaks and palms and privets, nearly two dozen buildings had been constructed or renovated in the past decade, including Bragg Stadium for football. This season it was getting lights for the first night games ever. The boom was partly the handiwork of the university's president since 1950, George W. Gore, a minister's son with a master's degree from Harvard and a doctorate from Columbia. But it was also, in no small measure, the result of official Florida's resistance to *Brown v. Board of Education*. The more impressive the FAMU campus, the more proof that separate was equal. Or so went the cynical calculation.

To begin practice, Gaither now called together the team for his tra-

ditional initiation. He crouched down, then went to one knee. The starters gathered in a circle around him, then knelt, and more concentric
rings formed around them, leaving the scrubs and newcomers on the
periphery. Gaither laid his hands on the shoulders of two players close to
him, and soon every player was similarly touching the shoulders of two
teammates. These eighty or ninety individuals formed, as their coach
intended, a single whole.

"Let's talk to the Old Man upstairs," Gaither said, bowing his head.
"Dear God of the Rattlers, a sweet and just God, the only God we know.
We submit ourselves humbly today for Your blessing. You have been so
good to us, much better than we deserve. We ask You for the ability to do
our best, so that every one of these kids gets every full measure. Let them
block, let them tackle, let them run like they've never run before. Grant
us the wisdom to know what plays to call and the strength to follow them
through. Help us, Lord Jesus, to transfer your strength and wisdom to
the game of life. This is my prayer."

Even though there was no opponent today, the veterans responded
with the traditional pregame chant: "We have wounded them. They have
fallen beneath our feet. They shall not rise. The Lord is my shepherd. I
shall not want. Hubba, hubba, hubba!"

Then, as Gaither's prayer had promised, they ran as they had never
run before, or at least as they had never run before experiencing summer
practice at A&M. They strode for two miles or more around the football
field and an adjacent baseball diamond, bugs buzzing into their eyes,
sweat already dripping. The assistant coaches, posted by Gaither at intervals along the course, made sure nobody dogged it. Some of the freshmen, softened by the off-season, began to wheeze and gasp. Limping to
the finish, they hung their heads, put their hands heavily on their thighs,
went faint in the face. "Getting the white eyes," it was called. One or two
threw up along the sideline.

There was nothing like the Florida sun, Gaither liked to say, to make
a team tough. If you could survive that heat, you could beat anybody. He
let the weather and practice routine cull the herd for him, too. Gaither

never cut anybody. Players cut themselves. Late at night in the dorm, you would hear the thump of somebody dragging his footlocker down the stairs, escaping in shame.

Just now, still catching breath, the players assembled in lines for calisthenics, led by the starters. With those exercises done, the sorting began. FAMU had three practice fields, and from the highest to the lowest their elevation designated a player's status. Borrowing a phrase from Winston Churchill, Gaither called his first, second, and third teams Blood, Sweat, and Tears, and he assigned them to the respective levels. The bottom field was the destination for dozens of incoming freshmen as well. They would serve as the scout team that imitated each upcoming opponent's offense and defense, and, not coincidentally, received the beating and humiliation doled out by the starters. Their field was called "The Pit." It also deserved the term Gaither used for football more generally: the "laboratory for manhood."

On this first day of practice, as on most of those to follow, Gaither busied himself with the offensive backs and observed the rest of the action from a deliberate remove. He did not curse or shout at a player; his way of dealing with a whopping mistake was to call it a "minor error." He never pulled a player out right after a blunder, because he knew that would rattle the boy's confidence. And he did call the players "my boys," transforming a phrase of racial disrespect into an endearment. When he addressed anyone individually, it was usually as "Baby."

Gaither was a delegator by temperament and necessity. Back in the 1940s, recovering from surgery on his brain tumor, he had been too weak to coach without plenty of help. So over the years he had constructed a staff that may have been the smartest and most loyal in all of college football. (Given the segregation on coaching staffs throughout the nation, upward and outward mobility was limited to other black colleges, few of which had a football program as renowned as FAMU's.) At a time when only 3 percent of black Americans held a bachelor's degree, every one of his six assistants held a master's degree, most of them earned at top research universities in the North—Ohio State, Indiana, NYU. The first among equals, defensive coordinator Pete Griffin, taught chemistry and wrote short stories.

Two years earlier, when Gaither had hired his newest assistant, he had drawn a play on his office chalkboard during a staff meeting. He asked the coach, Bobby Lang, if the play was right, and Lang said it was. After the other assistants left, Gaither asked Lang, "You trying to make a fool out of me?" He had designed the play wrong on purpose, to see if Lang would have the guts to object. "I don't need a ditto man, I don't need a yes man," he lectured Lang. "I need a man around me who's smart as me or smarter. And if you ain't, then get outta that chair. And let the door hit you where the good Lord split you."

Because nearly every assistant had played at Florida A&M under Gaither, they knew his system, too. Gaither was an innovator who had devised an offense called the split-line T. With it, the Rattlers of the late 1950s and early 1960s scored nearly forty-two points a game. Gaither had even written a book about it for a big New York publisher. In the split-line T, Gaither set back all his linemen a half step behind the center, and he widened the gaps between them so that the line's width stretched forty-eight feet, fifteen more than in a normal T formation. This design forced an opposing defense into impossible choices. If you played head on head along the line, within seconds a Florida A&M back was past you and through the hole. If you played the gaps, the blockers had the angle to knock you aside and clear the way for a sweep.

Instead of size, Gaither prized speed at every position. He stocked his offensive and defensive backfields with sprinters who could do the hundred-yard dash in less than ten seconds. Gaither's lean linemen could move downfield and his linebackers could race from sideline to sideline. By rotating Blood, Sweat, and Tears, Gaither could keep bringing fresh legs and lungs into a game. His gentlemanly nature ended with the opening kickoff. He wanted his teams to "kill a mosquito with an ax," to "run over a pig with a bus." He beat teams by scores of 76–0, 63–6, and 58–12.

The whole process started with the three-a-days of August and September—players on the field from six till nine in the morning, four till six in the afternoon, eight till nine at night. On this morning, a typically miserable one, by the time the distance run and calisthenics were finished, the sun was burning through the mist, evaporating the dew off the spiky centipede grass. Soon the temperature would be in the nineties, the humidity almost as high, waves of heat shimmering up off the turf. The thick air quivered with the sound of cracks, grunts, whistles, dry heaves. One of the defensive stars, Rudy Sims, had a shoe-lace tied around his neck, leading to a packet of smelling salts hidden in his pants. Some of the other veterans paid local kids a quarter to hang around the sideline with a cup of ice, sneaking a cube when the coaches weren't looking. Nearly everyone listened for the chimes of the campus bell clock, marking off each fifteen minutes of torture.

Pete Griffin might have his first-team defense crab-walking up the steep slope of "Horror Hill." Hansel Tookes and Bobby Lang, coaching the linemen, might have them pushing the blocking sled from goal line to goal line in a relay race. Costa Kittles would be putting the quarterbacks and receivers through routes and progressions, repetition after repetition after repetition. Shuffle drills, over-unders, running through tires—after all those, it was almost a relief when actual contact started, because at least then you could take out your anger at the coach on somebody. Of course, that somebody felt the same way about you.

Unit by unit, the first- and second-string offenses and defenses descended into The Pit to whack around the freshmen. They would still be staggering and struggling from the last combat, and eleven new faces in eleven clean jerseys would line up. "These guys hit you all kinds of ways," a tackle named Carlmon Jones put it. "You had to fight your way out." And all the while, the position coaches would be watching, mentally preparing their reports for Jake Gaither. Who are the "mules" who buck against orders? Who are the "racehorses" who listen, execute, and say, "Yes, sir"?

Sometimes Gaither himself would come down, just to enforce the hierarchy, to make sure no freshmen were showing up his starters. (And simultaneously to spot the ones who did, so they could be promoted from The Pit.) During one scrimmage, Gaither saw a first-year line-backer smash down a starting halfback. "Hell, who was that?" he asked. With improbable and insubordinate formality, the freshman said, "'Tis I, Coachie. I am the tackling man." Gaither called the same play, and this time the back ran over the defender. "Where's my tackling man now?" the coach asked.

The baptism only started in The Pit. The frosh had to submit to shaved heads or Mohawks. They had to carry the equipment from the lockers to the field. They'd be ordered to look at the same lightbulb for an hour. Or to talk to a telephone pole like it was their girlfriend. Or to run after a starter's car, going just fast enough they'd never catch up. Or to wear their helmets, with their jockstraps dangling around the neck, dur-ing team meetings. Or to carry an empty Coke bottle in the back pocket, and if an older player caught them without it, they weren't allowed to eat the next meal in the cafeteria.

The only other students who understood were the only other stu-dents on the campus at the time: the band. Even the football players had to admit that the Marching 100 practiced longer than they did. The band director, Dr. William Patrick Foster, otherwise known as "The Law," put his musicians through four-a-days on a former potato field called "The Patch." During any brief pause in football drills, the players could hear the rifle report of the snare drums echoing from Foster's domain. When the players trudged toward the locker room after night practice ended at ten, they could see the band still rehearsing under the lights.

Foster marked off the bare ground of The Patch into a grid, crossed one way by the five-yard lines of a football field and the other by stripes precisely twenty-two and a half inches apart. From his observation tower eighteen feet above the field, he called his charges to attention: heels close, feet together, hips level, shoulders square, eyes facing front, chin drawn in. Four paces between rows, three strides between ranks, exactly eight steps for every five yards, no more and no less: rehearsal was built on military discipline. Once it was instilled, Foster added his own dar-

The Laboratory for Manhood

ing kind of content—not just the usual Sousa marches but also jazz and R&B songs, not just block formations but also shifting shapes, not just high-stepping but also literally dancing. Foster had a FAMU professor of modern dance, Beverly Barber, teach his musicians how to move, demonstrating from atop a raised platform like a go-go girl. "It slides, slithers, swivels, rotates, shakes, rocks and rolls," Foster wrote of the band in his memoirs. "It leaps to the sky, does triple twists, and drops to earth without a flaw, without missing either a beat or a step." The aspirants who couldn't would be cut at the end of preseason rehearsals in a ritual called "the Shaking of the Tree."

They were in this thing together, Foster and Gaither. They burned with the same desire for excellence, the same fever to dominate any opponent. If anything, the Marching 100 had reached a national spotlight before the Rattlers, having played at halftime of two Pro Bowls and the 1964 NFL championship. Jazz aficionados knew that the Adderley brothers, Nat and Julian ("Cannonball"), had gotten their chops in Foster's conservatory. Lest any audience treat the Marching 100 as mere entertainment, Foster's band delivered another message with its repertoire. In addition to playing the "Star-Spangled Banner" before kickoff, the Marching 100 performed "Lift Every Voice and Sing" by James Weldon Johnson, commonly known as the Black National Anthem.

> *Sing a song full of the faith that the*
> *dark past has taught us,*
> *sing a song full of the hope*
> *that the present has brought us;*
> *facing the rising sun of our new day begun,*
> *let us march on till victory is won.*

With the sun high above the tree line now and the sky bleached white, the bell clock tolled. Gaither's players counted the chimes for nine o'clock. From all three practice fields, they straightened up from three-point stances, pulled back from the blocking sleds, and loped toward him. Encircling him, they jumped up and down in place, chanting in husky, raspy unison, "Dining! Dining! Dining!" After four hours awake, hours of exertion without food or water, they were ready for the double portions the cafeteria promised. They were, that is, except for the stragglers too weary even to eat, capable only of hurling themselves onto the mattress of a stifling dorm room, not an air conditioner around, nobody had that kind of money, and falling into a sleep more like a coma.

"Dining! Dining! Dining!" the call continued.

Gaither looked at them, his boys, and tried to hold back a grin.

"Ah," he said, waving one arm in mock disdain, "get outta here."

+ + +

In early March 1967, the off-season for college football, an item had appeared under the heading "Eye-Opener" in the *Atlanta Daily World,* the Southeast's major black newspaper. Marion Jackson, its sports columnist, reported rumors that Jake Gaither was going to resign. The implication, in fact, was that Gaither might even be pushed out. The coach was reduced to denying his own imminent departure.

Now, six months later, he was obviously still coaching. Yet the aura stirred by the column, the notion that Jake Gaither was past his prime, hovered over the coming season. Not since his first years at FAMU had Gaither and his team faced such skepticism, and for such legitimate reasons. In both the 1965 and 1966 seasons, the Rattlers had gone 7-3, cause for celebration at most schools, motive for disquiet at FAMU. In his first twenty years as head coach, Gaither had lost only twenty-five games, and in only one season had he lost more than twice. Now he'd been beaten six times in just two years. FAMU had lost a conference matchup for the first time in fifteen years (8–3 to South Carolina State in 1966), and it had been humiliated in black football's marquee game, the Orange Blossom Classic (36–7 to Morgan State in 1965).

For FAMU's foes, the inventiveness of the split-line T had grown familiar, which meant easier to defend. Opposing coaches had decoded the secrets of the method simply by buying Gaither's textbook or attending his clinic. As long as Gaither clung to the running game as first, second, and third choice, other teams could crowd the line with eight or nine men to outnumber his blockers, no matter how they were positioned.

The Gaither mystique was ebbing in other ways, too. No longer did his name and connections automatically deliver Florida's top black players. While southern white colleges still treated them as radioactive, coaches elsewhere were raiding the supply: Gaither had recently lost recruits to Oklahoma, Notre Dame, and Wichita State. Two of the best receivers in Florida, Harold Carmichael and Ken Burrough, shunned FAMU for Southern University and Texas Southern, respectively, black schools with sophisticated passing games.

Frustrated and irritable, Gaither uncharacteristically turned on his own assistants. On the Monday after a shutout loss the previous season, Gaither had found two of them lingering outside his office door, afraid to knock. "Gentlemen," he said, ushering them in, "you don't have to worry anymore about coaching the secondary. Hell, I'll do that. You don't have to see to it that someone is prepared to take over in case someone gets hurt and we have someone on special teams ready to take over who won't fumble the ball. Hell, I'll do that, too." This wasn't Gaither playing at being mad, a master actor calibrating the effect of a performance; this was Gaither in spontaneous fury, as the coaches had rarely seen or heard him. "I'll tell you what," he concluded, "I'll just coach all the positions and you all can pitch in when you want to."

With so much at stake for the 1967 season, Gaither had barely visited his fishing shack on the Gulf of Mexico that summer. He met almost daily in his office with Pete Griffin, the oldest and most trusted of his assistants. Sweating through socks and shirts, snacking on a drawerful of peanuts, chain-smoking in his sole vice, Gaither took stock. A restless sleeper at best, Gaither would call Griffin up at two in the morning with some nagging worry or lightning insight.

As always, the Rattlers had speed on the team: two cornerbacks and one receiver had been on the 440 team that won at the Penn Relays four consecutive years. As always, the Rattlers had capable runners on the team: a total of eight lettermen were returning to the backfield, including 1966's leading rusher, Hubert Ginn. The interior lines looked spottier, not deep enough for Gaither's liking beyond stars such as Rudy Sims and Roger Finnie, but switching a few underclassmen from offense to defense or vice versa could solve the problem.

The real challenge, it became apparent, involved strategy more than personnel. Maybe, at sixty-four, Jake Gaither had to break his routine. Maybe he couldn't run teams into submission anymore. Maybe he could no longer assume blowouts, or just plain victories. Gaither had been so sure of winning that FAMU didn't even practice a two-minute offense. He still had his receivers lining up in a three-point stance, as if they were interior blockers; for all their speed, they weren't a threat to catch any kind of pass until they straightened upright.

Meanwhile, opponents such as Tennessee State, Texas Southern, and Alabama A&M were running pro-style offenses and ringing up big points against FAMU—26, 29, 34, and 45 in games during the 1965 and 1966 seasons. Because the Rattlers threw the ball so sparingly in practice, their defensive backs were unprepared for gunslingers such as Eldridge Dickey and Onree Jackson. Griffin's defense had given up nearly nineteen points a game over the past two years, an embarrassment for a coach who had shut out twenty-five opponents between 1957 and 1962. So the answer to the offense's predictability was also the answer to the defense's vulnerability. Ending FAMU's sole reliance on the split-line T, Gaither began scripting plays from the I formation, which had been devised by one of the geniuses of the balanced offense, USC assistant coach Don Coryell. This year, the Rattlers would pass by choice, not rare necessity.

Gaither had, in effect, two starting quarterbacks in Ken Riley and Elroy Morand. In the 1966 season, they had set a FAMU record for passing yardage, though partly because the Rattlers were falling behind or surrendering too many points. This year, FAMU would pass to seize the advantage. What was the team slogan, after all? *We will strike! And strike! And strike again!* Morand gave Gaither the kind of classic drop-back quarterback he had rarely had; one of his many nicknames was "Rifle-arm." Riley brandished a rifle of his own—he could throw seventy yards—but his special talent was scrambling. He had rushed for 288 yards in 1966 and thrown best while improvising. For downfield threats, the quarterbacks had two sprinters as wide receivers, Melvin Jones and Eugene Milton, and an uncommonly swift and mobile tight end, John Eason. He had scored seven touchdowns on thirty catches the previous season, and received the unlikely nickname "Eydie" when Pete Griffin, mindful of the slinky nightclub singer, marveled during one practice, "That sucker has sweet moves like Eydie Gormé."

Perceptive as he was about human nature, Gaither knew how to productively exploit the rivalry between Morand and Riley, pit them against one another to elicit the best from each. The very day in 1965 when Riley had arrived in Tallahassee as a freshman, sophomore Morand had ordered the newcomer to unpack and hang up Morand's clothes. And what clothes Morand had—silk slacks, matching shirts, white shoes. He drove a Pontiac GTO. All the goods came from the money he earned working summers in a Detroit auto plant, and the style was celebrated in his nickname of "Sporty Mo."

Riley, in contrast, was studious and self-possessed. He spent his college summers hauling sacks of fertilizer, and used the evenings after preseason practice for writing letters to his hometown sweetheart, Barbara Moore. He picked up vocabulary from the Word Power column in *Reader's Digest.* Since his childhood years in church as the grandson of a preacher, he remembered, in order, the sixty-six books of the Bible. That prodigious recall helped him with both the FAMU playbook and his psychology classes. On the football field, though, Riley metamorphosed from humble to flamboyant, dodging the pass rush with twists and pivots, changing direction in a blink, swiveling his hips until it seemed like his thighs were parallel to the ground, leaving defenders' hands grasping at air.

The hometowns of each quarterback only heightened the competition. Riley was from Bartow and Morand from Ocala, a hundred miles apart in central Florida, joined by the main bus route. Each place had its own posse on the FAMU team. Eason, Milton, and guard Zeke Sims hailed from Ocala, while defensive backs Nathaniel James and Major Hazelton and tackle Donald Smith were from Bartow. All the woofing that went back to high school resounded among the Rattlers.

Throughout preseason practice and two intrasquad games, Gaither split the snaps between Morand and Riley. Though Morand had better statistics in the scrimmages—four touchdown passes and one touchdown run to one of each for Riley—what worked most effectively was the contrast between them and the way that contrast forced a defense to repeatedly adapt. There was no reason not to platoon quarterbacks, as Gaither saw it; he platooned every other position.

The two quarterbacks, for their part, deferred to Gaither's judgment. While they vied against each other, they never challenged him, never questioned his wisdom and authority. To run afoul of Jake Gaither was to risk losing your place on the team, and with it your college scholarship and the entire future a diploma represented. If you messed up at college, you disgraced your whole family, wasted every sacrifice your mama and daddy had made. On top of all that, you lost your student deferment from the draft, put yourself in line to be 1-A and shipping out soon for Vietnam. Against all that, neither Riley nor Morand could even dream of creating a controversy by demanding more playing time. For what? A better shot at playing in the pros? Everybody knew there were no black quarterbacks in the pros. But there were plenty of black teachers and coaches and principals in Florida who had ridden their FAMU football scholarship to a respected and respectable way of life.

In the second week of September, Gaither named Morand and Riley cocaptains. The next Saturday, September 16, FAMU opened its season against Allen University, effectively a warm-up against an overmatched adversary. The true test awaited the following Saturday, when South Carolina State came to Tallahassee in a revenge game for the 1966 upset.

The Laboratory for Manhood

+ + +

In more arenas than the athletic, Jake Gaither entered the 1967 season at
the risk of becoming obsolete. Everything he had believed and trusted
about his race and his nation, his lifelong commitment to gradualism
and self-improvement, suddenly looked insufficient, at least to his critics.
He had been born fewer than forty years after slavery ended, but his players had grown up in the civil rights era. And this summer, of all summers,
the patience of young blacks was running out.

Riots had struck Memphis, Newark, Washington, DC, Buffalo,
Milwaukee, Atlanta, Tampa, Cincinnati, and, most destructively of all,
Detroit. The *Pittsburgh Courier,* hardly a radical newspaper, published
a page of photographs under the cautionary headline "The Nation's
Ghettos Speak!" Two of Gaither's regulars, Elroy Morand and John
Eason, experienced the Detroit turmoil during their summer jobs in
the auto plants. Eason was driving through downtown when the violence broke out; he saw people running down the street with looted
TVs, and there were flames shooting out of store windows. The next
day, walking home from a playground basketball game, he was stopped
at gunpoint by the police. Every fear that his southern upbringing had
instilled about white cops set off internal alarms. But this incident felt
even worse because it took place in the North, where a black man was
supposed to be safe.

The month after Detroit's riot, a FAMU graduate named George Cal-
vin Bess vanished while organizing in Mississippi for the Student Nonvi-
olent Coordinating Committee. The presumption, soon confirmed, was
that he'd been murdered. Word spread in Tallahassee that SNCC's leader,
Stokely Carmichael, the sloganeer of "Black Power," would be coming to
campus. One of Carmichael's fellow firebrands, H. Rap Brown, had been
barnstorming the South all summer in advance of standing trial in New
Orleans for gun possession. Just a few weeks earlier, he'd proclaimed that
"violence is as American as cherry pie."

What Gaither probably didn't know was that many of his players, even as they revered him, could not resist a fascination with Carmichael, even a secret affinity, for giving voice to the anger they could feel welling up in themselves. They admired Muhammad Ali, too, who had just been convicted of draft evasion, and former Cleveland Browns star Jim Brown, who was talking about black athletes forming a union.

All this flux, all this change, all this anger Gaither put under the umbrella term "the new breed." The new breed was marijuana and militancy and Afros. The new breed was "kids who didn't have anything better to do than rebel against discipline, rebel against the establishment, rebel against the status quo." Gaither issued rules against beards and mustaches; he instructed his assistant coaches to find and punish the pot smokers. But he was a man trying to hold back a flood tide, and he was two political generations behind it.

In 1956, the year after Rev. Dr. Martin Luther King Jr. had led a bus boycott in Montgomery, blacks in Tallahassee declared a similar campaign. Then, in 1960, they sat in at the city's Woolworth's lunch counter. Three years later, they picketed the segregated Florida Theater—fittingly enough while the featured film was *The Ugly American*. In all those campaigns, FAMU students volunteered as foot soldiers. And in every battle, Jake Gaither, like most of the university's leadership, kept his distance. Only one time during the trial of Patricia Due, a student who helped lead the theater protests, did Gaither enigmatically appear at the county courthouse. Whether he was showing solidarity with idealists or keeping tabs on troublemakers, no one knew.

What Gaither knew was that Tallahassee's activists, even the ardent Rattler fans among them, privately disparaged him as an Uncle Tom. He resigned from the church pastored by local civil rights leader Rev. C. K. Steele and felt sufficiently defensive to remark in one speech, "There are no Benedict Arnolds in our race." During the bus boycott, Gaither told Bobby Lang, who was then a player, "I can't tell you what to do, but I plead to your conscience not to get in trouble." Even so, the provocations were too much for some of his players. A linebacker in the early 1960s, Alton White, joined the movement after seeing police pull a black girl out of church by her hair. During the picketing he was teargassed, beaten with a coatrack, and jailed overnight. One of the coach's favorites, Willie Galimore, made civil rights history as the first black person to register at the Ponce de Leon Motor Lodge in St. Augustine, the focus of major protests in 1964.

Nobody needed to lecture Jake Gaither on segregation's indignities. When he and Sadie drove north to visit relatives, there wasn't a gas station bathroom they could use until Washington, DC. Riding the team bus to road games, the Rattlers had to hide in orange groves to relieve themselves and get meals from a black mortician who sold takeout. After driving all night to Ohio for a coaching clinic, Gaither and Griffin had been refused service at a diner, and instructed to go the back way into the kitchen. "I don't eat in anybody's kitchen," Gaither answered, and they left, stomachs empty but principles intact.

Recognizing racism, though, was not tantamount to confronting it. Gaither knew firsthand that "trouble" could mean jailhouse beatings, burning crosses, the lynch mob's noose. He took seriously the vow he had made to his players' parents. Their boy would go to class, go to church, get his degree, become somebody. Not even a righteous cause could be allowed to interfere. Gaither sounded a lot like one of his idols, Booker T. Washington, when he said, "We must throw our shoulders back and feel that God gave us the potential to do an excellent job. If the Negro is a ditch digger, I want him to be the best in town. If he is a doctor, lawyer, teacher, or preacher, I want him to be the best in his community. If he is a carpenter, plumber, auto mechanic, or mason, I want him to be tops."

Gaither's antidote to white hatred was black institutions for black people. He would never concede that a black school or business or church was inferior to its white counterpart purely because of color. Even as he welcomed the legal victories over segregation, he worried aloud what their implementation would mean—the loss of everything black folk had spent decades building for themselves. Already, as schools in Florida belatedly and begrudgingly integrated, black principals were being bucked down to assistant, black teachers were being laid off, black coaches were being replaced. As black athletes got recruited by white colleges, Gaither despaired of them being treated as modern-day chattel, used up and thrown away. What white coach would care about his players as full human beings the way he did?

In his own way, Gaither was a black nationalist, so conservative he was simultaneously radical. It just didn't look that way in 1967. Middle-aged moderates such as C. K. Steele and Martin Luther King Jr. were being pilloried by the likes of Carmichael and Brown as accommodationists, pious windbags. How far behind the curve of history did that leave Jake Gaither, who was older and more cautious than the ministerial leadership of the civil rights movement?

The week before preseason football practice began, Thaddeus T. Stokes addressed this dilemma in his column in the *Atlanta Daily World*. "The 'middle class' Negro is really 'in the middle,'" he wrote. "He has not been accepted into the mainstream by those at which the social revolution is aimed. And now the revolutionists are beginning to reject him." He concluded the essay by lamenting, "The tragedy of the situation is that the middle class Negro is not the real culprit. He is a victim of his own insecurity."

In the face of such criticism, Gaither presented a steadfast face to his coaches and players. All of them, though, were being whipsawed. Day to day that summer, the news for black America veered between the hopeful and the bleak. The US Senate approved the nomination of Thurgood Marshall to be the first black justice on the nation's Supreme Court; but all eleven opposing votes were from southern senators, including supposed moderates such as Sam Ervin and Ernest Hollings. Fifteen black candidates won primary elections in Mississippi, but the state forced them into runoffs, which every one lost. The Supreme Court struck down the laws in sixteen states prohibiting interracial marriage, and the daughter of Dean Rusk, the secretary of state, was engaged to a black classmate at Stanford; but Rusk himself, a Georgian fearing political backlash, offered his resignation to President Lyndon B. Johnson. Bill Cosby was starring in the hit television series *I Spy* and Sidney Poitier in the movie *To Sir, with Love.* The deep soul music made together by blacks and whites in the studios of Memphis and Muscle Shoals—Aretha Franklin, Otis Redding, Sam & Dave, Booker T & the MGs—was topping both the R&B and pop charts. But the jazz singer and pianist Les McCann, in Atlanta for a gig, was turned away from the downtown YMCA.

In the late summer of 1967, Eddie Jackson, an army veteran in his midtwenties, was starting his second season as the sports information director for FAMU. Even as he threw himself into his "dream job," he chastised himself for it. "Always in the back of your mind—and sometimes in the front—is, 'What are you doing for the cause?'" he later recalled. "Then you wake up in the morning and go back to work. The belief that we were making black men—doing our best in an indirect way—seemed suddenly insignificant."

The tight end John Eason felt more confusion than doubt. "There were a lot of different messages," he said of the times. "There was a message from outside Florida A&M, which was a radical message. You were getting a message from white America that you're not good enough to go downtown. And in the community of A&M, you had Coach Gaither talking about your dignity and getting your education."

In the days before the Rattlers opened their season, the preseason polls for small-college football appeared. Coming off two disappointing years in a row, FAMU did not even rank. For a coach with Jake Gaither's record, the snub was a vote of no confidence, a more formal version of the verdict that Sadie had heard once from a heckler sitting near her in the stands: "Jake's getting too old." Those blows were only part of the problems he faced in a football season kicking off in the wake of the "Long, Hot Summer."

Jake Gaither needed his own kind of double victory to prove he still mattered, on the field and in the struggle. His new emphasis on passing with twin quarterbacks answered only one part of the challenge. But if FAMU could return to the top echelon of black college football this season, then Gaither would have the gridiron credibility to address the second part, the political and racial part. What nobody around him knew—not his friends, not his players, not his coaches, certainly not his critics, maybe just Sadie—was that Gaither had a plan to play his Rattlers against a white team, any white team that would take the dare. And he had a plan, too, for how to pull it off in the face of the South's persistent, defiant segregation. So maybe there was at least one advantage to being sixty-four. Jake Gaither had reached the age to establish his legacy.

3

SPARED FOR SOMETHING

Grambling, Late Summer 1967

n a Saturday afternoon during a stifling Louisiana August, James Harris planned a respite from his weeklong regimen of classwork and football drills. As quarterback and captain of the Grambling College football team, Harris had stayed on campus virtually all summer to prepare for his most important season yet with Coach Eddie Robinson. Until about Labor Day, when formal practices would begin and Robinson would be permitted under collegiate rules to participate, Harris was essentially serving as the head coach's surrogate, his instrument, leading practices after class every afternoon and until dusk fell.

On this particular weekend, though, Harris had brought his laundry and appetite home to his mother in Monroe, and now he set about rounding up a couple of college friends for a trip to Shreveport. Their classmate Ralph Garr, the star of Grambling's baseball team, was playing there in a small-college tournament game.

It was typical of Harris to take charge even of a road trip. Now twenty and heading into his junior year, he was the unquestioned leader among Grambling's players. He was sturdy enough for a lineman at 6-4 and 210, intense in his gaze. Even in high school, where he started for three years, teammates had called him "the Old Man." More often, people knew him by "Shack," the shortened form of another nickname, which had been bestowed by his minister father. It came from Meshach in the Book of Daniel, one of the three Jews so devout they were willing to be thrown into a fiery furnace rather than bow down before the idol of a pagan god.

For someone so young, Harris had already learned some firsthand lessons, too, about mortality. His father, Nashall, had died during Harris's senior year in high school. Two years before that, one of Harris's teammates had been stabbed to death inside school in an argument over a girl. It happened on the day the football players had received their state championship jackets, a day meant for celebration instead of mourning. Those losses had aged Harris, left him more measured, more resolute. The future, he understood, was not assured. You had to seize it and shape it.

Harris had a sense of his own destiny and a sober comprehension of all the obstacles in destiny's path. He had come to Grambling not only to win games and championships, which he could have done at plenty of schools. He had come to play quarterback, and to be groomed for playing quarterback in the pros, something no black man had ever been allowed to do for more than a few sporadic games. Quarterback, after all, was a thinking man's position, a position for grace under pressure. And black athletes, as the routine reasoning went, were all sinew and instinct, missing something upstairs. Whether Harris got the opportunity to prove otherwise, to make history in a real way, would depend mightily on the numbers he and Grambling put up in his final two seasons. Harris knew one truth, and it was true about a lot more than football: for a black man to get an equal chance with a white, that black man had to be twice as good.

So Harris had persuaded dozens of Grambling players to spend the summer of 1967 on campus, where they could work out informally until official practice with the coaches commenced. When one freshman receiver from downstate tried to back out and stay home, not realizing the importance of this extra training, Harris simply told him, "We want to win some games."

The player came and joined in the program, which was as austere as he'd feared. During the days, some of the players, like Harris, took courses toward their degrees. Others held jobs on campus, manual labor mostly, picking peaches in the college orchard or nailing tin roofs onto buildings or sweeping floors and hauling trash. Either way, as student or worker, the players were allowed to stay in the few dorms that remained open during the summer.

Five o'clock every afternoon, Harris gathered them on the practice field, a rectangle of sandy red-clay soil on the far side of Grambling's stadium, right next to the rolling, forested hills. Beneath a blanket of damp heat, the receivers, runners, linebackers, and defensive backs assembled in their cleats and gym shorts, and Harris ran them through seven-on-seven drills, essentially a passing scrimmage without interior linemen or tackling. Sometimes Grambling's head coach, Eddie Robinson, sat in the top row of stadium bleachers, a silhouette against the western sun, peering down over the railing onto the practice, ticking off the days until September, when he could take charge.

Harris tried to finish the drills before seven o'clock, because seven was when the cafeteria closed. If you missed your meal there, and if like most players you had no car and little money, you walked the quarter mile to "the village," a knot of stores along Main Street. Maybe you went in with some other guys on a pack of bologna and a loaf of bread; maybe you put down your quarter for a honey bun, which in a bittersweet joke everybody called "Grambling steak."

Once dinner ended and the sun went down, the only amusement

was what the players could create, as frugally as possible. They took turns feeding the jukebox in the student union for the latest hits by James Brown or the Temptations, five songs for a quarter. They shot pool. They played dominoes. They dealt out hand after hand of bid whist and penny poker and tonk, Harris's favorite card game. He required everyone he beat to sign a notebook he kept, admitting to defeat. Even a department chairman's signature was in it.

One night, Harris was bragging about how he could beat Essex Johnson, a swift running back, in a forty-yard dash. Johnson started jawing back about how everybody knew Shack wasn't a sprinter. Before long, all the players had clambered onto the street outside their dorm. "On your mark," someone called. Harris and Johnson lined up. "Get set." In the prolonged second before "Go," Harris took off, and Johnson was never able to catch up. And when he objected—*You cheated, man, you jumped the gun*—Harris imperturbably quoted from Coach Robinson. "The first one to draw is the last one to die," he said, as all the other players cracked up.

So the days and weeks went by, with this mixture of frat house and hermitage, and the underlying knowledge of the imminent season, the purpose for all the isolation and sacrifice. So the time went, anyway, until the particular Saturday afternoon when Harris decided to see Ralph Garr play ball.

He rounded up one of his Grambling roommates, Edgar Arnold, and a football teammate from both high school and college, Delles Howell. They piled into the ten-year-old Chevy that Harris's grandmother had helped him buy, and pulled onto Interstate 20, the fast new highway. Until it had opened, the drive from Monroe to Shreveport, roughly a hundred miles, took nearly three hours along two-lane Route 80. Route 80 was hills, curves, stoplights, and being stuck behind a lumber truck for what seemed like forever.

Interstate 20 had another advantage over Route 80, at least for drivers of a certain color. It was a federal highway, extending from South Carolina to Texas, with rest stops open to travelers of all races. It wasn't the province of shopkeepers who could turn away blacks or of local cops who could harass them. Another one of Harris's roommates, Leamon Gray, once had been driving on Route 80 with his father when their car was pulled over by an officer, who pressed a gun to the father's temple. The previous summer, on a stretch of Route 80 just outside the town of Calhoun, the Klan had burned a cross. This summer, with civil rights activity spreading into the backwaters of northern Louisiana, a car containing three young black men could easily attract the wrong kind of attention.

Steering free of it, Harris headed west on the interstate. Howell sat beside him in the front, and Arnold grabbed the middle of the backseat, leaning forward to join in the conversation. They talked some about Garr and baseball games they'd watched at Grambling. Mostly, though, they talked about football, the coming year. Grambling had gone 6-2-1 in 1966 and shared its conference title. For Grambling, for an Eddie Robinson team, 6-2-1 wasn't good enough. An Eddie Robinson team expected to win every time. Then there were the personal goals, the prospect of pro football. Delles's older brothers, Mike and Lane, had gone from Grambling to the NFL. Last season, Grambling had more alumni in the AFL than any college in the nation, beating out even Michigan State and USC. Something like thirty Grambling guys were in NFL or AFL camps this summer. And, of course, Harris had his dream of breaking the color line at quarterback.

As Harris drove, a drizzle began to fall. He dropped the speed from seventy, the legal limit, in deference to the slick road and the Chevy's worn tires. Then, changing lanes on the outskirts of Calhoun, the car abruptly fishtailed. Harris swung the wheel, trying to straighten out, but instead sending the car into a spin. In the backseat, Edgar Arnold started reciting the Lord's Prayer. Harris could feel the car rocking as it pinwheeled around, the tires starting to lift off the road. He fought with the wheel as if he were fighting with a snake, trying to force the car from rolling. Off the interstate's right shoulder, a ravine dropped thirty feet. That way was injury and the waste of the 1967 football season before it had even begun. That way was disability and the end of playing quarterback in the pros. That way was death.

Somehow the car skidded left into the center median, where the ground was soft and muddy from earlier rains. Sinking into the muck, the Chevy lurched to a stop. An oak tree stood inches from the front fender.

Harris and Howell and Arnold, none of them entirely sure they were still alive, stared into each other's astonished eyes. Their hearts beat wildly. This kind of pulse wasn't the rapid rhythm from doing wind sprints at practice; it was ragged, irregular, impossible to calm. For what seemed like a long time, the three friends said nothing, listening to their shallow, gasping breaths.

Finally, Harris spoke. "This is a message," he said. "We've been spared." He looked at Howell. "Del, if we didn't die, I know the Lord got something for us to do in September."

+ + +

Seven days into September and nine before the Grambling Tigers opened their season against Alcorn A&M, Eddie Robinson stalked the practice field. At age forty-eight, standing six-two and weighing two hundred, he still looked capable of suiting up. His muscles rose from waist to shoulders in a tapered triangle; his forearms retained their heft from his teenage years as a boxer; and he was nimble enough afoot for his unlikely hobby of tap dancing. Beneath a canvas hat, his eyes blazed. His gaze took in everything. Robinson didn't bother with the observation tower some head coaches favored, because he was temperamentally unable to stay still or detached for very long. He was dying to coach every position.

Robinson had scripted this practice, like every other, in meticulous detail. He carried a handwritten "Ready Sheet" listing the drills in fifteen-minute intervals and diagramming the particular plays he wanted to run through. He held a "Must List" of the skills demanded of players at every given position. He was not shy about stepping into the midst of a drill to correct a mistake by demonstrating the right way himself. One minute he would be riding the two-man blocking sled as linemen slammed it across the turf. Then he'd be wetting his fingers, shunting aside a quarterback, and throwing thirty passes in a row to receivers working on their patterns. Next thing, he'd jump between the dummies into a tackling drill to show a defender how to get the leverage to lay a runner flat.

With his whistle and clipboard, Robinson moved from station to station during the three hours of practice, covering every position group—linemen and backs on both sides of the ball, linebackers, special teams, the six or seven quarterbacks always in camp. Leaning forward, hands on knees, muscles tensing, he orchestrated every variation of scrimmaging—seven-on-seven, eleven-on-eleven, line versus line.

Through it all, Robinson kept urging, imploring, challenging, chiding. He scowled, clenched his fists, grabbed one player's jersey sleeve, whacked another's shoulder pads. As if working a wad of gum, his mouth never stopped moving. He did not curse, at least not more than "Damn it to hell," because he had a fuller and more correct vocabulary for motivation and manipulation, whatever the occasion demanded. The more insistent he grew, the higher his voice went, ending somewhere between a plea and a whine.

"He's big as a bear, mean as a honey bun," he might say of a defensive lineman. Or threaten a starter who'd been coasting, "I don't wanna bite the hand that feeds me, but don't let me find out I can win without you." Or turn his glare on the position coach for an oddly timid blocker and sputter in exasperation: "Coach him to do some *wrong*. Let him miss a day from Sunday school. Give him a brick, let him break the window out. I'll pay for it." Some of it was funny from a distance, or recounted later in the locker room, unless it was you who stayed on the ground too long to catch your breath after a tackle and Robinson grabbed a fistful of that sandy clay soil and hissed into your face, "Get up off the ground or I'll blind you."

When someone performed well, Robinson was just as quick and evocative in his praise. One time a backup receiver made a leaning, stretching grab on a square-out. "That kid looks like pork chops," the coach said, "but when he catch that ball, it's like sirloin steak." Robinson aimed to keep every player sharp and the fire of competition stoked. During the season he gave over Monday afternoons to a "grumblers' scrimmage" for all the reserves who complained they weren't getting enough playing time on Saturdays. On that proving ground, blood was known to flow.

Brutality, though, was never the point of an Eddie Robinson practice. Intimidation wasn't the point. The point was precision, precision and discipline, precision and discipline and execution. Even after twenty-six seasons and 162 wins, Robinson feared nothing more than carelessness. He was a man, after all, who wore a coat and tie on the sideline—people called him "the black pope"—and who still cut his own grass by hand with a push mower. Grambling had a playbook three inches thick, but the Tigers relied almost entirely on just twelve or fourteen plays. For nearly a decade by now, Robinson had used the wing-T offense created by Forest Evashevski, the coach of Iowa's Rose Bowl teams. The wing-T combined power plays such as fullback dives and halfback sweeps with misdirection trickery—counters that had a wingback running against the flow of the blocking. The few passing plays in Grambling's standard repertoire were play-action throws that tried to sucker a defense with fake handoffs.

After eight years of facing those same staples, none of Grambling's opponents was surprised by any of them. Robinson could not have cared less. His definition of dominance was to perform so flawlessly that Grambling could defeat a team that knew the Tigers' playbook by heart. More than defeat a challenger, Robinson wanted to break its will. During a game against Alcorn the previous season, James Harris had crouched under center only to hear the defenders shouting, "Here come the 126 counter." He called a time-out and jogged to the sideline to tell Robinson, "Coach, they know the play. They callin' out the play." Robinson grabbed Harris by the arm, pushing him back toward the huddle. "Coach, what play you want?" Harris asked, and Robinson answered, "126 counter." It went sixty yards for a touchdown. As Harris ran off the field, Robinson simply said, "Blocking and tackling. That's what the game is about."

So as the practice day proceeded, Robinson called for the seven-on-seven drill. He turned his Ready Sheet—actually a set of stapled pages—to the first of half a dozen plays selected for obsessive attention this day. He positioned himself five yards or so behind the fullback so he could see the offense unfold before him, the circles and triangles and arrows of his diagrams springing to life. The offense ran the play. He said, "Run it again." It ran the play a second time. He said, "Run it again." He might order fifteen or twenty repeats as the players and assistant coaches tried to correct whatever missed block or blown assignment had caught Robinson's eye, made him cry in that rising voice of his, "Boy, can't you see what you did wrong?" If the problems still persisted, Robinson would inflict his ultimate punishment: make the offense practice the trick play called "merry-go-round," which involved a triple reverse and a pass. By then the defenders were so angry and tired, someone would say in their huddle, "Let 'em run the play so we can go eat." Finally satisfied, Robinson would say only, "Let's move on."

The run-throughs culminated with the goal-line offense versus the goal-line defense, eleven on eleven. It was called a "thump" drill, because while tackling wasn't permitted, hitting anyone but the quarterback was. Sometimes, with the offense lined up, Robinson would call out the play to the defense. If anyone dared complain, he would say, "I don't care if they know it. Just execute it." Robert Atkins, who alternated between both sides of the drill as a safety on defense and a tight end on offense, got the message as indelibly as anyone. "We existed in this environment of indoctrination," he said in retrospect, "on what had to be done to win."

Last came the wind sprints. Robinson stood at one goal line, blew his whistle, and ten players went thundering a full hundred yards down the field. A few seconds later he blew again, and the next batch took off. Any player who'd broken Robinson's rule against cursing got an extra turn. With wave after wave, all those pounding cleats, a cloud of dust hung over the field. Through it, the players trudged toward the wood benches and wire-mesh stalls of the locker room, toward the liniment and salt pills and ice bags.

The linemen who had worn rubber suits to melt their off-season weight peeled them off now, and their sweat puddled on the floor. Others, undressing, winced at the slashes on their forearms and shins from sand burrs, the spiky weed that rambled over the practice field. Anyone who had been injured tried to hide the fact, because once you lost your position on a team as deep and talented as Grambling, you might never get it back. "We don't rebuild," Robinson put it. "We reload."

At six-thirty the next morning, Robinson marched through the players' dorms, clanging a cow bell and announcing, "Feet on the floor." After wake-up, he collected the players' meal cards, which could only be retrieved by showing up for breakfast. Once school got in session the next week, each position coach would be assigned to monitor the grades of his players. And every Sunday, Robinson dispatched an assistant to each of Grambling's churches to keep a list of which players attended. In these obligations resided no small amount of Robinson's autobiography.

+ + +

The most important addition to Grambling football during Eddie Robinson's years as head coach had never so much as put on a Tiger uniform. He was a marine veteran named Collie J. Nicholson, born and raised in the northern Louisiana town of Winnfield, who passed through Grambling in 1946 as he headed north to study journalism at the University of Wisconsin. Grambling's president, Ralph Waldo Emerson Jones, who doubled as the college's baseball coach, learned of Nicholson's skill as an outfielder and offered him a scholarship on the spot. He also assigned him to learn touch-typing from the college's business manager.

Typing skills aside, Nicholson was already a professional, and more than that, a politically astute pioneer. Ever since childhood, when he saw a playmate shot for accidentally venturing onto a white family's property,

Nicholson had refused to passively submit to racism. Serving in a segregated unit in the Pacific, he became the first black combat correspondent in marine history, syndicating his stories across America through the Associated Negro Press. Not long after moving to Grambling, he joined with a local minister and a shopkeeper to form the village's chapter of the NAACP. Even more bravely, Nicholson stayed in the NAACP after a state court in 1956 ordered the civil rights group to list its members, and the fear of retribution led the vast majority of them to quit.

Out of his talent and worldliness and racial consciousness, Nicholson concocted an audacious goal. Grambling could be for black Americans what Notre Dame was for Catholic Americans—an institution, deliberately parochial, that demonstrated its people's achievements and through them made the case for inclusion. Not Lincoln University, which had educated Thurgood Marshall and Langston Hughes; not Morehouse College, with its renowned presidents John Hope and Benjamin Mays; not Howard University, with Ralph Bunche and Alain Locke on its faculty—unassuming Grambling would represent the pride and hope of every Negro. And football, as at Notre Dame, would supply the means.

Very quickly, Robinson, Nicholson, and President Jones formed a triumvirate to plan and execute the strategy. Starting in the late 1940s, and for decades to come, they met for lunch in Jones's private dining room several times a week. Robinson's job was to field winning teams with student athletes who went to class and graduated. Jones's was to get money from the state, even if it meant debasing himself by manufacturing tears for legislators and bringing peaches and turkeys from Grambling's farm to the governor. Nicholson would sell, sell, sell.

He invented memorable nicknames for players. His articles added inches and pounds to their dimensions, straightened their wobbly passes into spirals. He sent dispatches about Grambling football by telegraph to four hundred black newspapers, and called in stories to the nearby white ones in Ruston, Monroe, and Shreveport that could not be bothered assigning a staff reporter to a Grambling game. Those articles, grandiose and florid in a Grantland Rice way, leaped off the page. Of one 1948 game, Nicholson wrote in emblematic fashion:

> The resurgent ghost of a fabulous Grambling College eleven, which only a week ago shedded its September stardust in the blow of an early October wind, hit the comeback trail here Saturday night in a most convincing manner, harpooning Texas State University, 61–0, with an auspicious display of power and speed.

The first major test of the plan involved a lineman named Paul Younger. After Younger scored an astonishing twenty-five touchdowns as a freshman on end-arounds from the single wing, Robinson moved him to halfback. Nicholson rechristened him Tank. He went on to compile sixty touchdowns in his career and to be named the black-college player of the year in 1948, his senior season. All of it would have remained invisible to the white sporting world except that one of Nicholson's articles made its way to the chief scout of the Los Angeles Rams. "I got me a plane ticket and a road map," the scout, Eddie Kotal, later recalled, "and I went to see that boy play."

Though the Rams did not draft Younger, and the entire NFL had only a single black player, Kotal went to sign him as a free agent. Robinson and Jones negotiated the deal by driving Kotal around the backwoods outside Grambling, pushing bottle after bottle of soda on him, and pretending they knew of no nearby toilet. Squirming in his seat, Kotal finally offered to pay Younger $6,000, making him the first player ever from a black college to sign with the NFL.

On the day Robinson waited with Younger at the Grambling depot to board the "Colored" train car for the journey west, the coach, not yet thirty years old, dared to speak with the sweep of history. "You have to make it," he told Younger. "If you don't make it, they can say they took the best we've got, and he wasn't good enough."

Even as Younger became a star, pro football integrated only in a fitful, halfhearted way, and Robinson and his college remained obscure.

+ + +

In 1955, after nearly fifteen years at Grambling, the coach finally could afford to buy a brick house and a used car. The same year, Robinson talked a sports equipment company into selling him a blocking sled on credit, the first one his team ever had. When Robinson began to attend conventions of the American Football Coaches Association in the early 1950s, one of the few blacks to do so, the mere name of his school would bring laughter. "Gambling College? Grumbling College? What college was that?" One Grambling player called Robinson from an NFL training camp, embarrassed that none of his teammates knew where Grambling was. "They'll know," the coach promised. "They will know."

Robinson set about locating those whites capable of treating him as an equal and advancing his football acumen. During several summers in the 1950s, he studied for his master's degree at the University of Iowa. In Iowa City, Robinson spent hours going over physiology with his faculty mentor, Charles McCloy, a former missionary in China, and learning the wing-T from the Hawkeyes' offensive coach, Jerry Burns, who had grown up in racially mixed Detroit. Doris met friends in a café with no color barrier, and the couple's son Eddie Jr. played pickup basketball on integrated courts. These seasonal tastes of freedom were not enough to entice Eddie Robinson to leave all that was familiar at Grambling—and Iowa, for that matter, had no blacks on its own coaching staff—but they taught him that the color line was not the determinant of human decency.

Even in Ruston, a place so hostile that many Grambling students and faculty avoided it, Robinson found a kindred soul in the form of W. A. "Dub" Jones, a hometown star in high school who went on to play halfback for the Cleveland Browns. Though he was a product of the segregated South, Jones grew to be appalled by seeing his black teammates turned away from the Browns' hotel every time they played in Baltimore. From Jones, Robinson picked up the intricacies of the Cleveland passing offense led by quarterback Otto Graham. From Robinson, Jones received tips on which Grambling players the Browns ought to draft, starting with a lineman on the 1955 team named Willie Davis. When the local Klan klavern heard of the men's friendship, it sent a member to Jones's home with a warning. Referring to the lumberyard that the family owned, the Klansman said, "You know, you got a lot of dry wood here."

Whatever it took to win, whatever it took to be better, that was what Robinson intended to do. Normally a creature of habit, he dropped any habit that cost him losses. The winter after Grambling had given up nearly 150 points in its last four games of the 1950 season was the winter when Robinson first joined the American Football Coaches Association for some expert instruction on defense. After a 14-13 mark over three seasons in the late 1950s revealed that his beloved single wing was archaic, Robinson installed the wing-T. In nearly a quarter century at Grambling, leading into the 1967 season, Robinson had won nearly 75 percent of the time, a record that compared well with Bear Bryant's or Woody Hayes's, not that much of the white world noticed.

Eventually, though, Robinson's results and Collie Nicholson's words drew the attention of the handful of black scouts in pro football. One of them, Lloyd Wells, had been Nicholson's roommate before the war. Another, Bill Nunn, doubled as a sportswriter for the *Pittsburgh Courier* and selected its Black All-America team. After retiring from the NFL in 1958, Younger began scouting for the Los Angeles Rams. Buddy Young did the same for his former team, the Baltimore Colts, until he was hired as the first black executive in the NFL commissioner's office. Some of the bolder owners and coaches in the NFL—Paul Brown in Cleveland, George Halas of the Chicago Bears, Vince Lombardi with the Green Bay Packers—began drafting Grambling players, though usually in the low-risk, low-pay low rounds. With the founding of the rival American Football League in 1960, mavericks such as Al Davis of the Oakland Raiders and Lamar Hunt of the Kansas City Chiefs aggressively competed for Grambling's stars. Willie Brown went to Denver and then Oakland, Ernie Ladd to the San Diego Chargers, Buck Buchanan to the Chiefs as the first pick in the 1963 AFL draft. The AFL, as Bill Nunn put it, was the closest thing pro football had to Branch Rickey.

Meanwhile, a sole white journalist was discovering Grambling. Jerry Izenberg had grown up during the Depression in working-class Newark hearing his father's stories of battling against anti-Semitism, sometimes literally, as the only Jewish baseball player on several pro teams. Adding ideology to intuition, Izenberg joined a Communist Party youth group while attending college. Although he soon dropped the dogma, he held on to his social conscience as a sportswriter for the *New York Herald Tribune* and the *Newark Star-Ledger* and a writer for television documentaries.

Looking over pro football rosters early in the 1964 season, Izenberg was astonished to discover that Grambling had more players in the leagues than Notre Dame, and he proposed an article to the *Saturday Evening Post*. Ultimately, the editors there, disinterested in what they disparaged as "sociology," killed the piece. But in the course of reporting it, Izenberg spent weeks with the Grambling team, getting to know Nicholson, Robinson, and President Jones. Back in the New York area, he talked about Grambling to his friend and sometimes collaborator Howard Cosell.

In the late fall of 1964, shortly after Grambling had finished its games for the year, Cosell invited Robinson onto his ABC radio show. Much like Izenberg, Cosell was a rarity for his time, a sports commentator with a Phi Beta Kappa key, a law degree from NYU, and an abiding interest in political issues. He also had a flair for provocation. All those traits came into play when he interviewed Robinson.

The coach and the radio host met as civil rights issues pervaded the news. By a vote of Congress and thirty-eight state legislatures, all but one in the North, a constitutional amendment was about to be enacted outlawing the poll tax that southern states had routinely deployed to turn away black voters. President Lyndon B. Johnson had thrown his legislative muscle and popular mandate into pushing through the civil rights bill introduced shortly before John F. Kennedy's assassination in November 1963. The measure, the most sweeping federal initiative for racial equality since Emancipation itself, was headed for a vote in the House of Representatives early in the new year.

Meanwhile, in the sporting world, the influx of black players in the pro football leagues over the previous decade, rather than ending the segregation of the game, had thrown it into more precise relief. The NFL and AFL still had no black players at the three positions that required the greatest intelligence and the most frequent on-the-field decisions. There was no black center, who would make the blocking assignments. There was no black middle linebacker, who would align the defense. And there was no black quarterback, who would call the plays and read the coverage and choose the right option under a defense's duress. Blacks, the unspoken assumption went, simply weren't smart enough. And the de facto ban on black players at these thinking-man's positions mocked every bit of optimism Robinson espoused about America.

"You've been in the profession some thirty or forty years and you've had pretty good success," Cosell said to Robinson, starting off innocuously. Then he tilted the studio microphone toward the coach and continued, "Do you feel, after this long tenure coaching, that you have the ability to train a black quarterback, a black American, who could go into the NFL?"

Robinson said yes.

"Well," Cosell said, persisting, "what do you base that on?"

Robinson could have spoken of his own prowess as a quarterback. He could have trumpeted his record at Grambling. Instead he thought back to the coaching clinics he had attended, back to the very first one, when he and Ruben Turner from Leland rode the train to Chicago, and Eddie, going north for the first time in his life, had a basket of fried chicken from his mother and a clutch of spending money pinned into his pants to protect it from big-city pickpockets. All those clinics over all those years were part of Robinson's endless campaign of betterment, the central mission of his life.

"I base it on the fact," Robinson answered Cosell, "that since 1941, every coach who was worth anything, I heard him. I've got a piece of everybody. If anybody could coach a quarterback, I think I could."

With that dare and that promise, Robinson flew back to Louisiana. Before driving from the airport to his home in Grambling, he paid a visit to the frame house at 1413 Dilling Street in Monroe.

+   +   +

On the Wednesday afternoon of August 28, 1963, James Harris sat in the living room of his family's home at 1413 Dilling Street in Monroe, staring into the black-and-white television. His grandmother Lorene had bought it with her earnings from a Laundromat, and as one of the few sets in the black neighborhood of Bryant's Addition it usually attracted a bunch of James's friends for popcorn and *Gunsmoke*. Now both of Harris's parents and his older sister joined him in the room, all of them keenly and quietly attuned to the scene on the screen—throngs of people, tiny as squares of confetti, gathered in front of the Lincoln Memorial in Washington for a civil rights rally.

Just a month past his sixteenth birthday, Harris hoped he could somehow spot the Brass brothers, his classmates at Carroll High School, the two kids his age already involved in the movement. His father, Nashall, a Baptist minister, looked on with warier eyes. He'd been hearing reports from his fellow preachers about the buses of activists from Louisiana that had been stopped on the way to Washington by Ku Klux Klansmen, claiming they were searching for "escaped prisoners." After a long silence Rev. Harris said, as much to himself as to anyone else, "It's a wonder a whole lot of people didn't get killed."

More than two hours into the rally, after Marian Anderson and Mahalia Jackson had sung, after A. Philip Randolph and Medgar Evers's widow had spoken, after some rabbis and priests had taken their turns at the microphone, the Reverend Dr. Martin Luther King Jr. rose to deliver his address. For the first ten or twelve minutes, he preached with the cadences and metaphors that Harris as a minister's son easily recognized. Then he started to repeat one particular phrase about having a dream. The dream he invoked, of equality and conciliation, reminded Harris of the sermons he'd heard from his father during worship services and revival meetings at St. Mary's Baptist. All his life in that church, he'd been hearing about how the Bible taught that everybody, all people, black and white, were God's children.

"I have a dream," King continued in his incantatory way, "that my four little children will one day live in a nation where they will not be judged by the color of their skin but by the content of their character."

Harris felt jolted. It was almost the way a backslider in church got "convicted" as he heard words in a sermon that were delivered to the whole congregation yet directed solely, specially, secretly just at him. King's words had not uncovered any sin or shame hidden in Harris, but rather his deepest, most impossible desire. In the coming month, Harris would begin his junior year at Carroll High School, returning as the starting quarterback for a team that had gone 12-0 as state champions the previous fall. His dream was to play professional football, and the reality that obstructed it was the absence of a single black quarterback in either league. Lately he had even been thinking of asking Carroll's coach to switch him to defensive back so he'd have a better shot someday at a major college and ultimately the pros. Now King's words told him change was coming, not in the hereafter, not in some distant, redeemed era, but in proximate, imminent time. "I had no chance, I knew that," Harris would explain much later. "But then I started listening to that speech."

Harris had grown up on the receiving end of conflicting messages from his parents about being black in a segregated time and place. He was supposed to be proud but also to be submissive, to know the rules but also stand his ground, to recognize injustice but turn the other cheek, and to do it all under the unique pressure of being a preacher's kid scrutinized by the whole chattering neighborhood. Wherever he looked, as far back as he could recall, Harris had seen the face of white supremacy. He had seen it in the crosses burned outside the Mount Nebo and St. Paul Methodist churches on the Saturdays that local bigots called "niggers' night." He had seen it in the hand-me-down books, no longer worthy of white pupils, that he got at school. He had seen it when the cops would barge into houses in Bryant's Addition on the pretext that somebody's dog didn't have a license, and before it all was over that somebody had been beaten up and the dog shot dead.

Even the subtler forms of inequality cut deep. On a lot of nights, Harris sat on his front porch with his friends and heard the faint echo of an announcer calling out the lineups from the baseball field in Bernstein Park. An irrigation canal, bisecting the park, defined the racial border in this part of Monroe. On the far side, the white side, American Legion teams played in real uniforms. Sometimes Harris sneaked up to the outfield fence, tantalized by the simple pleasures forbidden to blacks. Sometimes, with his buddies, he ventured onto the deserted diamond to scavenge a broken bat, which they would nail back together for their own sandlot games.

Harris's parents offered examples of perseverance, sacrifice, the long view. The son of sharecroppers from a family of nine, Rev. Harris worked days in a furniture factory while pastoring on nights and weekends. His wife, Lula, was the nurse for a white doctor, A. G. McHenry Jr., drawing blood and giving shots for the Negro patients required to come in through the back door and steer clear of the white waiting room. While neither of James's parents had finished high school, they equipped their home with a typewriter and a two-thousand-page dictionary, which Rev. Harris consulted every Saturday night as he drafted his Sunday-morning sermon. By the time James Harris entered high school in 1961, his older brother, Nashall Jr., was making a career in the army, and his sister Lucille was finishing nursing school. As for James, his parents repeatedly told him that he was expected to get a college diploma, the first one in the family.

So he diligently earned As year upon year, and he learned typing and penmanship from Lucille. After spending a couple of summers picking cotton—two dollars for a hundred pounds, and James could rarely harvest more than fifty, bent over in that withering heat—he appreciated the value of book learning in every aching muscle. "Get your education," Lula told James. "You don't wanna work in the kitchen. You don't wanna work in the fields. And you ain't no kind of mechanic."

He was, however, some kind of athlete, from early on. He started playing quarterback in pickup games in first grade, and taught himself to pass by throwing a biscuit can. During a touch football game in phys ed class early in ninth grade, Harris caught the eye of Carroll High's coach, Dorth Blade, who bought the boy his first actual football. Blade put Harris onto the varsity during spring practice of his freshman year. The coach built the boy's arm strength by requiring him to throw 150 passes a day from his knees, and sharpened his accuracy by having him stand and aim a couple hundred more at a tire swinging from a goal post crossbar. As Harris turned fourteen, he started a two-year growth spurt, rising five inches to his full height of six-four. Heading into his sophomore year in September 1962 and vying with an older teammate for the starting job, he won it in a coin flip from Coach Blade.

Only one small problem remained: Lula Harris did not know her younger son was playing football. Ever since Nashall Jr. had broken his collarbone in the sport years earlier, she had vowed of James, "I ain't having my son out there doin' that fightin'." Instead, his sister had forged Lula's signature on James's permission form for the Carroll team, and he explained his late arrivals home after practice as "working on a school project." With the first Friday-night game nearing, however, Coach Blade paid an abashed visit to the Harris home to ask Lula for her consent.

"He will not be out there with that junk on," she replied.

Coach Blade returned the next evening, this time with his assistant coach, who was a family friend of the Harrises. Mrs. Harris threw them both out. Before the third trip, Lucille Harris tipped off Coach Blade that instead of talking about football, he should talk about college, what a college degree meant, and how much college cost.

The coaches followed the script, and as they did, Lula Harris asked, "So how all these people go to college? Where they get that money from?" On cue, they uttered the magic words: football scholarship. That Friday, Mrs. Harris attended her son's first game as Carroll's starting quarterback and watched him put up twenty-eight points in an easy victory. The only thing she required, as she would continue to for three more years, was that James present himself to her at halftime to prove he hadn't been hurt.

In his own precocious way, James Harris knew the larger stakes of playing quarterback. He had followed his father's example and become a Dodger fan in homage to Jackie Robinson and Roy Campanella. In the month-old sports magazines Dr. McHenry handed over to Lula Harris, James read about Jim Brown and Bill Russell, a younger generation's emblems of black pride. Even as he obeyed the parental admonitions to steer clear of confrontation, Harris resented having to walk miles home from Carroll after practice, dodging the taunts of white men in passing cars, scrambling into the woods as they hurled rocks.

Every black person, though, had a limit. James remembered the day his own endlessly patient father learned that a bus driver had kicked off Lucille and Nashall Jr. for sitting near the white section, leaving them to walk three miles home. Rev. Harris had gone to the bus barn to register a complaint, and in case of trouble, he had pocketed the gun he normally kept behind the headboard of his bed.

Football could take Harris out of Monroe; the question was where. By the end of his junior year, having gone 24-1 as a starter while running up nearly thirty-five points a game, having led a pro-style passing offense while calling most of the plays, Harris began receiving feelers from colleges. He heard from Grambling, where Blade had played on the unbeaten 1955 team with Willie Davis, and from other black schools, such as Alcorn A&M. He heard from Houston, which was recruiting his friend Theodis Lee and a nearby star named Elvin Hayes to integrate its basketball team. And he heard from schools in the North and the West—Arizona State, Indiana, Wisconsin, and most persistently, Michigan State.

The choice was not so much among schools as between temperaments: hope or logic, aspiration or pragmatism. If he went to a black college, Harris recognized, he could play quarterback but would damage his chances of getting into the pros. If he went to a white college, he had to abandon his career as a quarterback but would be honed for the pros as a receiver or defensive back.

For all his intelligence, Harris had lived until now in an unsophisticated, circumscribed world. He had not traveled outside the Deep

South until his sophomore year at high school, when he visited Nashall Jr. at Fort Bragg in North Carolina. He had never seen a game film until Alcorn's coach, Marino Casem, ran a projector for Harris during a recruiting session. It was already dizzying enough to have coaches offering scholarships for Harris's best friends if he would sign with their school.

Only Michigan State held the potential for reconciling all the clashing voices in his head. Michigan State was a brand name in the NFL, and it had already recruited a black quarterback, Jimmy Raye, who was expected to start as a sophomore in the fall of 1965. The Spartans' head coach, Duffy Daugherty, was ready to fly Harris to East Lansing for a visit, and had Raye lined up to show him around. "Go eat that steak," Harris's friend and teammate Delles Howell urged, "and listen to what they have to say."

The first day in East Lansing, one of the assistant coaches brought Harris onto a practice field to throw. As they tossed the ball back and forth, Harris caught a few one-handed, just a little bit of showing off. Duffy Daugherty ambled over a moment later and asked the assistant, "What kind of arm does he have?" The assistant said, "He has a natural throwing arm, but great hands." Right then, Harris realized he was being sized up to play end.

That evening, the coaches paired off Harris with a white girl at a dance being held for the recruits. She kept talking to him, moving closer, and he kept sliding away. At one point, accidentally, he looked into her eyes and noticed they were blue. Until that moment he had never realized that white folk could have blue eyes, because all his life he'd been trained not to look white folk in the eye.

When the music started, the girl asked Harris to dance. He stiffly moved onto the floor, holding her at arm's length, pulling back whenever she laid her hands on his shoulders. All he could think about was what would happen if anybody took a picture of him with her, and if that picture found its way back to Monroe. All he could think about was Emmett Till, murdered in Mississippi at age fourteen on the mere rumor he had flirted with a white woman. The girl asked Harris why he was breathing so hard and he lied that he had asthma and was feeling sick and had to go. Back in the dorm where Michigan State was putting him up, he folded and unfolded the $50 the school had given him for "expenses," more money than he had ever seen in his life. He kept it closed in his fist until he handed it to his mother in Monroe.

Money was a big concern at that point during the fall of 1964. At the outset of Harris's senior year, several days before Carroll's season opener, his father had died abruptly of a heart attack at age fifty-two. With his two jobs and Lula's nursing, the family had been comfortable by the standards of black Monroe. Now, as James watched his mother fill out all the forms from Social Security and life insurance, he wondered how she would financially survive. He also grieved that his father would never see him in cap and gown receiving that college diploma. All of these forces thrust upon Harris, barely eighteen, an adult's responsibilities.

A few months later, with another state-championship season behind Harris, Eddie Robinson showed up at the front door, straight from Howard Cosell's radio show. Long before Cosell needled him about developing a pro-quality quarterback, Robinson had privately set himself that goal. Beneath his compliant exterior about segregation, beneath his absence of civil rights activity, he had already shattered two racial barriers. Tank Younger had been the first black-college player in the NFL, and arguably its first black star, selected five times for the Pro Bowl; Buck Buchanan was the first black-college player to be the number-one pick in the pro draft.

When James Harris burst into prominence as a sophomore, Robinson quickly heard about him. What he heard and then saw suggested that here was the chosen one. Harris was tall and sturdy, like a pro quarterback; he was a drop-back passer, like a pro quarterback; he was a student of the game, like a pro quarterback. By the end of his senior season in late 1964, Harris had thrown more than forty touchdown passes and twice been named to the black all-state team. He was so strong and agile that in his second sport, basketball, he had helped hold Elvin Hayes, one of the top high school players in the nation, to fourteen points. Most important, Harris had the temperament, the combination of intelligence and maturity, the self-possession beyond his years, to withstand the inevitable ugliness that would await pro football's Jackie Robinson.

Over the past three years, Eddie Robinson had visited the Harris family several times, always making a favorable impression with his coat and tie, his briefcase and Bible. Sometimes he studied Scripture with Lula Harris, and sometimes she baked him a cake. On a couple of trips to Grambling, James had seen Robinson in action on the sidelines, and he'd heard stories from Curtis Armand, Mike Howell, Dorth Blade, and many others. He regarded Robinson in a new way on this visit. He viewed him through the hole in his life left by his father's death, and Eddie Robinson fit its dimensions.

"I never met a man like Coach Robinson," Harris remembered years later. "A man with so much compassion, a nice man when you meet him off the field, but such a competitor on the field. I never met nobody with that. He can be a gentlemanly guy, a calm guy, a respectful guy. But at practice or during a game, I don't know if I ever seen that kind of competitiveness. He hated to lose. Coach hated to lose. That kind of combination I never seen."

Sitting in the living room, with Rev. Harris's favorite chair empty and his dictionary closed, James saw another form of Robinson's fervor. The coach talked about the Howard Cosell show, growing more agitated, and finally erupting. "Damn it to hell," Robinson said, "*he* asked *me* about producing a quarterback!" He paused, gathered himself, and went on, more composed but no less intense. "There's none playing now," he said. "But in four years, a black is gonna get a chance to play quarterback in the NFL."

Harris thought about what Robinson had said. He thought about what Martin Luther King had preached at the March on Washington. He knew he might be giving up his best shot at the NFL, which would be learning and mastering a new position at Michigan State. By the time he'd be drafted from Grambling, if he even got drafted, it might be too late to change. For some time he sat and lived with the choice. Against doubts, against safety, against history itself, he decided to trust Rev. King and Coach Robinson.

+   +   +

As Grambling went through final practices for Alcorn A&M, its opponent in the opening game of the 1967 season, two prophecies appeared in the form of preseason polls, and neither boded well for the Tigers. In the small-college rankings, Grambling didn't receive a single vote. Instead, among the black colleges, Tennessee State commanded national attention, including a feature story in *Sports Illustrated*. Riding a twenty-four-game unbeaten streak and led by the record-setting quarterback Eldridge Dickey, Tennessee State was headed into a showdown with San Diego State, the number-one team in the poll. Meanwhile, the coaches in Grambling's own league, the Southwestern Athletic Conference, overwhelmingly predicted that Southern University would be the champ.

Each of the slights cut deeply and personally for Eddie Robinson. Tennessee State's flamboyant and devious head coach, John Merritt, was the only opponent whom the mannerly Robinson could almost bring himself to despise, an emotion compounded by two consecutive defeats at Merritt's hands. As for Southern, it was Grambling's fiercest rival, committed not only to victory but also ridicule. Those Baton Rouge kids, so stuck up, so "siddity," just loved to crack about how country Grambling was. Didn't everybody know that Grambling girls had to use "overnight jars" to relieve themselves, and empty them in the woods every morning? And while Southern and Grambling had shared the 1966 conference title on paper, Southern had humiliated the Tigers by a 41–13 score on the field.

So Collie Nicholson was not being entirely tongue-in-cheek when he wrote of Robinson in a preseason column, "Glum Eddie will embark on the 1967 campaign with the usual pessimism" and noted the coach's "sour-grapes mumbling." Dissatisfaction may have been closer to the truth. Robinson viewed the 6-2-1 record in 1966 as evidence of complacency, a goad for him to return to those first principles of execution and discipline. A year earlier, in 1965, an 8-2 Grambling team had earned its first chance to play against a white school, North Dakota State, in a small-college bowl, only to be humbled 20–7. And the year before that, Grambling had gone into the Orange Blossom Classic against Florida A&M with a 9-1 record and limped home a 42–15 loser. Despite all the players he had sent to the pros, with this recent history, Robinson entered the 1967 season having to prove that Grambling's whole exceeded the sum of its parts. He would find out soon enough, because Alcorn A&M always went muscle to muscle against Grambling's running game, and featured an offense this year that had scored an astonishing 101 points in its first game.

Yet the team goals could not be separated from a goal that was simultaneously smaller and larger, individual and societal: the James Harris experiment. Every scrimmage, every film-study session, every coaches' meeting, whatever its overt purpose, contained a second, unspoken agenda. That agenda could not be separated from the broader racial and political climate. "Looking over your shoulder is the idea this guy can be playing in the NFL," one assistant coach later remembered, "and you want him to have every tool."

The experiment had started out bumpily. In Harris's freshman season of 1965, for the first time in four years, he had not started. That role went to the coach's son, Eddie Jr., who had been patiently waiting for his chance as a senior. The other quarterbacks on the roster neither knew nor cared about what Coach Robinson had promised James Harris some night in Monroe. *You shoulda gone to Michigan State,* one of them, a former all-stater from New Orleans, told Harris. *At Grambling, you'll be carryin' my clipboard.* Early in the season, though, Harris received the blue practice jersey that signified promotion to the varsity and the traveling squad. On passing downs, or in the second half of blowouts, Coach Robinson would insert Harris and a freshman end named Charlie Joiner.

For the first few games, that arrangement sated Harris's ambition. Then he developed a blood clot in one leg during the eight-hour bus trip to Nashville for the Tennessee State game and had to be hospitalized. Back in uniform two weeks later against Jackson State, ready to resume his designated role, he instead was left languishing on the sideline as Grambling glided to a 51–20 win, with Eddie Jr. building a big lead and third-stringer Wesley Bean doing mop-up duty. The next morning, Harris decided to quit the team. Without a word to anyone, he drove home to Monroe, a teenager acting his impulsive age just this once. When his sister Lucille saw him unloading his suitcases, she figured it was not an ordinary visit. The next day, learning the truth, Harris's mother called Coach Robinson.

By the time Robinson arrived at the Harris home after practice on Monday, James had gotten calls from Alcorn, Southern, and Arkansas A&I, all inviting him to transfer. It had never occurred to him that he could have discussed his discontent with Coach Robinson. You just didn't talk to adults that way; it was disrespectful. So Harris was stunned that Robinson had actually driven to Monroe to speak to him. This father figure, Eddie Robinson, hadn't waited for the prodigal son to return; he had gone out to rescue him. Robinson told Harris he hadn't been demoted; rather, after losing to Tennessee State, the coach had put all his emphasis into turning around the team. As for Harris, the plan was still the plan. "It gave me the sense of trust," Harris would later recall. "That he valued me as a player and he valued my future." By the next Saturday, at home against Texas Southern, Harris was back wearing his number 14.

As a sophomore the next fall, Harris became the starter, throwing for 907 yards as Joiner caught 9 TD passes, substantial numbers for a team that relied on its running game. Meanwhile, on all days except Saturday, the experiment proceeded in its deliberate way. Sometimes Robinson tried to manage the black-quarterback pressure by saying matter-of-factly, "It's a position like any position. Ain't we playin' football?" Sometimes he bluntly told Harris, "Don't expect life to be fair. Just be better."

Almost every afternoon of his Grambling summers, and at least once a week during each football season, Harris sat with Robinson at his office in the college gym. The coach invariably had some napkins or paper place mats or folded lunch sacks on his desk, each covered with diagrams of passing plays or notes about concepts—how to recognize the coverage based on a safety's location, how to "look off" a defender by turning your eyes away from your intended receiver until the last second. Whenever Robinson attended a clinic or addressed a banquet or visited a pro team's camp, he collected the latest wisdom on the passing game. Willie Davis, by now a fixture on Green Bay's defensive line, had given Robinson details about the throwing motion of Bart Starr, the Packers' star quarterback. Dub Jones, driving over from Ruston, demonstrated the way pro receivers ran patterns. Tank Younger, a scout for the Rams, brought playbooks from the innovative offense Sid Gillman had devised there and then taken with him to the AFL's San Diego Chargers—spreading the field with five receivers, using the pass to set up the run. With Harris the avid acolyte, Robinson took chalk to blackboard, or he showed film from pro games. They paid particular attention to Roman Gabriel, the Rams' quarterback, who except for his white skin was almost a match for Harris's body type and passing arm. "This is what they're doing in the pros," Robinson explained. "This is what you need to know."

In the here and now, Robinson surrounded Harris with talent, talent not just to win games but also to nurture a pocket quarterback. He hired a new backfield coach, Doug Porter, from Mississippi Valley State. There, out of the necessity of having small linemen, Porter had adopted a pro-style passing game and raised the team's points per game from ten to twenty-five. Robinson installed fleet Essex Johnson at wingback and backed him up with a freshman named Frank Lewis. He let a starting safety, Robert Atkins, also use his speed and mobility at tight end in passing situations. He had sprinters such as Coleman Zeno and Glenn Alexander ready to come off the bench at split end or flanker.

Most of all, Grambling had Charlie Joiner, a wiry and elusive end who had caught thirty-four passes and scored nine touchdowns in 1966. From the summer after high school, when they both lived on the Grambling campus, Harris and Joiner had clicked. They shared the same work ethic on the field; they shared the same serious purpose about academics. (Joiner majored in accounting.) They ran the fifteen-yard square-out until it was an unconscious reflex. To give both quarterback and receiver a taste of what to expect in the pros, Willie Brown of the Raiders would come back to Grambling for spring practice and subject Joiner to the tender mercies of bump-and-run coverage, stiff-arming the end's chest so hard he was gasping for breath and destroying the timing of the route.

For Grambling's own purposes, Harris refined his footwork and ball control for misdirection runs and play-action passes. He mastered the seven-step drop-back the Tigers used for their handful of deep passing plays. But because he was preparing for more than Jackson State or Texas Southern or any other college opponent, because he was preparing for a league in which only three blacks had ever taken a single snap at quarterback, he devoted hours of time and thousands of repetitions to mastering pro skills. Or, as he put it, "Customizing my game."

Harris worked on the "separation step" that took him away from the center and into immediate passing position. He worked on the three- and five-step drops, how to place his feet and square his shoulders for the most forceful throw. He worked on the "progression read," the split-second mechanics of checking your receivers in order of preference from first choice to safety valve—for example, split end down the sideline, then tight end crossing the middle, then flanker on a square-out, then running back in the flat. A pro quarterback had to see, analyze, and act; a pro quarterback had to find the open man. Harris learned how to read coverage, because in the pros his physical gifts alone would not be sufficient and because in the pros a lot of coaches and executives and fans would assume that a black quarterback was too dumb to outthink a defense. Is the cornerback up close or not? Is he favoring inside or outside? Is the safety set up for zone or man coverage? The brainwork started with diagrams on the blackboard, then it continued with walk-throughs on the field, and finally it moved to simulations at three-quarters speed.

There was one other little thing. Coach Robinson never let Harris be timed in the forty-yard dash. The quarterback could run a 4.6, and if any pro scouts found out, they'd plan for Harris to be switched to receiver or defensive back. Robinson had seen it most recently with Mike Howell, drafted out of Grambling in 1965 by the Browns as a quarterback, promised a fair shot at the position, then put at cornerback in training camp, never to return to his original position.

The Harris experiment went beyond the practice field and the coach's office. Robinson knew that the first black quarterback would have to be an exemplar. He would have to be a reconciler of contradictions—smart on the gridiron, humble with the press; fiercely competitive in the game, unflappably calm with the public. He had to be damn near perfect, with all the spikes-high intensity and preternatural composure of Jackie Robinson, just to have a chance. What Eddie Robinson had said all those years ago to Tank Younger at the train station echoed again with James Harris: *You have to make it. If you don't make it, they can say they took the best we've got, and he wasn't good enough.*

So Collie Nicholson put Harris through a different kind of training camp, a tutorial the publicist called "Interviews 101." With his tinted sunglasses and his sideburns, with his suits specially ordered from Dallas, with his subscription to *Esquire,* and with the vocabulary that led Robinson to call him "the man with the golden pen," Nicholson was Grambling's resident cosmopolitan and therefore the ideal person to impersonate the big-city reporters covering the NFL. He ran Harris through batteries of questions, he mimicked the staccato clamor of the postgame press conference, he laid out hypothetical situations that were all too realistic. How would you handle being racially heckled? What if they ask why you deserve to play quarterback? Then he critiqued each of his protégé's responses, a maestro fine-tuning a musician's pitch. Harris had to sound confident without sounding arrogant; he had to exude gratitude without groveling. He had to, in other words, hide essential parts of himself—the competitive flame that flared even in a hand of tonk, the swagger that talked trash across the line of scrimmage. "Don't ever let them see you angry," Nicholson said. "Don't ever show your anger." The last thing the white sports establishment wanted was another "black militant."

The cultivation of James Harris continued in an unofficial seminar that Robinson dubbed Everyday Living. It was adapted from a course titled Social Usage in Grambling's home economics department, and Robinson required all of his players to take it. What finishing school was for white children of affluence and pedigree, Social Usage was for these children of sawmill towns and cotton fields, reared in overalls and brogans. Harris had a certain head start. The son of a minister, the younger brother of a military officer, he didn't smoke, drink, or curse. After football practice he went straight into his homework as an education major, and when the card games in his dorm room dragged on too late, he just climbed into his bunk, pulled the bedsheet over his head, and fell sleep. Still, nothing in his life had prepared him for what Robinson envisioned for him: a career in big, fancy cities, where any unfamiliarity with the social graces would be construed as black ignorance.

For three hour-long sessions, Harris and his teammates submitted to the oversight of Mildred Moss, a young professor with training in art history and interior design. She handed out diagrams showing the correct format of table settings and thank-you notes. She deciphered the menus that Coach Robinson had brought back from restaurants in Los Angeles and Manhattan. She instructed her pupils to cut your meat one piece at a time, to take your seat from the left side, to tilt your soup bowl slightly to collect the last bit in your spoon, to walk with your girlfriend so you sheltered her from passing traffic.

With its rigid propriety, Everyday Living could hardly have propounded a more subversive idea, Eddie Robinson's idea. Black people, too, were worthy and capable of etiquette. Every Grambling football player, wearing a coat and tie, using the correct fork, could make an implicit case for racial equality. "The civil rights movement was helping to change laws," Robinson said in one of his mottoes. "Our goal was to help change attitudes."

+ + +

In the spring of 1967, a former Grambling player had paid a visit to Coach Robinson. In itself, the gesture was nothing unusual; lots of ex-players, now in the pros, returned to help with spring practice. But this particular alumnus, Frederick Douglass Kirkpatrick, had finished a brief pro career years earlier and had a different agenda. He wanted to know if Coach Robinson, with all the prestige and influence he held at Grambling, would support and endorse the civil rights group Kirkpatrick had helped to found, Deacons for Defense and Justice.

Robinson offered a few privately positive words to Kirkpatrick, nothing more. The whole conversation, in fact, proved just how far and fast events were moving from the bootstraps ethos that Robinson embodied. He approached civil rights with the same cautious, conservative attitude he did football, willing to wait for hard work's reward in the fullness of time. The Deacons for Defense, in contrast, were pushing well past the nonviolence and civil disobedience of Martin Luther King. With their rifles and .38s, they evoked a small-town version of the Black Panthers, who were then arming themselves in Oakland. The Deacons had joined together to defend civil rights workers from Ku Klux Klan attacks, and to turn the Klan's tool of intimidation against it. Just recently, the Deacons' chapter in nearby Homer had burned a Klansman in effigy. The Deacons, in fact, weren't even churchmen; inside a hollowed-out Bible, Kirkpatrick kept a derringer.

It didn't take such radicalism to leave Robinson looking outdated. For several years now, a gap had been opening between Robinson and his players, between Robinson and several of his assistant coaches, even between Robinson and his longtime comrade Collie Nicholson. Nobody ever addressed it, out of respect for the coach, but it was there. The landmark civil rights laws passed in 1964 and 1965 had created two new realities: the expectation, especially among younger blacks, of long-overdue equality, and the violent backlash by a resurgent Ku Klux Klan. A coach couldn't emphasize education the way Robinson did and not have his players follow the news.

On the television in their dorm lounge, Robinson's young men had seen footage of police battering the Selma marchers on "Bloody Sunday" in 1965; in the pages of *Ebony* and the *Pittsburgh Courier,* they had read about the shooting of James Meredith by a white gunman during a voting-rights pilgrimage in 1966. "We watched," Robert Atkins would later recall, "with fear, hatred, and sorrow." Collie Nicholson had driven to Selma for the third attempted march to Montgomery on March 21, 1965, bringing a cash donation from the Grambling NAACP. Four days later, he was driving along the same stretch of highway as a vehicle with a civil rights volunteer from Detroit, a white woman named Viola Liuzzo, when she was ambushed and shot dead by a carload of Klansmen. Nicholson drove straight back to Grambling, shaken and indignant.

No longer did Grambling itself afford a haven, some kind of Brigadoon or Shangri-la magically removed from the nation's racial convulsions. Fives miles away, in Ruston, 90 percent of black adults had been barred from voting for decades. The White Citizens Council maintained an active branch, espousing its policy of "massive resistance" to integration. Louisiana Tech University was desegregating only under a federal court order, and then expelling its first black student on a dubious allegation of theft. As President Jones of Grambling kowtowed his way through the annual ritual of securing funds from the state legislature, Nicholson lost his temper. "Someday we're not gonna have to do this, go down and beg for money," he said to his boss and mentor. "Someday we're gonna make big money with football and you can spend it on the school."

For now, though, sports was less a refuge than one more battleground. When Harris and Atkins and other players watched the college games on the dorm TV, they asked, "Why can't we play Notre Dame? Why can't we play USC?" The assistant coaches, most of them a generation younger than Robinson, complained that they'd never even be considered for an opening at LSU. They just had to look at Louisiana Tech's facilities to know that in football, as in academics, Louisiana only pretended separate was equal.

Facing a kind of mutiny—not against his authority, but against his worldview—Robinson offered what answers he could. He told the restive players who craved a game against ND or USC, "Someday we will." He told his chafing coaches how much worse things had been in the past, when as a boy he could only watch LSU games through a hole in the stadium fence. Rather than indulge his assistants in their complaints about what Louisiana Tech had, he assigned them to fertilize and seed Grambling's dusty, weedy practice field. "If you waste your time being bitter," he insisted, "you won't make any progress."

After a summer of race riots, amid the escalation in Vietnam, Eddie Robinson kept saying all the patriotic things he had always said. He said them because he believed them, but they also happened to be the words that white folk, especially in the South, wanted to hear. Collie Nicholson so loathed Ruston that he went there only for the Western Union office; Coach Robinson could walk down the Ruston streets and have one white person after another say hello, shake hands, tip his hat.

"Coach really waves that American flag," Harris said to his friends and teammates in the dorm. It wasn't exactly a compliment. Harris felt himself almost irreparably torn. The proof was all around him that white people were against black people, that everything was racial—why a black got a speeding ticket, why Grambling wasn't ranked in the preseason poll. Yet Coach Robinson, his mentor, his surrogate father, the man he most admired in the world, told him in every way that race didn't matter. Or maybe, knowing all too well exactly how ineradicably it mattered, Robinson wanted in a heartfelt and futile way to protect all his young men from the poison of the real world.

Coach Robinson had a program. Coach Robinson had a plan. Come to Grambling, play football, get an education, be successful in America. America was ready, he believed, even as his own players doubted. "Coach thought we had to exist within the system," Harris later recalled. "We thought the system was unfair. For a long time, there'd been no hope. We'd suppressed everything. But Coach gave us hope change was on the way."

Entering the 1967 season, Harris took the risk of trusting in that fragile, precarious hope. And Robinson, for his part, took the risk of engineering social change. With the James Harris experiment, he had chosen for the first time to explicitly join the civil rights cause. The question was whether he was doing it too soon for his nation or too late for his race.

4

SOMEBODY HAS GOT TO PAY

Florida A&M vs. South Carolina State, September 23, 1967

With 105 sets of cleats clacking, raising a racket like some vast teletype machine, the Florida A&M Rattlers strode out of their locker room in the school gym, entering a concrete plaza large enough to hold their number. They wore their home uniforms of green jerseys and white pants, both set off with orange piping, and carried their helmets in their hands. They assembled around Coach Jake Gaither, and then they knelt. It was a practical posture, allowing even the benchwarmers in the back to clearly see and hear the coach. There was something appropriate, too, in the team's aspect of penitence.

In less than an hour, in the home opener of their 1967 season and the first night game in FAMU history, the Rattlers would be meeting the South Carolina State Bulldogs, the team that had done more than any other to dispel the aura of invincibility around Gaither and his team. A year earlier, before a standing-room crowd on their field in Orangeburg, the Bulldogs had beaten FAMU 8–3, handing the Rattlers their first loss in the Southern Intercollegiate Athletic Conference since 1952, when Harry Truman was still president.

That 1966 win had vindicated the pregame promises of South Carolina State's head coach, Oree Banks. He had told the local newspaper in Orangeburg, "Florida A&M can be stopped and that's what we intend to do." He had told his players, "Forget about the legend. Jake Gaither's not playing." They had taken his word and throttled the Rattlers, holding A&M to 154 total yards, intercepting 3 passes, rushing for more than 200 yards. Had the Bulldogs not lost 3 fumbles of their own, the score would have been as lopsided as the statistics.

Most galling for Jake Gaither, he had been outcoached. Going into the 1966 season, he had abandoned his tradition of deploying the first-string defense for kickoff coverage. He decided instead to rest them and give the second-team players more time, since the Rattlers scored so often they kicked off seven or eight times a game. But South Carolina State's tailback, a sprinter named John Gilliam, raced through FAMU's back-ups for a 98-yard kickoff return and the game's only touchdown. The Bulldogs' defense was led by a linebacker, Tracy Hodges, who had been recruited out from under Gaither as a Tallahassee high school star. When Gaither, in a rare show of panic, inserted his third-string quarterback, Alonzo Gilbert, to try to spark the offense, South Carolina State trapped him in the end zone for a safety. Bill Nunn of the *Pittsburgh Courier,* the most important football writer in the black press, depicted the Bulldogs' victory as a kind of dynastic succession, declaring in his weekly column that "the Bulldogs are kings of all they survey."

In his midthirties, half Gaither's age, Oree Banks welcomed the Oedipal repercussions of the rivalry. A former assistant to Eddie Robinson at Grambling, Banks had also been mentored by Gaither. They met several times a year in Atlanta for conversations about not only football—with Banks following Gaither's example of recruiting players for speed—but just as crucially about the way a coach at a black state university had to handle relations with white politicians. Despite all that, Banks took special delight in toppling Gaither. He had devoted virtually all of State's preseason drills to preparing for FAMU, and in victory he had eschewed the public humility that was such a hallmark of Gaither's, declaring, "It's like beating your father in a contest."

The Rattlers' bus trip back to Tallahassee after that loss, eight hours through the night, proceeded with the silence of a funeral cortege. Whenever the team returned with a victory, as it usually did, the driver would roll through campus blaring the horn and drop the triumphant players on "The Set," the quadrangle that was the school's hub for friendship and flirtation. That Sunday dawn in 1966, the bus abashedly made its way straight to the gym, and the players staggered stiff-legged and morose into the locker room. "You don't make excuses," Gaither told them. "You don't give no quarter, and you don't get no quarter."

All that week, the players got chided by their classmates in the cafeteria line. Former Rattlers told the current ones, *You're not keeping up the tradition. We never lost to that team.* The worst part was that the critics were right. By the start of the 1967 season, and the rematch against South Carolina State, juniors such as Ken Riley had never experienced the storied dominance of FAMU. Even the seniors, key players such as John Eason and Elroy Morand, had been mere freshmen in 1964, watching from the sideline as a Rattler team featuring Bob Hayes went 9-1 and routed Grambling in the Orange Blossom Classic.

By this time, in the waning sunlight of the second day of autumn, an entire calendar year had passed since the 8–3 indignity in Orangeburg. The Rattlers had started their 1967 season the previous week by walloping Allen University 43–0 on the road. They were now ranked tenth in the small-college poll. But Allen was a perennial weakling, almost an exhibition game for FAMU. Everybody knew the season really began with South Carolina State, right here at home. "There's a mighty poor dog," Gaither said, "won't fight in his own backyard."

As if the point needed any underscoring, Gaither accomplished it by

Somebody Has Got to Pay

having the Rattlers practice in full pads with full contact from Monday through Thursday of game week, stoking a collective mean streak. He paced between the rows of players during calisthenics, saying, "Payback time." The captains, Riley and Morand, picked up the chant, then the whole team.

At other times during the week, Gaither summoned his top players into his office for individual meetings. "Like being called into the principal," Eason would later recall, "but the principal is a Baptist minister." As he spoke, Gaither rubbed a couple of coins between his fingers, like a hypnotist's pendulum, and he talked about how you couldn't rest on the laurels of the past. Those players, knowing full well the scuttlebutt that Gaither was past his prime, told themselves, *We can't disappoint him.*

Now the whole team gazed up at Gaither from the concrete plaza, awaiting inspiration. Gaither's way was never to scream or shout or curse, but he could fret and pluck the strings of the youthful psyche like a virtuoso. Sometimes he regaled the team with stories of the Buffalo Soldiers, the black troops in the US Cavalry. One time, trailing by several touchdowns at halftime, he said in a subdued, formal tone, "Excuse me, gentlemen, I thought I was in the Rattlers' dressing room. It appears I'm in the room with a bunch of black snakes." Gaither could generate tears when he thought tears would help, and he wasn't too proud to pretend at being abject, telling one Rattler team, "You're letting Jakey down." No matter what, when Jake Gaither held forth, all the coaches and trainers and players listened raptly, "so quiet you could hear a rat pissing in cotton."

So in this critical moment, Gaither squinted under his brimmed hat. Spectators were walking past the kneeling players. The drums of the FAMU band, marching through the campus, echoed in the twilight air.

"Somebody," Gaither said, voice firm, head mournfully bowed, "has got to pay."

Gaither's words carried both history and efficacy. The slogan dated to 1954, when an unbeaten A&M team faced Southern University in its final regular-season game, only to be embarrassed 59–20. When the team bus crept back onto campus, Gaither was stunned to find hundreds of students waiting on The Set. "Don't they know we lost the ball game?" he said to someone. "Didn't they get the message?" The students called for the team captain to speak, and after he did, they called for the coach. *Lord of Mercy,* Gaither thought, *what am I going to tell these kids now? I've messed up a perfect record. Went out there unbeaten and just got kicked all over the field.* So he told the truth, that the Rattlers had lost, that Southern had run all over them. Then, spontaneously, he added, "But I can tell you one thing." The students, shouting in unison like a church congregation in call and response, asked what it was. "Somebody's got to pay! Somebody's got to pay!"

The following week, in the Orange Blossom Classic, the Rattlers buried Maryland State 67–19.

The question on this evening in 1967 was whether the memory of an insult and the motive for vengeance would still be potent after a full year. One last time, this time proclaiming, Gaither said, "Somebody has got to pay." The Rattlers, to demonstrate that they had heard and heeded, chanted back, "Hubba! Hubba! Hubba!" Then they rose and formed ranks and headed toward Bragg Stadium.

+ + +

When Oree Banks arrived in Orangeburg in 1965 to take over as head coach of South Carolina State, he was carrying his membership card in the NAACP. His affiliation, begun while most southern states were attempting to outlaw the civil rights group, set Banks markedly apart from the leaders on his campus and in his profession. His predecessor at South Carolina State, George Bell, followed the apolitical example of his religious denomination, the Seventh-Day Adventists. The college president, Benner C. Turner, actively opposed students forming an NAACP chapter, even building a fence to separate the campus from an adjacent, all-black religious college, Claflin, lest students from each protest together. When students privately speculated about whether Turner was trying to pass for white, they were talking, metaphorically, about more than his fair skin.

Born in a central Mississippi town in the mid-1930s, Banks had come of age as the *Brown* case and the Montgomery bus boycott were shaking the foundations of segregation. Banks quickly lost his patience with the indignities in his own community, like the way black schools would be shut down whenever more field hands were needed for the cotton harvest. His service in the army and studies at Kansas State University provided him with a firsthand contrast between the Jim Crow South and the legally integrated North, however imperfect its version of tolerance. When Banks took his first coaching job in 1960, at an all-black junior college back in Mississippi, he struck up a friendship with Aaron Henry, president of the state chapter of the NAACP. The year before Banks went to Orangeburg, Henry led the insurgent, integrated slate of delegates from the self-proclaimed Mississippi Freedom Democratic Party into the Democrats' presidential nominating convention.

So when South Carolina State, a traditional hub of civil rights activity, began to roil again with student activism in early 1967, Banks did not do what many other black college coaches had done in similar situations: order their players not to participate. He reminded them of the importance of getting a degree, and of the prospect of being drafted if they got kicked out of school. He put them on an 8:00 p.m. curfew. Yet at the risk of his own job—as the employee of an all-white state government and its handpicked factotum, President Turner—he let the football players decide for themselves whether to join the burgeoning protests. "It wasn't easy for me," Banks recalled years later. "But I took the attitude that this is part of the change in our country. This was a change people needed to be concerned about."

The college campus and the surrounding community of Orangeburg had seen periods of protest against segregation in 1957, 1960, and 1963, the latter being quashed by local police wielding fire hoses in the manner of Bull Connor's cops in Birmingham. This newest round of protests began, in contrast, almost innocuously, with student complaints about the college's requirements that freshmen and sophomores attend weekly chapel, and that all undergraduates dress formally for Sunday dinner in the cafeteria. Wrapped in rhetoric about "student freedom" and "action now," however, those parochial concerns soon grew to encompass broader political issues, ranging from the mandatory course in ROTC to the flagrantly superior funding given to the University of South Carolina, which remained almost entirely white. Banks's players, in particular, paid attention to the construction of a new basketball arena called the Coliseum for the white university, one symbol among many of the state's racial inequality.

The breaking point came when President Turner dismissed two math instructors, both of them young white men from the North, who had been persistently raising the issue of inadequate funds and facilities at South Carolina State. In response, several hundred students, many football players among them, picketed on the front lawn of Turner's residence. He expelled three of the protest leaders, which resulted in an even larger demonstration, involving a third of the college's fifteen hundred students, and subsequently a two-week boycott of classes honored by 90 percent of the student body. The activists christened their effort "The Cause."

From the outset, several of Banks's players had been essential to it. The defensive back Willis Ham and the linebacker James "Diesel" Johnson had grown up in Charleston, where the civil rights movement was active, and were friendly from their home city with Isaac Williams, one of the leaders of The Cause. Johnny Jones, the starting quarterback, had discovered Malcolm X through an older brother who lived in Detroit. In his dorm, Jones kept an LP record of the late Black Muslim leader's speech "The Bullet or the Ballot."

As the campus protests escalated during the early months of 1967, the national program director of SNCC, Cleveland Sellers, came to Orangeburg with the goal of building The Cause into a more permanent group. Very deliberately, he set out to attract and enlist athletes. As Sellers well knew from his years of playing high school basketball, a team had built-in organization and recognized leaders. Football players, in particular, understood firsthand what it meant to persevere through pain, to compete, to win. Those virtues, Sellers believed, could be adapted from the gridiron to the struggle.

On many nights in the spring of 1967, Sellers spoke outside Bethea Hall, the dorm where most football players lived. Standing a lean six-two, wearing a goatee and a billowing Afro, he cut a figure both of physical force and political fearlessness. He orated on the theme of "consciousness-raising," speaking of socialism, liberation, and black identity.

Something was going on, and the football players were part of it. When Johnny Jones talked with Oree Banks about The Cause, the coach issued his standard admonitions about getting an education first and foremost, but he concluded on a fortifying note. "You're making history," he told his quarterback. "Don't be on the wrong side of history."

By the end of the spring term of 1967, The Cause had succeeded beyond its expectations. A federal court had reinstated the expelled students. No penalties were levied against the hundreds who had boycotted classes. Coach Banks still had his job. President Turner, however, had been pushed out, having lost credibility with his students for cracking down and with the white leadership for not cracking down harshly enough.

As the Bulldogs drilled in the late summer of 1967 for their rematch with Florida A&M, they no longer had the luxury of focusing single-mindedly on football. Cleveland Sellers—by now facing federal charges for refusing to submit to the draft, the same crime of which Muhammad Ali stood accused—was preparing to move to Orangeburg, where he would adorn his off-campus apartment with a poster of the Black Panther leader Huey Newton. The state police were dispatching agents to investigate Sellers and his followers. The entire temperature of Orangeburg, a town whose whites had well-known affinities for George Wallace and the Ku Klux Klan, was ticking up. But the football players, newly politicized, were not backing down. "There's an expression," Willis Ham recalled later of the mood at the time, "that it's better to ask forgiveness than to ask permission."

+ + +

Beneath the stands of Bragg Stadium, Pete Griffin gathered the Florida A&M defense around him. With pregame warm-ups over, and only minutes before kickoff, the Rattlers had jogged off the field and into the home team's dressing room, a cinder-block cave with bare wooden benches. Each position coach huddled with his players as oratorical inspiration gave way to sober strategy.

Where Jake Gaither played the preacher or the stem-winding lawyer, the professions to which he'd once aspired, Pete Griffin carried himself like an accountant. He was the X's-and-O's man, with horn-rim glasses, with pencil and clipboard, watching game films by the hour in his darkened office. "You win the game," Griffin always said, "on Monday, Tuesday, and Wednesday." He meant by both rigorous planning and ruthless practice. Griffin had started as an undersized center on A&M's unbeaten national championship team in 1938, and almost three decades later he held to his playing weight of 175, with bulging biceps and skin taut as a drumhead. He looked for versions of himself in his players, fleet and fearless, and when they clouted somebody, he would emit an approving sort of growl. "Hit that sucker" was about as verbal as Griffin got.

For the rematch against South Carolina State, Griffin, like Gaither, was seeking a kind of redemption. In the 1965 game, Oree Banks's very first as head coach, the Bulldogs had completed passes of sixty and eighty-seven yards against Griffin's vaunted defense, losing only 19–13. The next year, changing tactics, South Carolina State rushed for more than two hundred yards. Now Banks was boasting that the backfield on the 1967 squad was the best in the nation. It surely was one of the biggest, with the starters weighing more than 220 on average, while FAMU's middle linebacker went just 180.

So Griffin devised a game plan composed of equal parts aggression and guile, with the purpose of ambushing superior strength. He moved his three linebackers nearly onto the line of scrimmage. He drilled his linemen to "bingo"—a tactic in which they took their stance angled to one side, tantalizing the offense to run the other way, but then slashed back in that direction to shut down the gaps. Griffin assigned his safety to shadow the Bulldogs' wingback, a transfer from Ohio State named Benny Blocker, who ran the misdirection counters that Banks had learned from Eddie Robinson at Grambling. With nine of his eleven players committed to stuffing the run, just daring the Bulldogs to pass, Griffin instructed his two cornerbacks to bully the South Carolina State receivers into the middle of the field. That would take away the sprint-out passes toward the sideline that the Bulldogs favored.

Griffin called this alignment a "5-4 monster," the monster being the safety focused solely on Blocker. The name, though, also served as an inside joke, a pun, because the linchpin of FAMU's defense was middle guard Rudolph Sims, nicknamed "Monster." At 250, Sims was the heaviest starter on the team; he had built up massive arms and shoulders and developed deceptively quick feet from years of throwing the discus and shot-putting on the FAMU track team.

His ferocity was the stuff of team legend. One time, Coach Gaither sent Sims into a game with the order "Get vicious." After several sets of downs, Sims quizzically asked the defensive lineman next to him, "What's Vicious' number?" In another game, a Texas Southern blocker, lining up across from Sims, called him "sissy." The word was no accident; among the Rattler players, and evidently beyond them, it was persistently rumored that Sims was queer. On A&M, though, everyone knew better than to taunt him about it. His manhood mocked by Texas Southern, Sims shoved aside a teammate to have a better shot at the antagonist. Then he brought down his fist so hard on the guy's helmet that the blow split it like a walnut.

On the far side of Bragg Stadium, in an open area beneath the home team's stands, the South Carolina State Bulldogs made their own final preparations. Whether by design or convenient coincidence, the lack of a genuine dressing room for FAMU's opponents left them exposed to the sound of a belligerent crowd. The Marching 100, who actually numbered 164, were prancing around the perimeter of the field in the achingly slow pace known as the death cadence—one step every three seconds, one leg lifted at a ninety-degree angle, the musicians poised like a flock of herons. The drums tolled slowly as the procession went painstakingly onward. Then, abruptly, the drum majors' whistles shrieked and the snares rattled and the band members poured onto the field at 160 steps a minute.

With the crowd roaring, the stadium announcer declaiming, and all those whistles and drums sounding, the cacophony vibrated the ground beneath the Bulldogs and nearly drowned out anything Oree Banks tried to say. His plan, propounded during the past month's practices, was not to make mistakes. He always put his best players on defense, raiding the offensive ranks for conscripts when necessary, with the goal of shutting down the other team, keeping the game close, waiting for the turnover, needing only one or two scores from his own team to win. In the 1966 season, the Bulldogs had allowed opponents an average of barely forty yards a game on the ground and surrendered a total of just eighty-nine points. To Banks's benefit in this game, four of A&M's top runners had been hurt during the past week's intense practices, with injuries from pulled muscles to sprained ankles to cuts requiring stitches, and it was questionable whether any of them would play.

"Florida can be stopped," Banks had been saying all week. "We are not going to roll over and play dead."

How much the Bulldogs heard of their coach's final reminders, though, was uncertain amid the din from the Marching 100. For Jake Gaither's musical allies, pageantry doubled as a form of psychological warfare.

The stadium clock ticked down, and back over on the Rattlers' side, the brief pregame session neared its end. Griffin went player by player through his starting defense, standing so close they could hear the squish of his chewing tobacco. The coach had each player recite his responsibility in the 5-4 monster before going on to the next, like an officer moving down a line of paratroopers about to jump. When Griffin finished, as did the other position coaches with their charges, Gaither took center stage for what was always the culminating ritual, praying to the deity he worshipped as the "God of the Rattlers."

Then Ken Riley and Elroy Morand led the team onto the field. The previous week, in the rout of Allen, Riley had completed ten of thirteen passes, throwing for one touchdown and running for two more. Yet when FAMU started its first possession, Morand lined up at quarterback. Gaither had his system: Morand in the first and third quarters, Riley in the second and fourth. It was fair; it was equitable; it was stable. It was also the latest in a lifetime of reminders to Riley, so combative beneath his serene surface, that he still had doubters to disprove.

+   +   +

Two years after World War II ended, in a county seat called Bartow on the pancake-flat plain of central Florida, Ken Riley was born to a high school girl whose boyfriend soon left her to conveniently enlist in the peacetime army. While Beatrice Riley made her living as a maid, Ken's four grandparents took much of the responsibility for raising him. His paternal grandfather, Cornelius Wynn, was a minister who made extra money as a carpenter and by selling meat and hides from the game he killed. His maternal grandmother, Bessie Riley, was a domestic who exalted the kind of education that race and circumstance had denied her to the point of illiteracy. When Ken was learning to read from his "Alice and Jerry" books, she sat transfixed as he assembled letters on the page into simple stories.

The values Ken observed in those elders, of autonomy and aspiration, informed his own life from early childhood. He spent Sunday mornings in church, Sunday afternoons with the Baptist Young People's Union, summers in Vacation Bible School and accompanying his preacher grandfather on the revival circuit. In Union Academy, the black school in Bartow that spanned kindergarten through twelfth grade, Riley racked up As in the classroom and played cornet in the band. "I want you to do better than I did," his mother would tell him. "I don't want you to have no barefoot, snotty-nosed children." By which she meant, children Ken could not support as a responsible father.

The immediate world of Bartow offered clear alternatives for a child as observant as Ken. Two of his aunts, one on each side, had earned degrees from black colleges and become teachers; his mother, unsatisfied with a maid's lot, was taking classes to become a lab technician. So there could be a future; there were possibilities. For the blacks who didn't or couldn't grab hold of education's ticket, two coarse options awaited: phosphate mines and citrus groves. Those jobs paid better than teaching did, but they killed something in the soul. Ken paid attention to the way the miners and pickers drank or gambled away their money on the weekends, trying to spend their way out of dejection, only to find themselves back in the same place on every broke, hungover Monday morning.

For the whites who ruled Bartow, that social and economic structure was not disagreeable. Segregation established a steady, consistent order, an equilibrium of inequality. Whites ran the stores and offices downtown, while blacks lived in neighborhoods called "Coon Bottom" and "the Quarters," as if slavery had never ended. In a community of twelve thousand people, roughly a third of them black, theater seats and drinking fountains and even American Legion posts came in "white" and "colored" versions. Only when pressure periodically swelled up from civil rights advocates or the federal government did Bartow find it necessary to apply intimidation or violence as a reminder of who was in charge.

Back in the 1930s, Polk County police had killed a black war veteran for trying to organize a union. When the citrus groves ran short of workers early in World War II, the county's black schools were shut down for three months to provide cheap labor. After Bartow reluctantly expanded Union Academy in 1955, in all likelihood as a means of stalling integration under the *Brown* decision, the Ku Klux Klan planted several crosses on the school's lawn. Even without the symbolism, the evidence of Jim Crow lay literally across the street from Union Academy, within eyesight of Ken Riley's classrooms, where the municipal golf course spread languidly over the acres. The only blacks allowed on it were caddies.

"Don't you be whistling," Ken's grandfather sometimes advised him, meaning don't even *seem* to be showing interest in any white female. The admonition went beyond the sexual code of the South; it urged Ken in a broader way to stay within the safety, and the nurturing, of the black sections of town—the stores and churches and funeral parlors along Palmetto Street, the Blue Room club where Sam Cooke performed, and Union Academy, overseen by principal James Stephens, nicknamed "Wolfman" for his raspy voice and furious temper. Stephens demanded high standards of schoolwork and behavior, underscoring them with a wooden paddle he called the "Board of Education." More than a few students also thought Wolfman was doing white Bartow's bidding by keeping them in line.

As a sixth grader in Union Academy's band, Ken saw his first high school football game. Too young for the team, he practiced passing every day with a deaf classmate, a neighborhood bully who was devoted to Ken for not scorning him. Ken played sandlot games in what were literally vacant lots of loose, sandy soil, without realizing that those conditions were building strength and endurance in his modest frame. He was thirteen years old and the class brain of ninth grade when Union Academy's football coach, Claude Woodruff, spotted him starring in a playground game and informed him that the band was for babies. Ken stayed in the school orchestra for three more years, but he couldn't resist taking up Woodruff's challenge.

He started at quarterback as a sophomore and led his team to a division championship as a junior. In the process, Ken learned Florida A&M's split-line T offense, which Woodruff had picked up at Jake Gaither's coaching clinics. Woodruff put Ken on the track team to build up his speed and wind and gave him eye exercises to develop his peripheral vision. After football games, instead of celebrating, Woodruff brought Ken and other players to the cattle ranch where he held a second job, and put them to work baling hay. No opportunity for betterment, no reminder of humility could be missed.

One of Union Academy's assistant coaches, J. J. Corbett, taught Ken lessons of a racial and political sort. In a black infantry unit in World War II, Corbett had been allowed no closer to combat than Oregon and consigned to the rear ranks of a victory parade. On his way back to Bartow from the West Coast, he stopped in uniform at a restaurant in Texas, only to be denied entry, even as a tableful of German POWs were eating inside.

So the hopes for the civil rights movement in Riley's community were tempered by bitter experience. It took a federal lawsuit settled more than a decade after *Brown* for Polk County to even start to desegregate its schools. Meanwhile, as the county's white children walked to neighborhood schools in their hometowns, blacks from dozens of miles afield had to travel to Union Academy. After away football games, Union's team bus would wind its way across the map—Fort Meade, Mulberry, Bradley—to drop off players before finally getting back to Bartow. Every one of those tedious trips made segregation palpable and personal for Ken. Every one got him thinking about how white folks were so outraged about the idea of busing kids to faraway schools, unless, of course, those kids happened to be black. During Ken's last summer at home before going to FAMU, the municipal beach in a nearby town, Auburndale, admitted blacks for the first time. Incensed by the racial mixing, a bartender from Bartow drove there and shot a black teenager. "All my teachers said integration was coming," Riley later recalled, "and they would say, 'You're not going to be able to be as good as, you're going to have to be better, just to get an equal shot.'"

Riley spurned the inquiries he got from white schools such as Wake Forest, Southern Illinois, and Morehead State. As much as he craved every chance to prove himself, it wasn't in his guarded nature to be a test case. His passion and improvisation flourished on the field, but circumspection governed the rest of his life. He had achieved incrementally— the undersized athlete becoming captain of the football, basketball, and track teams; the shy bookworm being elected senior-class president; the teenager so wary of temptation he didn't even shoot pool. He courted a girlfriend, Barbara Moore, who was, like him, a child of the church, a loner, a self-described "stay-at-home kind of person."

Somebody Has Got to Pay

So on the day during senior year when Coach Woodruff said, "There's a scholarship for you," Riley unquestioningly accepted Florida A&M and Jake Gaither as his destiny. College football, in his view, wasn't about getting to the NFL; his scholarship represented the opportunity for a diploma and a future. Riley had never forgotten the way his grandmother Bessie looked at him when he read, and what the yearning in her face said about all the blacks who'd never had the chance he now did. It didn't hurt, though, to enjoy a sweet, private bit of satisfaction: Wolfman at Union Academy had always told Riley that he was too small to play college football.

One morning in late August 1965, Riley waited at the Greyhound station in Bartow for the bus that would carry him to a college he had never seen and a coach he had never met. Traveling three hundred miles and eight hours to Tallahassee, and not intending to return home until Christmas, he had only a footlocker of belongings and one of Barbara's homemade red velvet cakes. For company, a couple of former high school teammates, who were beginning their sophomore years as starters on the Rattlers, were taking the same bus.

As Riley stepped aboard, one of them, a defensive back named Major Hazelton, turned to Riley's mother and promised, "Don't worry, Miss Bea, I'll take care of him." The moment the bus lurched forward and beyond maternal view, Hazelton slapped Riley across the head. On the Greyhound's tedious, two-lane journey to Tallahassee, as it stopped in Lakeland and Leesburg and Ocala, other FAMU players climbed on and took seats, and each time Hazelton threw his arm protectively around Riley and said, "Don't y'all bother my homeboy." Then he slapped him again.

When preseason practice started the next morning, a different kind of hazing commenced. Riley received a pair of secondhand cleats, as all the freshmen did, and was assigned to the scout team and sent down to The Pit. He lined up with the scout team against the Rattlers' starting defense, a chunk of chum tossed to the sharks. There were three other quarterbacks in The Pit, among them an all-stater from Miami; on the upper practice fields, the Blood, Sweat, and Tears units had one quarterback apiece. In the Gaither system, those eight quarterbacks vied for one starting job. They were the "crabs in a barrel," as a popular black aphorism put it, each one trying to clamber to the top before being pulled down by someone else.

Except that Riley, so unprepossessing at 5-10 and 180, survived. He had speed enough to have run a 9.7 in the 100-yard dash, and he had skills less measurable than speed, an intuition for sensing a tackler closing in on him, and a balletic ability to escape. He spun, he reversed direction, he canted his hips to leave defenders swiping at air where his waist had just been. Then, having disoriented the defense with his antics, he would dart upfield or throw downfield for long gains. Nathaniel James, a starting cornerback who had known Riley since childhood in Bartow, found himself thinking of the rookie phenomenon on the Chicago Bears, Gale Sayers. On a team filled with nicknames—"Nature Boy," "Stick," "Palatka Red," "Pimp"—Riley got his: "Scrambler." On a team of fluent trash-talkers, Riley recalled later, "I talked my trash with what I did on the field."

During one particular practice, the quarterback coach, Costa Kittles, caught sight of Riley at work. "Who's throwing those passes?" he called down to Robert Mungen, who oversaw the scout team in The Pit. Mungen hollered back, "That's the boy from Bartow." After the scrimmaging ended that day, Kittles told Riley to come to the upper field and throw some passes under Gaither's observation. From then on, Riley would stay an extra half hour after every afternoon's practice so he could throw to the starting receivers. Kittles tutored him on timing, touch, motion, and footwork, mechanics that augmented a strong arm and separated a gifted savant from a polished master. On the Thursday before the Rattlers' first game of the season, Riley found a traveling bag hanging in his locker—pads, pants, and a game jersey with the number 3.

Even as a freshman elevated to the traveling squad, the top half of A&M's hundred-plus players, Riley was expected to subscribe to the hierarchy. On bus trips to away games, he sat on a jump seat in the center aisle. When an upperclassman demanded that Riley tell a joke, he told a joke, and if it was judged insufficiently funny, he was locked in the bus's toilet stall for the rest of the trip. He waited for playing time among several of those eight quarterbacks, waited until a game late in the season against Bethune-Cookman, when he came off the bench to throw two touchdown passes. Not long after, Gaither said to Riley, "Baby, you gonna ride with me."

The head coach's words were an anointing. Gaither never took the bus to road games. He drove his Lincoln. Or, more accurately, in recognition of his wavering control of the wheel, yet another lingering effect of his brain surgery, he let the team trainer George Thompson drive, while he conducted a rolling symposium for his passengers, the top several quarterbacks. Gaither would lay out a game situation and fire away the questions. *What play would you call? What play after that? What's the blocking scheme?* Gaither trusted his quarterbacks to call their own plays, which meant they had to know the offense as thoroughly as he did. If they got an answer wrong, he did not upbraid or embarrass them; he said in his calm, paternal voice, "That's not the way we do it. That's not the way you've been taught."

Sometimes, to give themselves a break, Riley or the others might ask Gaither about some historical marker the Lincoln had just passed. Next thing you knew, the coach was off on some tangent about the Pilgrims. Or Gaither might spot a landmark from his personal history, something of a grimmer kind. *That was where a lynching took place. That was a restaurant with a "No Niggers" sign.* He told his young men about the importance of avoiding downtown Tallahassee, the importance of saying "Yes, sir" and "No, sir" to whites. On one drive he said, "Two things don't live long. A dog chasing a car and a black man messing with a white woman."

Like the life lessons Riley had heard from his grandparents, Gaither's offered a tangled mixture of black pride and black deference. It took a figure of the coach's stature to hold that contradiction in suspension, to keep a player such as Ken Riley, the product of an era of rising expectations, from tuning out. Then again, from age eighteen, Riley had commended his future to this man.

Away from home for months that first fall in Tallahassee, Riley keenly felt the pressure of measuring up, and not only on the football field. He missed his mother and his girlfriend. Having come from a high school of five hundred students, he sat anonymous and adrift in lecture classes with a hundred or more. He had to manage his time—studying after practice till midnight, getting to class on time the next morning at eight. In his first semester, he got a 2.29 grade point average, a C. It was more than enough to keep him eligible, more than enough to satisfy Coach Kittles, who was assigned to monitor all the quarterbacks' attendance and marks, but not nearly enough to satisfy Riley himself. He took the classroom as yet one more proving ground, motivating himself with the mantra *Don't tell me there's something I can't do.*

Sure enough, he lifted his grades back to the familiar As and Bs, and in his sophomore year won the Rattlers' scholastic award for the highest grade point on the team. He also moved into the regular lineup during the 1966 season, sharing the starting position with Elroy Morand. Riley told himself he had no basis for complaint; you couldn't be selfish on a team with so much talent. For a part-timer, he compiled solid enough statistics—36 of 74 passing for 601 yards and 6 touchdowns, as well as 288 yards rushing, third best on the squad—for a team that much preferred for its quarterback to hand off to his running backs. Yet Riley rarely played for more than a quarter at a time, sometimes for as little as one possession. He struggled to fall into a rhythm, into a zone where knowledge and preparation and reflex and intuition merged. In some games, just when Riley was finding that feeling, Gaither decided it was time to send in Morand.

So when spring practice rolled around in early 1967, the start of preparations for Riley's junior season, he did something uncharacteristic. He skipped the drills one day to check out the coeds on The Set. Heck, he knew the offense already; he'd been using the split-line T since high school. Busy admiring the scenery, Riley didn't notice a certain Lincoln creeping up from behind, though he did wonder why the other players with him suddenly scattered. Then he turned to see Jake Gaither, who looked him up and down and slowly drove away.

Somebody Has Got to Pay

The next day, the coach called Riley to his office. "Baby, you supposed to be the leader," he said. "You supposed to be my coach on the field." He paused, let those words penetrate. "If you're lying to me, baby, who can I trust?"

All it took was that one whiff of disappointment: Riley never defied Jake Gaither to ditch practice again. Neither, though, did he abandon his private ambition to be the one and only starting quarterback.

+ + +

An offensive tackle named Horace Lovett, who did improbable double duty as Florida A&M's placekicker, made his stiff-legged, hulking way toward the tee and knocked the opening kickoff into flight. Near South Carolina State's goal line, R. C. Gamble gathered in the ball and headed upfield. In the Rattlers' loss in 1966, John Gilliam's kickoff return had beaten them, and even though Gilliam was by now in the NFL, Gamble was similarly lanky and strong and swift, and had racked up nearly a hundred yards rushing against A&M the previous year. Within seconds, everyone in Bragg Stadium would get the first clue as to whether the rematch would be a repeat or a reversal.

Gaither's coverage team, known as "the Headhunters," swarmed over Gamble at the fifteen-yard line and, in the pile, added a few punches for emphasis. "Let them know what it's like to be hit by a Rattler," Gaither had been preaching all week. "Rattle him from his head to his toenails." On first down, the Bulldogs lined up in their slot-I formation, and the Rattlers answered with their 5-4 monster. Pete Griffin squatted along the sideline, peering through his horn-rims down the line of scrimmage, spitting out arrows of tobacco juice, waiting to see how his formula would work.

Crouching under center, the quarterback, Johnny Jones, struggled to shout his signals above the noise of the crowd and the band. The Marching 100, strategically placed at the Bulldogs' end of the field, blared their brass and pummeled their drums and broke into a favorite chant: *You may be slick, you may be sly, but you can't slide on barbed wire.* When Jones looked over the Rattler defense, his eyes met those of Monster Sims. "Oh, Big Red," Sims said, referring to Jones's height and tawny skin. "I been waitin' on Big Red."

He didn't wait long. Two plays in a row, Sims smashed into the Bulldog backfield, causing losses and bringing up a long third down. Oree Banks, not wanting to risk a pass, not wanting to let A&M set up for a punt return, ordered a quick kick. But Willie Grate, the running back who was supposed to boot it, bobbled and lost the ball, and when the pile was untangled, the Rattlers had recovered the fumble on the Bulldog three. Two plays later, barely minutes into the game, Hubert Ginn slashed in for the touchdown.

It was exactly what Banks had feared and inveighed against: mistakes and turnovers, turnovers and mistakes. And it was exactly what Gaither had wanted: an early lead. "Don't make it close," he'd been saying in practice. "Because if it's close, they think they can win."

Several plays following the subsequent kickoff, South Carolina State fumbled again, this time on its own twenty-nine. Runs by Morand and Ginn took FAMU to the ten, and a pass interference penalty put the ball on the one. On first and second downs, the Bulldog defense held, but then Ginn squirted through for his second score. Riley ran for a two-point conversion, and the Rattlers were leading 15–0 in the first quarter. Early in the second, A&M blocked a State punt, and added a field goal for an 18–0 bulge.

By then, Banks's game plan was irrelevant, obsolete. Dominate the line, run the ball, use only short passes, get a lead and protect it: that was his method. He often told his quarterbacks, "All you got to do is don't lose it," meaning the ball, their composure, and the game. Instead, his team had already lost the first two and was headed toward losing the third.

Pete Griffin jammed nine defensive men close to the line, just plain outnumbering the Bulldog blockers, and ordered bingo stunts to baffle them. From his spot in the offensive backfield, R. C. Gamble could see his linemen hesitating, not sure whom to hit. He and Grate and Blocker could hardly get out of the backfield before being gang-tackled, and getting an earful of trash talk in the pile. *You keep running in here, you gonna get hurt.* And Gamble had to admit it: he was slowing down, ducking from the blows, trying not to get injured. Between plays, the Rattler defenders could hear the sounds of recrimination drifting from the Bulldog huddle. *Man, you gotta hold your block. . . . I'm working on it. They keep coming at me.*

Besides the eleven A&M players on the field there were another ninety-four Rattlers stretched along the sideline, an intimidating sight for South Carolina State's forty-man traveling squad. Griffin sent defenders in waves—the Blood unit on one possession, the Sweat Team on the next, the Tears Squad on the one after that. They shuttled in so quickly that A&M never needed a time-out, which might have given South Carolina State a moment to regroup. Instead, one of the Bulldog linemen, trudging off the field after yet another turnover or punt, said wearily to Banks, "Coach, I don't know what's going on. Every time I look up, someone has a fresh jersey."

For months now, Oree Banks had been telling his players that they could go unbeaten in 1967. It was a realistic prospect after a 16-3 record over the previous two years. Even as this game unraveled, he was trying to transfuse confidence into them, saying after each error, "They're not that much better," and, "Just don't make the same mistake." Now all that confidence, all the swagger, all the necessary arrogance were collapsing into a sinkhole of self-doubt.

Jones, the Bulldog quarterback, was paying the price for the way he'd spent the summer. Instead of devoting it to football practice, as he had every year since seventh grade, he went to Trenton, New Jersey, where three of his brothers worked in a Ford plant. Though he, too, put in hours on the assembly line, off-duty he caught the scent of the hippie movement, what the newspapers were calling the "Summer of Love." He rode the train into Manhattan and found his way to Greenwich Village, listening to the poets and folk singers in Washington Square Park, discovering a band named Iron Butterfly. Meanwhile, Oree Banks had been phoning Jones's mother in Greenville, asking where the heck he was and when he was coming back. For a while that magical summer, Jones doubted he would. Ultimately he reported back to Orangeburg, but fifteen pounds above his usual playing weight. When he sweated off the flab in a rubber suit during preseason practice, he felt weak and winded.

So by the third quarter against Monster Sims and the rest, Jones was woozy and bruised, anticipating hits even before he received them, completely out of rhythm. Banks benched him in favor of a sophomore, Robert Scott, who was better at reading defenses but too slow to escape the Rattler pass rush. He, too, got the hook, as Banks tried inserting a defensive back, Milton Nicholson, who had started his college career as a quarterback. It was the mirror image of Jake Gaither's jitters the year before in Orangeburg.

The whole game, in fact, inverted the 1966 upset. With one last touchdown, FAMU won 25–0. The Rattlers outrushed the Bulldogs 174 yards to 23, outgained them in total by 319 to 53, caused 5 turnovers, and didn't allow State across midfield until late in the third quarter. Not since the 1964 season, when the Rattlers routed Grambling in the Orange Blossom Classic, had a Gaither team so humbled such a quality opponent.

With its overpowering defense against South Carolina State, Florida A&M needed its quarterbacks only to be efficient and error-free. Even so, Ken Riley had a mixed game—long gains on several scrambles, a two-point conversion run, but also an end-zone interception and a fourth-down incompletion that blunted Rattler drives. If he didn't lose any ground to Elroy Morand in the starting quarterback sweepstakes, then he certainly hadn't gained any. The pair remained yoked together, each the first-stringer for half the time.

As a reward for their revenge victory, Jake Gaither gave his players a day off from practice the next Monday. Later that week, when the newest Associated Press small-college poll appeared, the Rattlers had climbed a notch, to ninth. South Carolina State didn't even rate an honorable mention. Between Gaither and Banks, it was clear once again who was the man of the house.

+ + +

In the carpeted room he had named "the Rattlers' Den," Jake Gaither welcomed the guests who were streaming in for a victory celebration. He and Sadie hosted an open house after every A&M home game, and the mood of this one was especially buoyant. Their brick bungalow, a few blocks off the campus, filled up with assistant coaches, alumni, college administrators, church deacons. There were the professors with whom Gaither played cards in a group called "the Benedicts," for a reason nobody could remember anymore, and his fellow members in the Tallahassee chapter of Sigma Pi Phi.

As always, Sadie Gaither had fried up chicken as crispy and dark as Jake liked—"Don't give me nothing that ain't brown," was his standard instruction—and loaded platters with collard greens, sandwiches, cookies, and cakes. Rum and gin and vodka flowed, though Gaither, a teetotaler, drank only ginger ale. For public amusement, he and Sadie put on their well-practiced version of *The Bickersons,* with her complaining about his play-calling. An English instructor at FAMU during the week, she spent football Saturdays in the stands, critiquing her husband's game plan as rigorously as a student's composition.

On a shelf in the Rattlers' Den there stood photos of Jake and Sadie in their college days, when they were courting, she with hair bobbed like a flapper's, he pensive in coat and tie. The inscription under her portrait read, "She Must Have Been A Beautiful Baby." Nearly forty years into a childless marriage, the Gaithers presided over an intentional family, the A&M players whom he coached and she taught, the surrogate children who loved and revered them as parents. Like a proud father, Gaither had decorated the room with their photos—a *Sports Illustrated* cover of Willie Galimore hurdling over several Green Bay tacklers; Bob Hayes breaking the tape to win the hundred-meter dash in the Tokyo Olympics; Al Denson and Clarence Childs with their respective pro teams in Denver and New York. The coach also displayed a framed portrait of a doctor in a lab coat, who as a FAMU student had played on the 1951 football team. "To Coach and 'Mom' Gaither," read the doctor's inscription. "Thank you for the opportunities and for your example."

As the party hummed along, a bank of headlights swept across the front of the brick house, and a red light pulsed through the night air. Several car doors opened, then slammed shut. From experience, Gaither and his guests knew what these signs signaled: the governor had arrived. The current one, Claude Kirk, was in his first term; before him, there had been one term apiece of C. Farris Bryant and W. Haydon Burns and two of LeRoy Collins. To a greater or lesser degree, each one was a fan of Rattler football, each one was a regular at the postgame open house, and each one was a defender of racial segregation in Florida. Kirk had won election as a Republican one year earlier by disavowing the party's Lincolnian legacy, its death knell in the South, and capitalizing on white backlash against President Lyndon B. Johnson, a Democrat who championed civil rights.

Tall and gregarious, Kirk moved through the living room, a tumbler of Jack Daniel's in hand. He called Gaither "Coach" and Gaither called him "Governor," and they painted a picture of comity. But for some of the younger members of Gaither's staff, and some of the more politicized professors, all the mutual backslapping provoked a quiet, private kind of disgust. Sure, it was a compliment of sorts that the governor had shown up for the party; certainly the head coach saw it that way. Outside the front door, though, a state trooper's cruiser was parked in the spot it always took when a governor came calling: on the front lawn. The Gaithers had put such care into their home, built from scratch with their two salaries, that they had even remade the floor plan to spare a favorite tree. Now, with its tires cutting furrows in the grass, the police car treated the house like some backwoods shanty, and Jake Gaither, despite all his gridiron achievements, as someone beneath ordinary respect.

THE BEST QUARTERBACK TONIGHT

Grambling vs. Tennessee State, October 7, 1967

The team bus pulled out of Grambling early on Friday morning, while the rest of the college slept, and it rolled through the ground fog across valleys and creeks on its way to an appointment in Nashville with Tennessee State. In the first row, right behind the driver, Eddie Robinson sat with his briefcase at his feet. It held his game plan and Ready Sheet, as well as a set of barber's clippers, should any of his players look insufficiently groomed. Earlier in the week Robinson had admonished them, "You're representing Grambling and you're representing your family," two obligations he considered nearly sacred. To a man, each player on the traveling squad was wearing the required coat and tie, some purchased by Robinson himself. Many of the veterans, familiar with the tedium of travel, had also come equipped with pillows to nap away the time.

There were nine hours and five hundred miles between Grambling and Nashville, and then a full day of practice, meals, fitful sleep, and mounting anticipation before the Saturday-night kickoff. Over all his years in the Deep South, navigating the hostile white terrain that separated the archipelago of small black colleges, Robinson had learned to devise road trips that were both frugal and free of confrontation. On this journey, the team would debark only once along the way, to eat lunch in the employee cafeteria of a black-owned insurance company in Memphis. Even with such precautions, the coach reminded his young men not to answer any jeers or slurs they might encounter along the way, maybe at a gas station, maybe at a traffic light. That kind of baiting had happened enough times before.

Inside the team bus as it pushed northeast through the Arkansas Delta, each cluster of players or coaches settled into its own chosen distraction. By superstitious routine, Robinson sat as usual beside Fred Hobdy, an assistant coach who had played for him on the unbeaten team back in 1942. The men shared a language of shorthand and inside jokes, starting with their habit of calling each other "Lefty." Across the aisle, Doug Porter and Melvin Lee, the assistant coaches who had scouted Tennessee State, reviewed their strategy. James Harris, as quarterback and captain, merited a seat behind the coaches, next to his Monroe homeboy Delles Howell and his favorite receiver, Charlie Joiner. Harris spent some time with his books, preparing assignments due on Monday, and some time talking trash. As he always said, at black schools like Grambling trash talk was the only publicity you got. Deep in the back rows, where some of the guys were playing bid whist or tonk for a nickel a hand, two massive tackles from New Orleans, Robert Jones and Clifford Gasper, started singing Motown hits. Gasper, a sophomore weighing nearly 300 pounds while most college linemen were 220 or less, was called "Big Tiny." That nickname somehow captured the unlikely magic of this behemoth hitting the falsetto highs on "My Girl." Pretty soon the whole bus joined in the chorus.

Until the season's first away game, two weeks earlier against Alcorn in Mississippi, many of the younger players in the bus had never been outside Louisiana. The Delta landscape of this trip, cotton fields and rice fields, shotgun shacks and juke joints, had them staring out the window like tourists. Harris liked to jive the new players about how elegant life was on the road. Didn't they know Grambling always stayed in a motel? There was the "gym motel," the "bleacher motel," the "barn motel," wherever the opposing school put up the visiting team on its campus. And as the Grambling players were falling asleep the night before the game, you could be sure some windows would have been mysteriously left open for the mosquitoes to swoop in or that the band would just coincidentally be rehearsing outside.

None of the diversions on the bus, though, could last through the morning, and none of them could obscure the sense of urgent purpose. Over the 1965 and 1966 seasons, Tennessee State had eclipsed Grambling (and Florida A&M, and every other school) at the apex of black college football. It had gone 19-0-1 while winning consecutive national black championships and trouncing a northern, mostly white school, Muskingum College, in a small-college bowl game. Eleven players from the last two Tennessee State teams had already been drafted by the pros, and the 1967 squad featured more than a dozen prospects. While Collie Nicholson was still struggling to persuade newspapers in Ruston, Monroe, and Shreveport to assign a reporter to cover Grambling, Tennessee State had been the subject of a feature article earlier in the fall in *Sports Illustrated*.

That was plenty, but there was more. As much as Coach Robinson taught that football was a team sport, won or lost as a unit, the game against Tennessee State also devolved to two personal rivalries, one between the head coaches and the other between their starting quarterbacks. Down each bench and through each lineup, the passion ran so deep it seemed fitting that both teams claimed the same mascot, the Tiger, as if to say the other was just the paper variety.

Many were the reasons why Eddie Robinson loathed John Merritt, and they only began with Tennessee State's growing mastery over Gram-

▼

bling on the field. Merritt had beaten Robinson twice in a row, six of the last ten times, and had done it in a style calculated to infuriate: the Flim-Flam Man fleecing the Boy Scout. Where Robinson went recruiting Bible in hand, Merritt arrived in a luxury sedan, sporting sunglasses, multiple rings, and an El Producto cigar. Of his tactic, Merritt once explained, "A boy who lives on a dirt floor is bound to be impressed by a man who drives a Cadillac and dresses well." While Robinson prided himself on an intricate understanding of every facet of his team, Merritt rarely visited practice sessions and barely knew the playbook. His self-appointed role was as showman, impresario, ringmaster of a sporting entertainment he simply called "The Show."

And if The Show wasn't going quite as planned, Merritt could turn for intervention to particular referees who regularly worked Tennessee State home games. A certain amount of home-field advantage, including in the officiating, was expected among the black colleges, but as far as his opponents were concerned, Merritt was not willing merely to benefit from a few favorable judgment calls. He wanted to orchestrate them; he wanted to write the script. Merritt had been known to call out from the sideline for a helpful penalty, seemingly ordering clipping or interference like a burger and fries. After one exasperating game in Nashville, Robinson informed Merritt that he would only play there again if the officials were hired from the Ohio Valley Conference, an integrated league to which neither team belonged. At Grambling's next game in Nashville, there, again, were two of Merritt's regulars, in uniforms adorned with the OVC logo.

On at least one occasion, the antagonism between the head coaches had nearly turned physical. Just before kickoff of the 1965 game in Nashville, Merritt had strolled into the Grambling locker room, a complete breach of football etiquette, apparently to sneak a look at which players were being taped and wrapped for injuries. "Get out of here," Robinson demanded, seething. As Merritt blithely continued his inspection, the Grambling coach spat in his palms and rubbed them together, readying the first punch. Only then did Merritt retreat, evanescent and unsettling as the gremlin on the wing, having succeeded in disrupting Robinson's pregame preparations. Tennessee State proceeded to blow out Grambling 40–7, as lopsided a defeat as Robinson had ever endured.

The competition between James Harris and Eldridge Dickey, the dueling quarterbacks, was of a different nature. For two years they had been circling each other, aircraft on the same radar screen, without yet having collided. Harris had missed the 1965 game because he developed a blood clot in one leg from being squeezed into a bus seat for the long trek to Nashville. He still remembered the way the nurses in Nashville's black hospital, some of them Tennessee State coeds, had teased him about Grambling's loss. The next year, with the game in Grambling, Harris guided his team to a 16–0 lead before suffering a knee injury. Sidelined for the second half, he watched helplessly as Dickey threw for 343 yards and 4 touchdowns to rally Tennessee State to a 31–23 victory. Games like that typified Dickey's career. Heading into his senior year in 1967, he had posted extravagant numbers: 64 touchdowns, more than 4,700 yards passing, a 68 percent completion percentage. Lithe and sinewy at 6-2 and 190, he could throw the ball 60 yards with either hand, and punt or placekick farther than anyone on the team. His IQ was in the high 130s. Always eager to promote his product, Merritt awarded Dickey the nickname "The Lord's Prayer."

Harris was filled with both admiration and envy. He could not help rooting for Dickey to break the color barrier at quarterback in the pros, even if that accomplishment would deprive him, a year younger, of the chance to make history. When the Houston Oilers' general manager, Don Klosterman, declared in *Sport* magazine that "Dickey can definitely make it as a quarterback" in the NFL or AFL, black newspapers from the *Los Angeles Sentinel* to the *Chicago Defender* picked up the story as civil rights news. Dickey himself spoke with a daring candor that Eddie Robinson and Collie Nicholson never would have allowed Harris, announcing that he would require a contract guaranteeing him the right to play quarterback, as protection against the pros' habit of switching black quarterbacks to other positions. "If they won't give me a real chance," he told a black newspaper, "I'll be working on my master's degree and watching pro football on TV."

Even though he felt solidarity with Dickey, Harris hungered for public confrontation, side-by-side comparison. For the past two seasons, he had read all the headlines in black papers—"Dickey Dazzles for Tennessee State" . . . "Dickey Stars in QB Role for Big Blue" . . . "Dickey Paces Tennessee Romp." Harris had seen Dickey named twice in a row to the *Pittsburgh Courier* All-America team. While Harris could hardly begrudge the selection, he had waited with a clock watcher's vigilance for the weeks and months to pass, for the 1967 game to come around. He craved a showdown in which he could prove he was as great as the great Dickey, and just maybe better.

"This was truly the only time I was interested in showcasing my talent," Harris recalled years later. "The other games I played in, I was aiming to win. When we played Tennessee State, I had to put my skill on the line against Dickey. It was the only game I played where I was thinking it was me against the other."

The comparison, however much Harris welcomed it, put him at a built-in disadvantage. Tennessee State had designed its entire offense to exploit Dickey's passing, recruiting receivers with sprinters' speed and splitting them wide on nearly every play. Harris, in contrast, had willingly sublimated his quarterbacking ego for the sake of an offense built around running and physical domination, seasoned with short passes off play-action fakes. On the rare occasions when Harris lined up Grambling in its deep-passing formations, the "East" and "West," every single opponent knew immediately from years of experience the handful of downfield patterns that Eddie Robinson preferred. It was a lucky day for Harris if Charlie Joiner was getting only double coverage instead of triple.

And if 1967 was going to be the season for Grambling to open up its offense, that certainly hadn't happened yet. The Tigers had won their first two games, against Alcorn and Prairie View, while scoring a grand total of twenty-six points. With Alcorn, perhaps, the struggle could be ascribed to Coach Marino Casem's habitually strong defense, and to an injury that knocked wingback Essex Johnson out of the game. There was no excuse for the futility at home against middling Prairie View: six holding penalties, three drives that stalled inside the twenty-five-yard line. The winning margin, a short touchdown pass from Harris to Joiner, came after Prairie View had fumbled away the ball on its own five. It was no wonder that Grambling had vanished from the AP's most recent small-college poll, not receiving a single vote.

It also was no wonder that in the week leading up to the Tennessee State game, Doug Porter and Melvin Lee had been mulling over some ways of rejuvenating the offense. One thing they knew from experience was that Tennessee State was too strong and aggressive on its defensive front for Grambling to expect to outmuscle it. The problems started with Claude Humphrey, a 6-5, 250-pound defensive tackle who was surprisingly quick and mobile on his bowed legs. During the 1966 game, Humphrey had spent so much time in the Grambling backfield that Robinson paced the sideline muttering, "We've got to get someone on him." A reserve lineman called out, "Coach." Robinson ignored him. The player shouted again, "Coach, put me in." Again, Robinson said nothing. "Coach, let me try." Finally Robinson turned to face the reserve and in his most exasperated voice, the one that was almost a whine, said, "I got somebody *trying*. I need someone to *block*."

The usual offensive logic against aggressive linemen such as Humphrey called for using their speed and momentum against them. When they rush forward fast, catch them in a trap block. When they pursue laterally, run counters in the opposite direction. Grambling specialized in precisely those plays, but they hadn't worked well against Tennessee State the past two years. Instead, Porter and Lee were pondering the apostasy of a pass-first, run-later game plan. In scouting Tennessee State, they had identified its defensive weakness as the secondary, which had lost all but one starter to the pro draft. In its opening game of the 1967 season, against San Diego State, Tennessee State had surrendered the game-winning touchdown pass to a third-string quarterback. How much more damage could a gifted, experienced, confident passer such as James Harris do?

Sitting together on the team bus, kickoff drawing closer by the minute and the mile, Porter and Lee talked about using more than the predictable East and West formations, doing more than splitting out just Charlie Joiner as the only receiver the defense had to worry about. Eddie Robinson had the plays in his playbook to stretch the field; it was a matter of convincing him to call them. For all the head coach's emphasis on painstaking execution and minimal mistakes, the qualities that Robinson emulated from Woody Hayes's teams at Ohio State and Vince Lombardi's in Green Bay, both Porter and Lee knew that Robinson also had a soft spot for the long bomb. In the right situation he was willing to go deep three times in a row in the hope of completing one, preferably for a touchdown. When that happened, Robinson had a way of saying with a wistful sigh, like a suitor remembering a romantic night, "I love to see that scoreboard light up."

During the long ride to Nashville, Harris alternated between stretching his legs into the aisle and standing in place. He was already nursing a sore ankle from a basketball injury over the summer, which made it difficult to plant his feet when he passed. No way was he going to miss another Tennessee State game with another blood clot. When Porter walked back for a visit, though, Harris sat and listened. It turned out that he, too, had been thinking about a Plan B. The coaches and the quarterback agreed on one more thing: with Merritt's chosen officials calling the penalties, Grambling needed to make sure the game wasn't close. Only a passing offense could supply enough points.

Late on that Friday afternoon, the Grambling bus pulled up outside Tennessee State's gym, where the team would be put up overnight. Several dozen students were waiting. As the Grambling players walked out on stiff legs, their dress clothes rumpled after so many hours, the hosts began taunting. *We're gonna send you back home.*

After a brief practice in the stadium and dinner in the university cafeteria and a team meeting, the Grambling players repaired to the cots that had been set up for them in a phys ed classroom. At some point in the night, Delles Howell heard whispering from Big Tiny's direction and asked what was going on. "There's a pimp downstairs," someone said. "He's got three or four girls. He wants to know does anybody want one." The Grambling players, imbued with Mildred Moss's lessons about being gentlemen and Coach Robinson's lectures about representing their college, called out that nobody had that kind of money, trying to get the pimp to leave. When he still lingered with his girls at the bottom of a stairwell, several players hurled down chairs to make the point more emphatically. Finally the pimp took his business elsewhere, leaving behind a sleepless team and a lingering question: Was this just one more of John Merritt's little tricks?

+   +   +

At the same time that Grambling's bus had been nearing the Tennessee State campus, another vehicle was making its way through Nashville. This one was a new Cadillac, painted in a shade called autumn rust and driven by a burly man with a floral tie and a dangling cigar, John Merritt. He steered the Cadillac onto a stretch of sunbaked dirt set beside a cow pasture and a machine shed, what sufficed as a practice field for the Tennessee State team, and glided to a halt on the fifty-yard line. Then, as he did at the conclusion of workouts on the Friday before every home game, Merritt stood like a stumping politician with his players around him and declared, "Gentlemen, the hay is in the barn."

At 6-3 and 250 and possessed of a booming baritone voice, Merritt turned his gaze to Eldridge Dickey and said, "Dickey, you owe me." He stared at Claude Humphrey and said, "Humphrey, you owe me." As the hubbub built, Merritt shouted, "I want my pay today!" He meant the victory he thought he deserved for inviting these young men to star in The Show. Nearly all of the time, they obliged.

For all the excitement that Merritt ginned up with this ritual, it also attested to a certain hypocrisy. Except for these Friday crescendos, when he could command all the attention, Merritt hardly ever favored the practice field with his presence. Sure, he might turn up at the end of drills on other days just long enough to order wind sprints, the emperor among the commoners. But the deeper into the lineup he went past marquee players such as Dickey and Humphrey, the less likely he was to know anyone's name. His signature greeting, "How you feel, baby?" neatly covered his indifference to such details.

Merritt put the details in the hands of two brilliant assistant coaches, Joe Gilliam Sr. on the defense and Alvin "Cat" Coleman on the offense. He had hired them to work with him in 1955 when he was the head coach at Jackson State in Mississippi, and brought them with him to Tennessee State in 1963. Over several intervening summers, while studying for his master's degree at the University of Kentucky, Gilliam had been mentored by the school's football coaches, among them Blanton Collier, Chuck Knox, and Don Shula, all of whom later led NFL teams. In the generation younger than Eddie Robinson and Jake Gaither, Gilliam may well have been the most talented defensive coach of any color in the nation. He worked, though, for the most covetous of bosses. Whenever Gilliam received coaching offers from other colleges, Merritt made sure to undermine him, telling their athletic directors, "You can't handle Gilliam. Can't nobody handle Gilliam but me."

In exchange for his coerced loyalty, Gilliam got to function as the de facto head coach six days a week. He oversaw all the practices, and he instilled Tennessee State's trademarks of conditioning and ferocity. Gilliam adapted the training techniques that Tennessee State's track coach, Ed Temple, had used with his women's team, the Tigerbelles, to develop Olympic medalists such as Wilma Rudolph. To that emphasis on speed and endurance, Gilliam added a disciplinarian's rigor. As a professor, he was known for locking his classroom door to any tardy students. As a coach, he meted out a penalty called the "two-five-five": the offending player had to logroll himself from goal line to goal line twice, then run five hundred-yard sprints, and finally five fifty-yard sprints. Gilliam especially applied the punishment to Humphrey, building up a rage to be unleashed on each Saturday's opponent. Only once did Gilliam miscalculate. The day after an especially harsh practice, Humphrey caught sight of the coach's teenage son Joe Jr. on a shopping street off-campus. Humphrey shoved the teenager and instructed the bewildered boy, "Tell your daddy."

Perhaps because he had played quarterback in college, earning Black All-America honors at West Virginia State, Gilliam understood exactly how to destroy an opposing offense. He varied the number and placement of defensive linemen incessantly during a game to confuse the blockers, and he ordered his cornerbacks to play "bump and run" against receivers, stiff-arming them at the line to disrupt pass patterns before they even got under way. He taught a defensive philosophy like a sequence of Latin declensions. No touchdowns. No big plays. No consecutive first downs. Turnovers. "We will be an offensive defense," he demanded. "We're gonna attack you. We're not gonna react."

Cat Coleman, in contrast, was reassuring in a pedantic sort of way. Having earned a master's degree in biology from the University of Michigan, he taught genetics at Tennessee State and enjoyed chatting about molecular structure. He brought a scientist's logical mind to the gridiron as well. In the sophisticated style of a pro team, Tennessee State ran multiple variations off its basic formation—shifts, men in motion, empty backfield, three or four or five wide receivers. Coleman taught Dickey how to quickly analyze coverage by dividing the defensive backfield into four quadrants and then taking aim at the most vulnerable one. To use Dickey's combination of intelligence and instinct, Coleman let him call almost every play at the line of scrimmage. The results of this experiment were recorded in Dickey's gaudy statistics.

As for the absentee landlord Merritt, he busied himself with a few chosen duties, most of which involved his talent for mind games. He courted journalists. He lined up "sponsors" to give players summer jobs and travel money. He insinuated himself into Nashville's segregated political scene, and white candidates sought his endorsement as a key to black votes.

Most crucially, Merritt provided Gilliam and Coleman with the raw material to mold into championship contours. He recruited the top prospects, and when his Cadillac and clothes didn't seal the deal, he had a habit of reaching into his pocket for a roll of cash—fifty singles, there for deceptive bulk, wrapped inside a visible $100 bill. When he sent his main recruiter, Shannon Little, on the road, Merritt specified the type of player he coveted, ideally a lanky and agile basketball player, as Humphrey had been in high school, who could add thirty or forty pounds of muscle in college. And it had to be muscle. Merritt ordered no uniforms with waist sizes larger than thirty-four inches, announcing, "Not a belly on this team but the head coach." When a player plumped up, "Big John" felt no hesitation in ordering him onto a "T-day diet," meaning no food on Tuesdays and Thursdays.

Whatever Merritt didn't know about X's and O's, even his own team's, he did know about manipulating his young men. Instead of enlisting players' families as his allies, he played in an almost Faustian way on their distance from home. "All you guys," he often said, "when you left home, your mama broke your plate and tied your bed up. I got you now. You're here with me."

Merritt imbued the team with his own braggadocio and swagger. Tennessee State players didn't just tackle an opposing player, they stood over the fallen foe, boasting. The team's linebackers and defensive backs specialized in "clotheslining"—whacking a forearm across a receiver's neck to lay him out flat. Though the move looked more like a karate chop by Oddjob in the James Bond flick *Goldfinger* than a football maneuver, it was devastating and, for now, legal. Not that the rulebook had ever restrained Merritt much, anyway. He gladly tolerated penalties for unnecessary roughness, accepting a fifteen-yard mark-off in exchange for the aura of intimidation that a cheap shot imparted.

Yet the coach also knew how to pluck tender chords. At halftime of a game against Southern University in Baton Rouge in 1965, Tennessee State was trailing 36–7. Dickey, then a sophomore, had thrown six interceptions. The homecoming crowd was jeering. Entering the locker room, Gilliam and even Coleman were prepared to breathe fire. Merritt pulled them aside and explained, "I know you two damn guys are upset. Let me tell you something. If you go in there and give 'em hell when they're down 36–7, an undefeated season is out the window. Tell them what they can do to *win* this game." The men took Merritt's advice, and Tennessee State charged back to win 40–36 on its way to a 9-0-1 record.

Something, though, had been misfiring so far in the 1967 season. The year had begun with a small-college version of a "Game of the Century"—second-ranked Tennessee State, riding a twenty-four-game unbeaten streak, taking on number-one San Diego State. It was no embarrassment for Merritt's team to narrowly lose on the road against a higher-rated squad. But scoring just one touchdown in a 16–8 defeat came as a shock. In Merritt's four previous years at Tennessee State, the Tigers had never put up fewer points; the 1966 team, with almost the identical lineup on offense, had averaged forty points a game.

Coming off the opening-day defeat, Tennessee State reverted to its commanding form, shutting out North Carolina A&T 35–0 in Nashville. Then, the following week, Tennessee State faltered again, losing 14–10 at Texas Southern. Instead of showing off in his home city of Houston, Dickey took such a pounding that the Nashville newspapers speculated that he might sit out the next game, against Grambling. Of course, Merritt could have been feeding such disinformation to reporters to throw off Eddie Robinson.

With twenty-eight returning lettermen on Tennessee State, the problem wasn't a lack of talent. If anything, the team had too much talent, with too little supervision. Ever since summer practices had begun, Joe Gilliam had noticed some unfamiliar white faces around campus— lingering outside Merritt's office door, idling in front of the athletics building. These men weren't pro scouts, because all the pro scouts who surveyed Tennessee State were black men whom Gilliam knew. These men weren't any of the handful of white professors at the college, all of them familiar by name or face. These men, the coach surmised, were agents, and they shouldn't have been anywhere near players until the season had ended and the seniors had used up their college eligibility.

Soon Gilliam spotted several players inexplicably driving new cars.

Then a particular linebacker led a boycott of the afternoon session of two-a-day practice. Even after Gilliam quelled it with the threat to kick the ingrates off the team, a pattern of defiance had been set. Word leaked back to Gilliam that the agents were telling their prospective clients that Tennessee State practiced too hard. Why risk getting injured? Why blow your chance at the big bucks of a pro contract?

As Gilliam watched the first three games of the 1967 season, he recognized the subtle differences, the way a certain running back wouldn't strain forward in the final lunge for a first down on a third-and-two play, the way a particular defender didn't throw himself into the blocking wedge on kickoff coverage. "It destroys the chemistry," Gilliam would say years later, remembering the frustrations freshly enough to speak in the present tense. "You got guys who think they're above the law, above the team."

So the game against Grambling offered Tennessee State its best and perhaps last chance to salvage its season, to reestablish its dominance. The team had not lost a home game since 1963. W. J. Hale Stadium, better known as "the Hole," sat in a natural ravine, helping the spectators and marching band drown out an opposing quarterback's signal count and audibles. The decibel level promised to be even higher for the Grambling game, with five thousand seats newly added to the existing nine thousand. For all its stumbles and subplots in going 1-2, Tennessee State remained number eight in the small-college poll, and Grambling was uncharacteristically overlooked. But only one of the Tigers would emerge from their tangle as the top cat.

+   +   +

James Harris and Eldridge Dickey stood almost back to back at midfield of the Hole, each quarterback limbering up his arm in the final moments before kickoff. Within eyesight and earshot of the pair stood another set of antagonists, the black scouts Tank Younger and Lloyd Wells. Younger, of course, was a Grambling alumnus, Eddie Robinson's first star, who was now working the black college circuit for the Los Angeles Rams. Wells did the same for the Kansas City Chiefs, driving from campus to campus in a convertible painted with the team's red and gold.

Marine veteran, professional photographer, a reporter for black newspapers, and a civil rights activist in sports, Wells was already a legendary figure in his early forties. People called him "Judge" for his appraising eye, "Seldom Seen" for his habit of quick exits, "Outta Sight" for his favorite term of praise. Compared to Younger, an establishment type in the Robinson mold, Wells was a dapper dandy, an operator. Everyone in black college football knew the story of how he'd almost literally stolen Otis Taylor, a wide receiver from Prairie View A&M, for the AFL's Chiefs. Posing as a photographer for *Ebony*, Wells had sneaked him out the window of a motel where the Dallas Cowboys of the NFL had him sequestered until he signed their contract.

Normally, Wells evaluated players without regard to sentiment, loyal only to his employers on the Chiefs and to his goal of furthering the integration of the AFL. He had guided the Chiefs to drafting such future stars as Buck Buchanan from Grambling, Willie Lanier from Morgan State, and Emmitt Thomas from Bishop College. As a Houston native, though, Wells could not remain professionally detached from the showdown between his homeboy Eldridge Dickey and James Harris.

"There's the best quarterback," Wells said to Younger, indicating Dickey.

"We'll see tonight," Younger replied.

As Harris eavesdropped on the banter, he heard the scouts make a bet.

Then, with warm-ups over, Younger pulled aside the Grambling quarterback and laid a hand on his shoulder pads. "You got to go out today," he told Harris, "and shut Lloyd Wells up."

Hearing the order was one thing; executing it against Joe Gilliam's defense was another. On Grambling's first possession, Harris found seven defenders crowding the line, and often a cornerback and safety as well, creeping forward. From his crouch, Claude Humphrey could glare right up into the quarterback's eyes. Flanking Humphrey on one side was his roommate Tommie Davis, 270 pounds of defensive tackle. All week in the dorm, they'd been jawing about who'd hit Harris first, who'd get more sacks. On Humphrey's other side, defensive end Joe "Turkey" Jones pressed his cleats into the turf for traction. He was 6-6 and 250, yet supple enough to perform double-gainer dives in the college pool. Better yet for Jones, Grambling's usual starter facing him at right tackle had been injured, and was being replaced by a converted defensive lineman.

With its aggressive alignment, Tennessee State was daring Grambling to pass. Gilliam, knowing Robinson's penchant for routine, reckoned that it wouldn't. And he reckoned right enough. Grambling threw a couple of safe square-outs to open the game, getting a first down. But Joiner, the only wide receiver, was being double-covered. James Marsalis, Tennessee State's most experienced defensive back, was shadowing Essex Johnson when the wingback went downfield. By Grambling's third pass attempt, Humphrey and Jones were overpowering Grambling's linemen and Tennessee State's linebackers were bolting past the Grambling running backs assigned to pick up the blitz.

Harris managed one first down on a survival scramble, retreating almost twenty yards before escaping up the sideline to gain fifteen, but on the next set of downs he was sacked and had a pass batted down before Grambling punted away. Pinned inside its own five on the subsequent possession, after Eldridge Dickey had been intercepted, Grambling returned to its commonplaces, and Tennessee State was waiting for them. Humphrey and Davis swallowed up Johnson on counters and Henry Jones on fullback dives. After heaving a long incompletion from the end zone on third down to avoid a sack and a safety, Harris heard the trash talk. *Shack, I got you lined up. . . . You can't block me. . . . I'ma getcha next time. . . . I'll be back to see you, Shack.*

Harris jogged off the field and approached Robinson. It was a rare thing, a straining of protocol, for him to speak to the coach in midgame unbidden. With his clipboard in hand and a phone connection to Fred Hobdy in the press box, Robinson was readying his defense. Though he was relentlessly restless during practice sessions, during games Robinson stayed almost stationary, focused as a searchlight's beam on the field, emitting short phrases of compliment or concern as players shuttled past him. *That's the way to go after him. . . . Son, you got to do better than that. . . . That's the way to hit him. He'll remember your name next time. . . . Damn it to hell.*

But Harris felt compelled to try something. He and Doug Porter had been discussing it all week. He and Joiner had been talking about it throughout the first quarter as they compared notes on Tennessee State's pass coverage. In this decisive game, Harris could no longer wait compliantly for permission. So he told Robinson, "Give me Atkins."

Robinson turned to Porter and asked, "Do you believe in it?" Porter nodded.

Robert Atkins started at safety for Grambling, and also backed up the first-string tight end, Billy Ray Newsome. Newsome was a blocker, not much of a receiving threat. Atkins had 9.6 speed and soft hands. If he split out a few yards from the line, Marsalis would have to cover him. A stocky sparkplug with powerful hands and shoulders for the bump-and-run, Marsalis matched up well against shorter, lighter Essex Johnson. But he gave away four inches, a dozen pounds, and a half step of speed to Atkins.

As Harris, Porter, and Robinson talked, Atkins was playing defense on the field, where Dickey had Grambling on its heels. Eight plays after a short Grambling punt, he handed off to Wayne Reese for a five-yard touchdown run. With 1:25 left in the opening quarter, Tennessee State led 7–0. "The last to draw is the first to die," Eddie Robinson liked to say, quoting a favorite cowboy movie. Against the toughest foe in the most hostile stadium on Grambling's schedule, his team was now on the wrong side of that aphorism.

When Atkins trotted off the field with the defense, Robinson grabbed him by the arm. He told him a play he wanted called. Then he pushed him over to join the offense.

The substitution did not surprise Tennessee State. During the previous week, in fact, Merritt had posted a sign in the locker room, the football equivalent of a *Wanted* poster: "Robert Atkins #84 The Man." Gilliam now implemented his solution. Rather than reducing the pass rush to provide more coverage on Atkins, he added even greater pressure on Harris, sending defensive backs on blitzes.

On first down, Tennessee State sacked Harris yet again. But on second, as Harris backpedaled under the assault, he softly lofted a screen pass to Charlie Burkins, a sophomore halfback, who scampered for seventeen yards and a first down. Two running plays and a defensive penalty later, Harris called signals at the Tennessee State twenty-six-yard line. Atkins lined up tight on the right side, with Johnson flanked outside him, drawing Marsalis in coverage. At the snap, the cornerback instead shot across the line, bearing down on Harris. The quarterback watched Atkins dash downfield, then angle right toward the end zone on a corner-post route. Marsalis leaped toward Harris, stretching out his arm to block the pass. The ball barely cleared his fingers. Atkins beat a safety to it for the tying touchdown.

Gilliam on the sideline and Humphrey on the field began to come to the same maddening realization: unlike most quarterbacks they attacked, Harris was not panicking. He was strong enough to stand in the pocket against the onslaught, mobile enough to evade it when necessary, and, most important, composed enough not to choke.

Dickey put Tennessee State back ahead halfway through the second quarter with a short touchdown pass to Wayne Reese after Grambling had fumbled away a punt. And right then, with a 14–7 lead, Tennessee State had several chances to pull away. But Dickey was intercepted by Delles Howell on Grambling's five. Three plays later, the halfback Burkins fumbled on Grambling's ten-yard line, amid three Tennessee State defenders. Falling to the ground, he stretched out an arm and managed to recover the ball. On the next play, with Grambling punting out of its end zone, Tennessee State surged offside, giving Harris a new set of downs.

With less than two minutes remaining in the half, he started cautiously, with a run by Burkins. Tennessee State piled on for a fifteen-yard penalty. After Harris slipped on his weak ankle while dropping back, re-sulting in a ten-yard loss, he tried to hit Joiner on a fly pattern down the right sideline. A defensive back interfered, and the penalty took Grambling to the Tennessee State twenty-eight.

Now, barely a minute shy of halftime, Tennessee State hoped to force Grambling into a long field goal. The kicking game was Robinson's weak spot, the one part of Grambling's game that received little attention in his hands-on, coach-every-position leadership style. Grambling, after all, was not supposed to have to punt very often; Grambling was not sup-posed to be in a game close enough for a field goal to matter.

So Gilliam called for a prevent defense, dropping his linebackers into pass coverage and deploying all four defensive backs deep to guard against a long gain. Atkins split wide right, with Marsalis awaiting him. Harris dropped back, tall enough to see over the encroaching rushers. Atkins raced straight downfield, with Marsalis rapidly skipping backward to keep the play in front of him. But as Atkins threatened to burst past him, Marsalis turned his back on both quarterback and receiver to break into a run.

From all their informal summer practices with Willie Brown, the Grambling alumnus now starring as a cornerback in the AFL, the team's receivers had learned to wait for that exact moment, when the defender pivoted and was briefly as disoriented as a driver losing sight of a passing car in the mirror. Atkins cut diagonally left toward the goal line, gaining a stride before Marsalis could locate him. Harris arched a pass toward the back of the end zone, where only Atkins could possibly reach it. Inches from the end line, with just fifty-seven seconds left in the half, Atkins reeled in the ball for a touchdown. The extra point tied the game at 14–14, and the half ended that way.

To Harris and Atkins and the rest of the team, the deadlock felt more like a presentiment of victory, proof Grambling could hold its own in the Hole. Heading into the Tennessee State locker room, in contrast, John Merritt had reason for concern. Gilliam's defense had been playing with such reckless fury that it had racked up nearly seventy-five yards in penalties, despite the presence of hometown officials. On offense, Dickey had been throwing with unusual impatience, far from the suave aplomb of The Lord's Prayer. He suffered from the absence of his favorite receiver, John Robinson, who had been injured against Texas Southern, and inadequately replaced against Grambling by a newly converted defensive end. Dickey was also facing two defensive backs, Howell and Atkins, who had been studying him in films of the 1965 and 1966 games. They knew Dickey had a habit of locking onto one receiver, so they read his eyes to position themselves. They knew, too, that Dickey tended to float his passes to be easily catchable. It also made the ball just a little bit slow, and the Grambling cornerbacks were poised to react fast and beat the receivers to it.

Grambling's preparation and Tennessee State's penalties, though, explained only so much. More was wrong with Tennessee State than any scouting report or game plan could rectify.

+ + +

During the early 1950s, when he was coaching and teaching at a black high school in Winchester, Kentucky, Joe Gilliam Sr. led three family rituals. One was to listen together to *The Shadow* and *Fibber McGee and Molly* on the household radio. Another was supper after church on Sundays, with Gilliam making fried chicken, collard greens, and his special potato salad. Last, and most cherished, was the Friday-night talent show. Gilliam tap-danced. His sons Craig and Joe Jr. oiled their bodies for muscle-flexing exhibitions. And his daughter Sonia sang.

Her choice must have especially pleased the contest judge, Gilliam's wife, Ruth, for she adored classical music. She filled the Gilliam home with LPs of Chopin, Beethoven, and Tchaikovsky, and on weekends drove her children the hundred miles to Louisville to sit in the segregated balcony for Philharmonic Society concerts. A college graduate who had chosen to be a homemaker, a rare luxury for a black woman of her place and time, Ruth Gilliam joined her husband in imbuing their children with culture and aspiration, and in waiting for America to make good on its promise to reward those traits, irrespective of color.

By the summer of 1967, the advent of the football season, the Gilliams were in most visible ways enjoying the comfortable existence of a faculty family, residing on the college campus, moving among the black elite of Nashville. Their elder son, Craig, had just graduated from Tennessee State and been drafted by the Pittsburgh Steelers in recognition of his illustrious career as a defensive back. His younger brother, Joe Jr., was the starting quarterback for Nashville's black high school in the second year of an integrated city league. The youngest Gilliam child, Kimberly, was turning seven. And Sonia, a twenty-year-old heading into her senior year at Tennessee State, had blossomed into the star of the family—dean's list student, drum majorette, vice president of the band, member of the Spanish honor society, volunteer counselor, selection for *Who's Who Among Students in American Colleges and Universities.*

What almost no one outside this proud, accomplished family knew was that during the summer Sonia had tried to slash her wrists. Outside public view, she had been struggling with depression for several years, while her parents sought counseling and therapy for her. Those efforts, the slashing made clear, had failed. In the wake of Sonia's suicide attempt, the Gilliams had her committed to the teaching hospital affiliated with Meharry Medical College in Nashville. A black institution that had been founded almost a century earlier by the United Methodist Church, Meharry had for decades offered the best option for a black patient anywhere in the South. Even with segregation officially outlawed, the Gilliams were reluctant to have Sonia admitted at Vanderbilt University Medical Center, part of an overwhelmingly white university.

So during the late summer of 1967, Joe Gilliam Sr. stinted on practices to spend time with his daughter in the hospital. Even after she was released, and seemingly returned to her academic routine, he felt distracted with worry. Players such as Claude Humphrey could see the distant stare behind Gilliam's black-framed glasses, could hear in Gilliam's flat tone that the coach wasn't being his "usual ornery self." One of them, a defensive back named Bob Askew, understood especially acutely; he was Sonia's boyfriend.

Then, in late September, several majorettes' uniforms were stolen, and the episode threw Sonia into disproportionate despair. Early on the Wednesday afternoon of October 4, three days before the Grambling game, she crawled onto a window ledge on the sixth floor of a women's dormitory. Four friends, together in the room, pleaded with Sonia to come back inside. Instead, she rolled herself off the ledge and fell to her death. When Joe and Ruth Gilliam, already distraught, approached their pastor, he told them that the church could not perform a funeral for a suicide.

Amid all the grief and anger, Gilliam still tried to prepare his defensive team for Grambling, and he intended to be on the sideline as usual for the game. John Merritt, in an uncommon moment of humility, admitted to a Nashville newspaper that he couldn't be of much help, saying, "Coach Gilliam is the only man on the staff who knows our complete defensive system."

For the Tennessee State players, though, Sonia Gilliam's death and her father's mourning offered a profound motivation for victory. "We felt sorry for Coach Gilliam and wanted to win the game and see if that would make him happier," Humphrey recalled years later. "As young ballplayers, we didn't know that nothing was going to make him happier."

+   +   +

In the third quarter, the scoring stopped on both sides. Robert Atkins and Delles Howell each intercepted Dickey for a second time, and as Atkins was tackled near the Tennessee State sideline, he heard someone, presumably Merritt, shout to his players, "Y'all get him. Get him!" Tennessee State, for its part, now knew to expect passes from Harris, and curtailed its blitzes for the sake of better coverage.

The strategy worked well enough to have Grambling trapped at its own five-yard line late in the quarter. Harris reverted to a tight formation and conservative plays, calling two runs for a total of two yards. On third and eight, with only Joiner split wide, it looked like more of the same. This time, though, Harris faked a handoff to his fullback, and from a shallow drop, just three steps, he flung a pass far upfield and toward the right sideline, where it dropped into Joiner's arms at Grambling's forty. He had beaten three defensive backs on the play. In short succession, Harris hit Joiner three more times, each on a fifteen-yard square-out, the play they had practiced until they could do it by reflex.

Grambling lined up with a first down at the Tennessee State nineteen. Then, as Harris dodged a strong pass rush, a penalty flag flew—clipping against Grambling on what appeared to be a clean block, a fifteen-yard mark-off back to the thirty-four. After two long incompletions, Robinson sent in his kicker, a reserve quarterback named Wesley Bean, for a fifty-one-yard field goal. It fell laughably short, not even reaching the goal line.

Dickey responded by moving his offense down the field to the Grambling twenty-three. From there, Tennessee State's reliable kicker, Roy Meneese, knocked through a forty-yard field goal. It put Tennessee State back into the lead, 17–14, early in the fourth quarter. It also confirmed Joe Gilliam and Cat Coleman in their analysis that Tennessee State held an edge, possibly a decisive edge, with its kicking game. All that had to happen now was for the defense to keep its unspoken promise to Gilliam, to stomp and stifle Grambling, to ameliorate his personal loss with their collective victory.

Harris summarily tore the promise to tatters. On a second-down play after Tennessee State's kickoff, he connected with Atkins for twenty-five yards on a post pattern. Over the previous few offensive series, Harris had seen the Tennessee State linemen growing ravenous to hit him, hurtling headlong into the pocket. Because Grambling had rushed to such little avail so far, Humphrey and the rest had stopped holding their positions against the run. So, on the next play, Harris dropped back to pass. The Tennessee State stampede began. As it closed in, Harris slipped the football into Henry Jones's chest on a draw play. The fullback rambled for twenty-five yards, Grambling's longest run in the game, putting the team at the Tennessee State twenty-seven. From there on a third and ten, Harris found Atkins on the right sideline, wide open at the fifteen, and the tight end was finally dragged down at the two. On the next play, Essex Johnson scored on a counter. Crossing the goal line, he spiked the ball in jubilation and audacity.

He had celebrated too soon. Bean's extra point was blocked—yet another failure in Grambling's kicking game, and an especially costly one. Tennessee State trailed by just three points, 20–17, when it took over with 9:42 left in the game. All Merritt's men needed was a field goal to tie, and Meneese, unlike Bean, had proven he possessed the requisite leg. As it turned out, he didn't have to use it. Helped by four Grambling penalties, Dickey led Tennessee State to the go-ahead touchdown, scoring on a quarterback sneak.

Then, with barely five minutes left, with the crowd on its feet and howling, with the Tennessee State band on the sideline at Grambling's end of the field and blasting its fight song right into the huddle, James Harris called the first play of what might well be Grambling's final possession. He had spent his entire athletic life preparing for such a moment. He had waited two injured years for his shot at Tennessee State. Every important black scout in pro football—Tank Younger, Lloyd Wells, Bill Nunn, Marion Motley, Buddy Young—was watching. Whether or not they had come to watch Harris, the presumed second fiddle to Eldridge Dickey, they were watching him now. He was number 14 in a gold jersey, the color that Eddie Robinson in his superstitious way had insisted Grambling wear both home and away. And the Hole, John Merritt's domain, was as away as away got.

On first and ten from his own twenty-seven, Harris dropped straight back, looking for Atkins on the same sideline pattern that had worked on the previous drive. This time, rather than shoving his way forward, Humphrey stood upright at the line of scrimmage and then jumped like the basketball player he had once been, forcing Harris to throw high and incomplete. On second down, Joiner split wider than usual on left. On the other side, a freshman named Coleman Zeno was flanked out. Robinson had sent him in to replace Essex Johnson because Zeno was taller and faster, a better deep threat. And because Zeno was in his first year and had seen little game action through the season's first three games, Tennessee State had not prepared for him.

At the snap, Zeno bolted from the line, streaking past the cornerback and safety assigned to him. Harris shuffled backward in a seven-step drop, waiting for Zeno to cross into Tennessee State territory, holding his ground even as the defensive end Joe Jones looped past a Grambling tackle, the replacement who had been conscripted from defense. Harris tried to anchor his cleats in the turf, but his injured ankle was too weak for the leverage that a long throw required. Though his pass sailed nearly sixty yards in the air, it descended just short of Zeno. Somehow the receiver managed to adjust, stopping and turning to reach back for the ball. The two defenders, heads down and legs pumping to catch up to him, could not brake in time to intercept. They brought down Zeno at the Tennessee State twenty-two.

Had Grambling not blundered twice earlier with its kicking game— the blocked extra point, the missed field goal—it would have been able to win with a field goal. Instead, trailing by four points, Harris needed a touchdown. With the clock running, he could not waste much time on runs. After surrendering the long pass to Zeno, Gilliam's defense still had a chance to redeem itself. Just one sack would reverse the momentum and put Grambling into desperation mode.

Harris dropped back on first down, once more seeking Atkins on the sideline. Humphrey sliced past a Grambling guard and into the backfield. There he lost his footing, tumbling and rolling toward Harris, swiping at the quarterback's feet, barely missing. His pressure was enough, though, to make Harris toss the pass deliberately out of bounds. With Tennessee State sure to expect another throw on second and ten, Harris called a fullback dive. Henry Jones got only five yards and the clock kept ticking. Instead of going for the points, Harris decided to settle for getting a first down and with it four more chances. He threw to Joiner in the left flat along the line of scrimmage, depending on him to run for the needed yards. Not fooled, two Tennessee State defensive backs spun Joiner down for the loss of a yard.

Fourth and six at the Tennessee State eighteen, two and a half minutes remaining: the entire game rested now on one play. If it could stop Grambling, Merritt's team would take possession and almost surely run out the clock.

In the huddle, Harris called the play: Wing right open X post Z curl. His first choice would be Atkins on a crossing route over the middle. The quarterback made his medium drop, five steps, and watched Atkins run forward seven yards, then cut sharply left, moving parallel to the line of scrimmage. Just as Atkins was breaking free, just as Harris was about to throw, the linebacker James Greer clotheslined the tight end. *Y'all get him. Get him!* Atkins lay on the turf, rigid as a corpse.

By this time, a defensive end, Harold Rice, had broken free and was bearing down on Harris from the left side. The quarterback retreated a few paces on his gimpy ankle, then drifted toward the right sideline, strangely light-footed, almost gliding. Rice swung his arms, stretched his fingers, grasping at him. And in the next few seconds, Harris drew on everything he had learned—from Dorth Blade in high school, from Doug Porter and Eddie Robinson at Grambling.

Those lessons had been aimed at preparing Harris to be a pro quarterback, showing the skeptical white world he was not a scrambler who could be denied the chance. They happened to be ideal lessons, too, for fourth and six with a defensive end snorting and panting after you. *Don't try to run. Just run enough to buy time. Get to a spot where you can plant your feet to pass. Keep looking downfield. Keep going through your progressions.* Now backed up to the thirty, Harris spotted Glenn Alexander, a reserve flanker whom Robinson had inserted for this play, lifting an arm to show he was open in the center of the field. Tennessee State had put the correct coverage on Alexander, a cornerback with a safety's help, but as Harris eluded the rush and lengthened the play, the receiver had finally wormed his way free.

Harris stopped, aimed, threw. Alexander gathered in the pass at the five-yard line. As safety Willie Johnson got a hand on Alexander's waist, the receiver pivoted, shook loose, and dashed into the end zone. Johnson dropped to his knees, banging his palms against his helmet, feeling responsible, perhaps, for more than a football defeat. His posture was one of mourning, of sackcloth and ashes.

+ + +

When he awoke on the morning after the Grambling game, Joe Gilliam Sr. realized he could not remember much of it. He knew Tennessee State had lost, but he was unable to recall very many plays or the strategic decisions he had made. He watched the game film less as a coach than as an amnesiac straining to recover memory. After Gilliam was done, he called his defensive players together and told them he could see how hard they had tried to win the game. He could tell they had been trying to win it for him.

The next day, Joe Sr. and Ruth Gilliam buried their daughter. After three different churches had refused to hold the homegoing ceremony, as a funeral is called in the language of black Christianity, the pastor of St. Andrew's Presbyterian Church offered his sanctuary. Once Sonia was interred, Ruth Gilliam stopped attending church. Joe Sr., in contrast, began paying his weekly tithes to St. Andrew's.

Then, with a game coming up against Jake Gaither and unbeaten Florida A&M, he went, with a broken heart and a shattered family, back to work.

+ + +

On the bus heading home to Grambling, flush with their 26–24 victory and 4-0 record, Eddie Robinson's young men talked long into the night. The final statistics provided a very pleasurable math lesson. James Harris had thrown for 264 yards and 3 touchdowns, while Eldridge Dickey, The

Lord's Prayer, had been intercepted 5 times. It was both the biggest game and the finest game so far in Harris's career. He had upstaged the star of The Show.

Rolling through the dark, Harris regaled Delles Howell and Charlie Joiner, his closest friends on the team, with the story of coming upon Tank Younger while leaving the field. "I *told* him," Younger had exulted, referring to Lloyd Wells. "I *told* him." Howell, too, had a story. As he was heading into the locker room, he had passed within earshot of an old man, a Tennessee State diehard. "I thought Eldridge Dickey was the best quarterback I ever saw in college," the man had said. "But that number fourteen from Grambling, he might be better."

6

DIPLOMACY WITH DOWNTOWN

Jake Gaither, the Governor, and the Regents, October 1967

On the Thursday afternoon of October 12, two days before Florida A&M's homecoming game against the sacrificial victims of winless Morris Brown College, Governor Claude Kirk paid a visit to the Rattlers' football practice. He strode the sidelines in his business suit, hair piled into something like a pompadour, palming a football as photographers and reporters duly recorded the scene. In just ten months in office, Kirk had earned a reputation as "Kissin' Claude" for his flesh-pressing style with voters and "Claudius Maximus" for his imperious manner with most everyone else; he described himself as a "tree-shakin' son of a bitch." Kirk had recently married his third wife, and he treated governance as a perpetual campaign. The Rattlers' practice field was one more whistle-stop.

Kirk had Gaither call together the players, and then the governor asked how many were from Florida. All but a half dozen of the hundred young men raised their hands. "We're going to have plenty of jobs in Florida," Kirk assured them. Why, he'd even find jobs in Florida for out-of-state players. The governor apologized to Gaither for having to miss the homecoming game, already being committed to attending "a sailboat race down in Miami." But if the Rattlers would beat Morris Brown for him, then he promised to attend another game. In fact, he announced unprompted, he wanted to sit on the team's bench for the Orange Blossom Classic in December. Then, before departing with the press entourage in tow, Kirk posed for photographs with Gaither and eight top players, including Ken Riley. The snapshots would ultimately be published, like targeted political advertisements, in black newspapers.

For gridiron reasons alone, Gaither was glad enough to play host. His Rattlers were 3-0 and hovering near the Top Ten of both the AP and UPI polls. On the previous Saturday, FAMU had avenged yet another of its 1966 defeats, beating Alabama A&M 45–36 on the road. Riley had led the comeback victory, scrambling for long gains and then throwing to John Eason for the go-ahead touchdown with less than three minutes left in the game. Now the whole Tallahassee campus was abustle with homecoming activities—the Coronation Ball for the queen, the fraternities' step shows, the Rattler Strikes pep rally, the mock funeral for a coffin labeled "Morris Brown."

The upbeat mood could only serve Gaither's hidden agenda. In less than half a football season, the veteran coach had sized up the new governor, with his flamboyance, his self-importance, even his frustrated-jock yearnings. Gaither knew to stock bourbon, Kirk's favorite drink, for the postgame parties. He was planning on presenting the governor with his own set of cleats, no small gesture when all the Rattler freshmen had to settle for secondhand pairs. Later in the month, it had already been decided, Gaither would appoint Kirk honorary chairman of the Orange Blossom Classic, a ceremonial role that provided copious publicity in exchange for minimal duties.

For his part, Kirk could not resist pretending to be part of the team. During another appearance at a Rattlers' practice, doing what he thought coaches did to motivate players, Kirk cursed at one. Gaither, of course, never swore. Neither, though, was he about to confront the governor. So Gaither shouted at Robert Mungen, one of his assistant coaches, "You can't be cursing here with the governor on the sideline." Mungen looked baffled for a moment, since he had said nothing, and Gaither rarely raised his voice in anger. Then the assistant realized the reprimand had been subtly intended for Kirk.

Such incidents revealed not only the evolving relationship between Gaither and Kirk but also the way the coach interacted with the power structure. Gaither had spent decades mastering the fine art of finessing the white man, and he had been rewarded with stature and access greater than almost any black person in the entire state. He was the one whom governors asked for help and advice. He was the one who could go downtown to cash a check and wind up in the bank president's office, legs crossed, amiably chatting away. He was the one who had a golf course and a gym named for him, who got salary raises above the university's official budget request to the legislature.

Gaither's standing, however, came at a price. When his A&M colleagues said, "Jake can go downtown and take care of things," their words often carried a judgmental tinge. Gaither's former sports information director, D. C. Collington, put it almost scornfully: "He'll always let you know that he can call Mr. Charlie and get what he wants." The resentment arose not simply because Gaither had attained access but also because of how he had attained it—in no small measure by staying publicly silent on the subject of civil rights. While Gaither was enjoying approval and largesse from white Tallahassee, the black minister who led the local movement, Rev. C. K. Steele, was being repeatedly arrested. While Gaither was being honored with that golf course and gym, vigilantes were shattering the windows of Steele's home and burning a cross on his front yard.

In the years since the *Brown* decision and the Montgomery bus boycott, the twin catalysts of the civil rights movement, Gaither had managed relationships with four different governors of Florida. He had coped with them amid the ambiguity of the state's racial politics, and of his own. Florida's recent governors, though not the more raucous and populist legislature, had aspired to what passed for moderation: rejecting the integration of schools and public facilities but avoiding the truculent model of George Wallace, Orvil Faubus, Ross Barnett, and Lester Maddox. Dependent on the tourism industry, booming with an influx of former northerners, Florida literally could not afford the public-image nightmare of "massive resistance," a reincarnation of Civil War secessionism. Nevertheless, in its genteel way, without turning fire hoses and police dogs on marchers, without physically barring the schoolhouse door, Florida sought the same results.

"We will have segregation in this state by lawful and legal means," maintained LeRoy Collins, who was elected governor six months after *Brown*. During his six years in office, Collins paid lip service to "the fact that the Negro does not now have equal opportunities, [and] that he is morally and legally entitled to progress more rapidly." He described resistance to Supreme Court decisions as "little short of rebellion and anarchy." Yet he unwaveringly insisted that the *Brown* ruling did not require school integration. He supported the state's lengthy and expensive court case against a single black man seeking admission to the University of Florida law school, characterizing it as a "battle to protect our state's customs and traditions." By the time Collins left office in 1961, Florida had desegregated exactly one school district with a total of four incoming black children.

Only after he retired from campaign politics and was freed of the need to please an overwhelmingly white electorate did Collins become a prominent southern civil rights supporter for the Kennedy and Johnson administrations, even joining in the Selma march. His successors in Tallahassee, meanwhile, perpetuated the former governor's contradictory combination of dignified rhetoric and tactical obstruction. C. Farris Bryant, who served from 1961 to 1965, pledged in oxymoronic style to "maintain segregation by every honorable and constitutional means."

W. Haydon Burns subsequently won a two-year term in 1965 by paint-
ing his liberal opponent as "candidate of the NAACP," an organization
that Florida politicians routinely lumped together with the Communist
Party. In his previous political incarnation, Burns had been a moderate
mayor of Jacksonville who was popular with both races. Reborn as an
advocate of "law and order," a code phrase for the racial status quo, Burns
lost the black vote by a 25–1 margin. Then came Claude Kirk, who side-
stepped the issue of race relations by saying, "I won't even admit there's a
problem. We don't have color in Florida."

Jake Gaither did not choose Collins, Bryant, Burns, or Kirk. They
were the cards he was dealt. As in his poker games with his faculty buddies in the Benedicts, he had no choice but to play his hand to greatest
advantage.

On one occasion, Collins telephoned Gaither with a report from
the state police that a busload of young blacks, armed with clubs, was
heading for Tallahassee to attack whites. What did Gaither know about
it? The coach informed the governor that the blacks in question were
the baseball team from Tuskegee, equipped with bats for that afternoon's
game against A&M. Humorous as the episode sounded in retrospect,
Gaither's calming intervention likely stopped an erroneous rumor from
igniting a violent confrontation.

During the tensest periods of civil rights activity in Tallahassee—
the bus boycott in 1956, the lunch-counter sit-ins in 1960, the picketing of movie theaters in 1963—Gaither urged his players not to
participate. In part he was acting as surrogate parent and protector,
ensuring that the young men entrusted to him would not be harmed,
arrested, imprisoned, expelled. But political expedience also entered
in the calculus. Florida A&M was simultaneously a bold expression
of black self-determination and the ward of an all-white state government. Gaither never let himself forget it. Nor did his closest internal
ally, FAMU's president, George Gore. As Gore wrote during the 1956
protests, which included hundreds of A&M students, "I am frankly
worried about what will happen when our appropriation request goes

before the next legislature. It behooves us to keep our heads to keep this ship from going under."

Gaither did more than fight rearguard actions. He actively insinuated himself into the good graces of Florida's rulers. He donated money to the Democratic Party during the Collins years. Along with Gore, he gave prominent politicians tickets on the fifty-yard line for A&M home games. One home game each season was designated "Legislative Recognition Day." The campus hosted an inaugural ball for Burns with Gaither as chairman. The coach wrote to governors to thank them for "your kind consideration," "your kind help," "the generosity of you and your friends." After Bryant delivered the first major speech of his term to the legislature, having scrupulously avoided even a single mention of civil rights or desegregation, Gaither sent a letter complimenting it as "sound, practical, and progressive."

All this praise and all this flattery were bestowed on men who were upholding and defending the legal architecture of white supremacy. Perhaps they genuinely did see Jake Gaither as an equal, but if so he was the exception that proved the rule, the grateful, gracious, uncomplaining "credit to his race," the counterpoint to all those marching militants. The movement blacks, for their part, had a term for accommodationists such as Gaither: "Jefferson Davis negotiators." Few phrases could have hurt Gaither more. His father, born into slavery, had been named by his owner for Jefferson Davis and had spent his adult life hiding that humiliating fact behind the initials J. D. In defiance, he named his own sons for bishops in the African Methodist Episcopal Church.

What Jake Gaither thought about the white man, and what he wanted from the white man, was infinitely more complex than either the governors or the activists realized. He had a memory full of humiliations suffered, all the ways he had been belittled in front of his wife—refused coffee at roadside cafés, forced to eat on a folding table in a restaurant kitchen, reduced to urinating in the woods on vacation trips. "You start the day happy, in good spirits," he once put it, almost abjectly, "and then something happens to spoil the day."

He had learned to cloak or bury his anger. Speaking on one occasion about "the Negro's sense of humor" in the face of hatred, he may well have been trying to explain and defend his own seeming passivity. "It might be interpreted as lack of interest, or doesn't matter that much, it's inconsequential, so why take it so seriously," he said. "Another attitude might be that it's a defense mechanism. He's learned to smile and bow in delicate situations as a defensive mechanism. If he assumes the attitude he really felt, it might result in some type of reprisal. So ofttimes that attitude of humility may be a defensive mechanism that he learned over the years to use. Our parents learned it in slavery."

Nothing in Gaither's privileged position as of October 1967 had made him oblivious. But nothing had made him any less of a realist. "When I look around me," he said, "and I see all the money is centralized in the hands of the white man—he controls the bank, he controls the courts of justice, he controls the running of the United States of America—the only way in the world I can progress as a citizen of this country is somehow I've got to work out a relationship with the man in control."

Gaither also harbored genuine doubts, for very plausible reasons, about how Florida would choose to comply with Supreme Court rulings and Lyndon Johnson's civil rights laws. Gaither supported desegregation, which meant striking down the legal machinery of inequality. It was the actual process of implementing integration that worried him. Gaither recognized that integration, for all its virtue, shared one tenet with racism: any entirely black entity was automatically deemed to be inferior. Integration was the solvent for dissolving every institution black people had created for themselves. The son of a black minister, the graduate of a black college, the member of the Boulé honor society of black professionals, the resident of a black faculty neighborhood called College Terrace, Gaither had spent his entire life in a realm that was separate by choice and fiercely convinced of its equality.

His ethos, and that of his closest friends, was of self-help. It wasn't so different from what he said about his sport. *You don't give no quarter, and you don't get no quarter.* With college football in the South rigidly segregated, Gaither held coaching clinics so renowned that white coaches broke the color line to attend. When Tallahassee closed its municipal pools rather than integrate them, Gaither's longtime assistant coach Pete Griffin bought a vacant lot, dug it out to install a pool, and drove through town picking up black children to swim there. When black families were losing their homes because they had fallen behind on tax payments, Costa Kittles, another of the Rattler coaches, bought the properties from the city and rented them back to the previous owners.

From what Jake Gaither had seen so far, Florida was enacting integration in the selective and destructive way he had feared. Since 1962, the state had been trying to shut down the FAMU College of Law, perversely assisted by a civil rights lawsuit. In May 1967, the state stopped funding FAMU's hospital, which for decades had been the only one within a hundred miles that treated black patients, hired black doctors, and trained black nurses. Rumors persisted that, as the state opened new public universities in Tampa and Boca Raton, it intended to close Florida A&M. The alarm reflected more than paranoia. Florida had already shuttered all twenty-eight of its black junior colleges in the name of civil rights, and not one of those schools' presidents had been given a comparable position at an integrated junior college.

No less a civil rights hero than the Reverend Dr. Martin Luther King Jr. himself had expressed precisely the concerns that were chewing up Jake Gaither. "I favor integration on buses and in all areas of public accommodation and travel," King put it in a conversation with two of his church members in Montgomery, Alabama. "I am for equality. However, I think integration in our public schools is different. In that setting, you are dealing with one of the most important assets of an individual—the mind. White people view black people as inferior. A large percentage of them have a very low opinion of our race. People with such a low view of the black race cannot be given free rein and put in charge of the intellectual care and development of our boys and girls."

So on the very rare occasions when Jake Gaither cashed in all the goodwill he had built in the governor's office, he did so to advance his people and his university rather than himself. He asked for a new gymnasium to replace the decrepit aircraft hangar that had been serving as one for decades. (Gaither wanted it named not for himself, but for Willie Galimore, a former A&M star killed at age twenty-nine in an auto accident.) He appealed to Governor Bryant for money to send Bob Hayes, a star receiver and world-record sprinter, to California for a track meet against the Soviet team. He lobbied Governor Burns to grant a pardon to Hayes, who had been given ten years' probation for a minor robbery committed when he was seventeen.

With all those goals achieved by 1965, and with plenty of currency still in the favor bank, Gaither set about executing his most audacious plan. It would be integration the Gaither way: through the game of football, from a position of strength, with the white world coming to him. He wanted the State of Florida—specifically the Board of Regents, which controlled higher education—to permit Florida A&M to play against a white team.

Such a contest had never occurred in the South. There had been controversy enough on the rare occasions when one of the all-white southern powers, such as Alabama or Georgia Tech, took on an integrated northern team in a bowl game. Two teams from the North—all-black Morgan State from Baltimore and integrated West Chester from the Philadelphia area—had played before a small crowd in a small-college bowl game in Orlando in 1966. For years Gaither, his coaches, and their players had believed they could compete against any college of any color, and for years they had had no way of testing that belief. Within Florida alone, there were three major universities with prominent football programs, natural opponents for the Rattlers except for the racial barrier. By the indirect calculus of the pro football draft, Florida A&M indeed looked to be their equal. Over the decade leading into the 1967 season, Gaither had sent nearly as many players into the AFL and NFL (nineteen) as had the University of Miami (twenty-one) and nearly twice as many as had Florida State and the University of Florida (ten apiece). All that was missing was all that had never been allowed: the game itself.

"We must face the sad fact," Martin Luther King had once put it, "that at the eleven o'clock hour on Sunday morning when we stand to sing, we stand in the most segregated hour in America." He may have been only half right. In the South, a region that treated college football as a kind of religion, kickoff on a Saturday afternoon was just as starkly separated by race. For a man so often ridiculed as an Uncle Tom, a man seemingly so obsequious in the presence of white power, a man whose outer compliance with Jim Crow had all too effectively masked an inner resistance, Jake Gaither behind the scenes was now attempting to overturn at least one part of an immoral social order. And in so doing, he intended to alter the direction of history.

+ + +

Several weeks after Claude Kirk and his entourage visited football practice, another delegation from downtown arrived on the FAMU campus. It was composed of the nine members of the Board of Regents, who conducted one meeting yearly at each of the state universities they oversaw. All of the regents were white, and eight of them were male. The chairman, Chester H. Ferguson, was an attorney who had married into wealth and power; his wife's family owned shipping and citrus businesses and was among the largest land barons in the state. Ferguson's colleagues on the board had grown prosperous on banking, insurance, phosphate mines, and cattle ranches. They served at the pleasure of the governor, so it was no surprise that several of the most recent appointees had raised six-figure sums for Kirk's victorious campaign.

Until 1965, the Board of Regents had been formally known as the Board of Control, and that earlier name was the more truthful. The board held complete control over the budget for public higher education, and, acting at the behest of various governors, also handpicked university presidents, favored particular campuses for construction projects, and canceled faculty raises in fits of pique. In the pecking order, Florida A&M fared poorly, even as the state's economy boomed and tax revenue flowed as if by aqueduct into the state's coffers. Not only were FAMU's law school and hospital endangered, the university was also losing faculty members because of its low salaries. In one emblematic piece of business, when President Gore asked the board in 1965 for $1 million in research grants, the school received one-quarter that amount.

Gore must have felt some slight relief alongside his chronic anxiety as he welcomed the board members on the Monday morning of October 30. The meeting was being held on his campus, in a setting he could stage-manage, right down to the luncheon with napkin holders and gold-rimmed goblets, culminating in ice cream tinted the Rattler colors of orange and green. Too many times during his years as president, Gore had attended board sessions held at white schools or in state buildings that had no bathroom for a black man to use, no restaurant where a black man could eat. Sometimes he would sit in a hallway before being summoned in by the Board of Control to be informed of the FAMU budget and sent home, no questions invited, no discussion allowed.

Even as he played host on this day, even as he held the credential of a Columbia PhD and the title of a university president, Gore recognized that in the eyes of the regents he was subordinate to Jake Gaither, the football coach. Gaither had not usurped the prime position; he always treated Gore with palpable respect. But next to the president with the timid, halting voice and the slender, almost frail frame, Gaither could not help but exude magnetism and charisma—an eloquent orator with a common touch, a robust presence despite his unseen infirmities. By every outward indication, the regents placed greater import on a black man who turned out winning football teams than on a black man with a doc-torate from the Ivy League. In an ironic acknowledgment of the upside-down hierarchy, Gore once had told the board, "I would like to build a university that Coach Gaither and our football team can be proud of."

Gaither rarely attended Board of Regents meetings but always ar-ranged to be nearby just before they opened and just after they closed. With that calculated proximity, he cultivated relations with individual members. He was, one regent later remembered, "a very smooth lobby-ist." Another recalled, "He would ingratiate himself to his audience very well, and he usually got what he wanted." Now that Gaither knew what he wanted—a football game against a white school—he was not about to let his carefully tended clout go to waste.

He had begun the covert campaign of persuasion two years earlier. Haydon Burns, then the governor, had appointed Clifton Dyson as the first black member of the Board of Regents. Dyson was impeccably respectable and certifiably moderate—air force veteran, former chemistry professor, real estate broker in the black community of West Palm Beach. He also happened to be a friend of Jake Gaither's. So, upon Dyson's appointment, the coach did two things. He wrote a letter to Burns extolling him on such a wise choice. And he began talking with Dyson about how unfair it was that Florida A&M was banned from playing white teams.

Though Dyson's term on the board ended in early 1967, when Kirk took office, the subject had at last been broached. Gaither pursued it with the two youngest members of the board—Burke Kibler, an attorney, and Louis Murray, a physician—whom he had correctly discerned as moderates on civil rights. Gaither had long ago built ties to Chester Ferguson, the chairman and most powerful member of the board. A trial lawyer by trade, Ferguson used his litigator's amalgam of persuasion and aggression to dominate the others. He was hardly a leader on the subject of racial equality, but like the man who had appointed him, LeRoy Collins, his private beliefs were more tolerant than his public statements. No ideologue, he understood that Florida could not drag its feet on integration forever. At least Gaither's plan was for a voluntary form of racial mixing, not the court-ordered kind that was politically explosive.

Even so, the prospect of a black-versus-white football game was hazardous enough. To put two hundred black and white players onto the same field, to put tens of thousands of black and white spectators in roughly equal numbers into the same stadium would be the largest single act of integration in Florida history. What if Florida A&M wanted to play against Florida State, the overwhelmingly white university with the all-white football team, barely a mile away in Tallahassee? What if Florida A&M won? A football game, with all of its passion and intensity, could provide the pretext for setting loose Florida's unresolved, often unadmitted racial tensions. There could be riots. "They were being cautious," Gaither later recalled of his conversations with the regents. "No governor wanted to assume responsibility for something happening. . . . It wasn't that they didn't want to have the game; they were afraid of the repercussions that might have come."

To counter that fear, Gaither applied all his leverage. He told the board members he was getting old, his career was coming to an end. He told them this one game was all that he wanted, presenting it almost like a deathbed request. He told them it wasn't about integration, he didn't care much for integration, it was about football. And he assured them that "nothing would go wrong, everything would go right." Truth, half-truth, sugarcoated lie—he used every trick, short of tears, that he had refined during decades of pregame pep talks and halftime exhortations.

Gaither's pitch was painted with artifice but endowed by idealism. Deep in his soul, as a devout Christian, he believed in the possibility of conversion. He believed a hard heart could soften. He believed justice could triumph in the end. He had always said his favorite Bible verse was Micah 6:8: "What doth the Lord require of thee, but to do justly, and to love mercy, and to walk humbly with thy God?" He was not inhumanly patient. In one unguarded moment, admitting to the attraction of divine vengeance, he told a friend a joke about a white child who could speak to his father in hell: "The boy said, 'You know, I'm really giving these niggers hell, just like you told me. I'm really giving them hell.' The man said, 'Take it easy on them. You know the fireman down here is a nigger.'"

Still, as the regents weighed his request, and as he waited for their answer, Gaither did not want revenge. He wanted results. And he had one more reason for hope. It was the same reason he could never bring himself to hate.

+ + +

Twenty-six years earlier, when Jake Gaither was still an assistant coach, Florida A&M had defeated Tuskegee in the Orange Blossom Classic to triumphantly end the 1941 football season. Without his absence being much noticed, Gaither excused himself from the celebration. For several months he had been suffering intermittently from headaches, nausea, dizziness, ringing in the ears. On this day he felt so ill that it took him two hours to finally hobble aboard the team bus for the ride back to Tallahassee. Once there, he contacted an elderly white doctor in Thomasville, just over the state line in Georgia, a German immigrant who was known to treat the occasional black patient. A general practitioner possessed of more decency than expertise, the physician diagnosed Gaither with Ménière's disease, a disorder caused by excessive fluid in the inner ear, and assured him the symptoms would subside with time.

Except that they did not. Walking home one night from an A&M basketball game several weeks later, Gaither found himself helplessly wobbling from side to side down the street, as if his legs were not listening to his mind. Another time, sitting in the stands with his wife, Sadie, during a basketball tournament at Tuskegee, he blurted, "I feel so lonely." She asked him what he was talking about. "I don't know," he replied. "I just feel like I'm alone somewhere."

As months rolled past and the 1942 football season neared, and with Gaither no better, the college's then president, J.R.E. Lee, shifted him from the strenuous outdoor job of assistant coach to the office duties of a dean. Gaither was driving back to Florida from a meeting of black-college administrators at Hampton Institute in Virginia when he realized with alarm that he was seeing double. He managed to make it as far as North Carolina, where he spent the night at his brother-in-law's home, and the next morning he tied a handkerchief over one eye so he beheld just one steering wheel, one center line, one lane for oncoming cars.

He returned to the Thomasville doctor, who reiterated the diagnosis of Ménière's. So did a doctor in Jacksonville. For two weeks of that June, Gaither hardly rose from his bed. Then, one day in July, he slipped into convulsions. Admitted into the college hospital, pain hammering his skull, seizures coming in waves, Gaither let out shrieks that could be heard down the corridors and out onto the campus. The doctors, thinking he was having a nervous breakdown, sedated him. But during one lucid moment the coach gazed up to Sadie at his bedside and spoke.

"You better get Earl Odom," he said. "If you don't get Earl Odom, I am going to die."

Earl Odom had been a classmate of both Gaithers' at Knoxville College. Since graduating, he had earned his medical degree from Meharry Medical College in Nashville, done advanced studies in cardiology at the renowned Massachusetts General Hospital in Boston, and then returned to Meharry as a professor. Sadie telephoned Odom, and, based on her report, he speculated that Gaither, not yet forty years old, had a brain tumor. Odom took the next train from Nashville to Tallahassee and arrived there to find his college friend—the champion debater, the rugged football player, the natty dresser with pomaded hair and a pencil mustache—barely conscious and unable to speak.

Odom proposed bringing Gaither to Nashville for treatment. President Lee argued against it. The trip would be long and arduous. The doctor in Thomasville was more experienced than Odom, and besides, he was white. "He's not getting better here," Sadie told Lee. "And if he dies" under Dr. Odom's care "I will know that I did what he asked me to do."

As the ambulance carrying Jake Gaither pulled away from the college hospital, and people on campus found out who was inside, some began to weep. The next day, having reached Meharry and Nashville, Odom placed a call across town and across the color line. Its destination was a neurological surgeon at Vanderbilt University Hospital named Cobb Pilcher. The outcome of that call was by no means certain.

Nashville fancied itself an enlightened city, the self-described "Athens of the South" with a scale replica of the Parthenon, a total of seventeen colleges and universities, and a comparatively moderate attitude toward race relations. Signs of "WHITE" and "COLORED" were indeed rare in the city. Prior to the Civil War, Nashville had included a sizable population of black freedmen. By the early 1940s, a substantial black professional class had sprung up around a critical mass of black institutions—Meharry, Fisk University, Tennessee A&I, and the American Baptist Theological Seminary. Mutual racial progress with minimal public discord was "the Nashville Way."

Beneath the seemingly amicable surface, however, familiar fissures existed. No restaurant or hotel downtown would serve a black customer; no white bank would give a black applicant a loan. A black doctor such as Odom, irrespective of his skills, was barred from joining the local branch of the American Medical Association, which meant he could not practice in Nashville's white hospitals. A black patient with an emergency, at least an emergency such as Gaither's that was beyond the resources of Meharry's teaching hospital, had to rely on the pity of a white physician. Sometimes it never came, and sometimes it carried a degrading price. One black postal worker was made to wait in a white doctor's broom closet before being seen.

The Meharry faculty, in contrast, functioned as an island of integration, with black and white doctors serving as colleagues and equals. Cobb Pilcher's brother-in-law was one of several Vanderbilt University School of Medicine professors to teach part-time at Meharry. These ties spoke to something in Pilcher's temperament, the part that, as one of his neighbors put it, was "at soul an artist and humanitarian." More than racial tolerance, though, had brought Pilcher to Odom's attention now. Pilcher was a lifelong prodigy—admitted to Vanderbilt at age fourteen, graduated from its medical school at twenty-two, trained in his specialty by the greatest neurosurgeon in the nation, Harvey Cushing of Harvard. Odom had correctly diagnosed Gaither as having a brain tumor, and Pilcher had researched and written extensively on the subject. Slight in build, almost fragile, yet tireless and driven in his work, Pilcher particularly sought the challenge of "massive brain tumors in patients who were poor surgical risks," as an admiring colleague put it. Gaither's case fit that grim bill.

For three days, Pilcher stabilized and strengthened Gaither, returning him to a conscious state. Then, starting at six o'clock in the morning, he shaved the coach's head, applied spinal anesthesia, and began cutting a portal through the skull into the brain.

Five hours later, Odom emerged from the operating room to tell

Sadie Gaither, "It was beautiful. Dr. Pilcher was great." She shot back, "I don't care about that. Tell me about Jake."

The surgeon soon arrived to deliver that report. He had found two tumors, both of them malignant. If the cancer recurred, Gaither would have, at most, two years to live. As it was, the surgery left the coach blind and disoriented for several weeks. When Sadie asked her husband, "How do you feel?" he could only parrot back the words. Even after his sight returned, his delusions persisted. Gaither once tried to climb out of a third-floor window, saying he wanted to visit a friend in town.

Pilcher prescribed follow-up treatments with X-rays and radium, and released Gaither to a rehabilitation center run by the Seventh-Day Adventists. Just before Thanksgiving 1942, about a year after those first inexplicable headaches, Gaither left Nashville. He walked with a cane, feet set widely apart, a once-athletic man turned into a three-legged stool. When he spoke loudly, his eyes protruded. And because Pilcher had decided against replacing the missing piece of skull with a steel plate, which might irritate Gaither's brain, only a layer of skin separated it from a crippling, even fatal blow. Sadie winced every time he climbed into or out of a car, knowing it would be so easy for him to bump his head.

As Gaither returned to Tallahassee, Pilcher turned to another gruesome specialty, repairing the brain wounds suffered by GIs in World War II. Florida A&M's head coach, Bill Bell, went off to fight, and Gaither yearned to fill the position. President Lee, convinced that the pressures of coaching had caused the brain tumors, instead assigned Gaither to be a political science professor. Without him, the Rattlers went 1-4-2 in 1943. By the start of the 1945 season, though, President Lee had died and the football coach, Herman Neilson, had left for a job at Hampton Institute. With his military service over, Bell became athletic director at North Carolina A&T. Reluctantly and belatedly, Florida A&M's new president, William H. Gray, offered Gaither the position of head coach. Acting like a man who had options, acting like his old self, Gaither replied that he would consider it only if he could select his entire staff. Gray conceded. Gaither accepted. In 1945, his first season, the Rattlers went 9-1.

In the years between then and 1967, when he pressed his case with
the Board of Regents for an interracial game, Jake Gaither had shown
several lasting effects of his brain operation. He drove shakily. He walked
unsteadily. He had trouble stepping quickly to the side. His hair first went
gray on the site of the incision. And whenever anyone asked Gaither why
he didn't hate white people, after everything they had done, he replied,
"How can I hate white people when this white man saved my life?"

+   +   +

The proposal by Jake Gaither that Florida A&M be permitted to play
against a white school never appeared on any agenda of the Board of
Regents. The decision by the board to allow it was never recorded in the
official minutes of its meetings. These omissions were not oversights. The
regents decided, almost certainly with Governor Kirk's approval, not to
leave any record of their landmark decision. If the game ultimately did
set off racial violence—and there were high school games in the supposedly enlightened North, games of far less consequence, that provided the
annual occasion for black-white brawls—neither the regents nor the governor wanted to look responsible for it. This would be social change by
way of a wink and a nod, social change without fingerprints, or without
the fingerprints of anyone other than Gaither.

The only written clue to the regents' decision turned up in the minutes of the October 30 meeting on the Florida A&M campus. One item
noted innocuously that President Gore had invited the regents to attend the
Rattlers' game on November 25 against Texas Southern as "special guests."
Interestingly, the game was being played in Tampa, rather than on A&M's
home field in Tallahassee; and it was being called the "Tampa Classic," as
if it were something more than the annual meeting with an every-year opponent.

For the past few years, Gaither had been mulling over the possible
locations for a black-versus-white football game. It would have to be a
neutral site. It would have to be a sizable stadium. It would have to be

in a tolerant place by Florida standards. Miami, the state's most sophisticated and liberal city, already hosted the Orange Blossom Classic. The Tampa Bay region, though, had arguably the most courageous newspaper in Florida on civil rights, the *St. Petersburg Times*. It had a population swelling with migrants from the integrated North, especially from the Midwest, where Gaither and many of his assistants had gone to graduate school. The game against Texas Southern, with the regents in attendance, would be a stealthy dry run for the history-making game to follow, perhaps as soon as the next year.

Only one element was missing: an opponent. Given Jake Gaither's record and reputation, was there any white coach in Florida willing to take him on? And was there any brave enough to risk the consequences of losing to a black man and his black team?

+ + +

Amid all of Jake Gaither's single-minded maneuvering with the governor and the regents, all of his concerted diplomacy with the political powers collectively known as "Downtown," he still had a football team to coach. The Rattlers had routed Morris Brown as expected in their homecoming game, scoring offensive, defensive, and special-teams touchdowns in a 44–0 win. Then, on October 21, Gaither and his team had traveled to Nashville to play Tennessee State. Smarting from its home loss to Grambling, Tennessee State took vengeance on A&M, coasting to a 32–8 victory. The Rattlers' only touchdown had come thanks to some typical John Merritt hijinks: as an A&M defensive back was running up the sideline and toward the end zone with an intercepted pass, a Tennessee State reserve jumped off the bench and bolted onto the field to deliver a sucker punch of a tackle. Even Merritt's officials had no choice but to award FAMU six points in compensation.

The defeat ended the Rattlers' unbeaten streak. Still, at 4-1, they remained on track for Gaither's best season since 1964, and would face a feeble opponent in their next game, North Carolina A&T, with its

1-4-1 record. "Shake it off, baby," Gaither told his players during the bye week after the Tennessee State loss. In private with his assistant coaches, though, Gaither was less sanguine. Despite his plans to pass more this season, the Rattlers had slid back to the old habit of relying on the run. And despite his plan to alternate two quarterbacks, and the nearly equal statistics each had compiled, one of them was emerging. He had qualities that numbers could not capture: a unique explosiveness, a gift for improvisation. Something, Gaither realized, had to change. On November 4 against A&T, he would start Ken Riley.

Florida A&M did not need to keep winning to earn a berth in the Orange Blossom Classic; it hosted the game. But for the Classic to be what Gaither envisioned—the de facto championship game in black college football—then Florida A&M had to do more than invite the highest-ranked opponent, which so far looked to be Grambling. With games later in November against two of the stronger black teams in the country, Southern University and Texas Southern, the Rattlers would have to prove they belonged in a title match.

7

THAT'S MY BLOOD

Grambling vs. Texas Southern, October 28, 1967

Winding their way through the Grambling College campus, passing tigers made of chicken wire and crepe paper, coursing around lawn signs promising victory, several hundred students reached their destination, the redbrick bungalow that was the home of their president, Ralph Waldo Emerson Jones. It was early on the Monday evening of October 23, the start of homecoming week, and the procession was an annual ritual called "serenading." The crowd gathered around the front steps of Jones's house and called in unison, "Speech! Speech! Speech!"

Savoring the ceremony, Jones gradually made his way to the door. He was an unexceptional physical presence, five-foot-nine and portly, bald and bespectacled, and starting to show a double chin. Sixty-two years old, he had spent his entire adult life at Grambling, arriving as a math professor at twenty, rising to the presidency when he was just thirty-one. He had led Grambling since 1936, before any of these undergraduates on his front lawn had even been born. They called him, like almost everyone else did, "Prez." And Jones loved little more than strolling across a quadrangle or through the bleachers, hearing his students call out, "Hi, Prez," with a mixture of familiarity and adulation.

No man, perhaps, had been more aptly named. Like the original Ralph Waldo Emerson, Jones embodied the virtue of self-reliance, and, even more so, the philosopher's observation that "an institution is the lengthened shadow of one man." In his forty-two years at Grambling, Jones had expanded the school from 120 students, 17 faculty members, and 9 buildings to 4,200 students, 410 faculty members, and 41 buildings. He had done it, when necessary, by begging and sobbing before the white politicians who controlled the budget, by sending them turkeys and peaches from the Grambling farm. Rather than challenging segregation in the wake of the *Brown* decision, Jones had adroitly manipulated the state government into funding a building boom for the campus just to show those Yankees that separate really was equal. Jones had even provided the college its present name in 1946 by appealing to the legislature in calculatedly folksy fashion: "When we are playing football and the other team has the ball on our five-yard line, the other team has scored by the time our cheerleaders can say, 'Hold that line, Louisiana Negro Normal and Industrial Institute.'"

Everything was personal to Prez. He managed the college through a daily lunch meeting with his "cabinet," half a dozen valued allies, including Eddie Robinson. He coached the Grambling baseball team, amassing nearly seven hundred wins. A widower with two grown sons, he expressed his familial instinct on his students. He counseled them on marriage and household budgets; he advised them to quit smoking. There was one student in the 1950s, a coed named Mildred, who worked in the business manager's office and attracted Jones's concern for her severe acne. "She sure is a nice young lady," Jones told the administrator, "but her face is all messed up. We gotta do something for her." Sure enough, he paid for Mildred to see a dermatologist in Monroe, thirty miles away, and recommended that she switch to a diet light on fried foods. For Jones, Grambling was and always would be the school for striving people from simple homes. Every year on the eve of Christmas vacation, he addressed the student body, and he delivered the same piece of advice about showing thanks for sacrifice: "Kiss your momma. Kiss your daddy. And kiss the mule."

As Jones stood in the portal on this Monday night in late October, having delivered his usual homecoming pep talk, the students asked on cue, "Which cheers do you like, Prez?" He named a favorite, and they chanted it for him. Then they asked him to lead the alma mater, and he joked about how he could never get the pitch right. So he listened as they regaled him, these children of stevedores and sawmill hands, sharecroppers and maids, the first in their families ever to attend college. They had learned, in the model of the famous Fisk Jubilee Singers from that black university, to perform compositions from European lieder to Negro spirituals with care for elocution and musicianship, to sound every bit as refined as an Ivy League ensemble, to have every lifted voice make the implicit case for equality.

Old Grambling, dear Grambling,
We love thee, dear old Grambling.
We're loyal to thee, our dear old school.
We'll fight for thee for evermore.

Then they bid him farewell, and Prez Jones basked in satisfaction. All seemed right in his world. All needed to be right in his world, because Grambling had never known such a crucial homecoming week. The game itself was significant enough. After running its record to 4-0 on October 14 by trouncing Mississippi Valley State 68–0, with James Harris throwing four touchdown passes, Grambling had stumbled a week later, losing 20–14 to Jackson State. The defeat left the Tigers trailing Jackson

State in the Southwestern Athletic Conference standings, at risk of not receiving a bid to the Orange Blossom Classic. The homecoming game pitted Grambling against Texas Southern, a 4-1 team ranked fifth in the UPI small-college poll. A Grambling victory would mean staying within striking distance of Jackson State, the conference title, and the Orange Blossom Classic. A loss would dash all of those goals. It also would damage James Harris's prospects of playing quarterback in the pros. No fewer than twenty-seven scouts, white as well as black, would be attending the Texas Southern game.

One additional element, though, really ratcheted up the level of anticipation: the impending arrival of a television crew from ABC. The outspoken sportscaster Howard Cosell had wangled a budget of $13,000 from his reluctant network to make a documentary about Grambling football. The idea actually belonged to Jerry Izenberg, a sports journalist whose affinity for Grambling's struggle arose from his left-wing Jewish background and who had been writing about the Tigers for several years. Izenberg and his three-man crew were due to fly into Shreveport on Wednesday and film at Grambling for the remainder of the week.

Even more than Prez Jones, Collie Nicholson recognized the stakes. For nearly thirty years as Grambling's sports information director, he had dreamed of turning the college into a national symbol, a black Notre Dame. He dreamed of it even as he knew all the obstacles in publicizing a small, segregated school, far from any large media market, ignored by the white newspapers and television stations in its own vicinity. "We've got to take it to the people," he said over and over. "Because the people can't come here." Nicholson had tried to create a big-city bowl game several years earlier, raising enough money from a group of black businessmen in New Orleans to hold a game called the Sugar Cup Classic. It turned into a fiasco—a boring rout of Bishop College, played in a downpour on a high school field, drawing a crowd of only two thousand, losing the entire investment. After one more try, the "Classic" died.

The only good thing to come out of the whole mess was Jerry Izenberg. He had covered the Bishop game, befriended Nicholson, and spent a subsequent week in Grambling, kindling his ongoing passion for the school and its story. Now, three years later, fruition was at hand: national publicity with the celebrity imprimatur of Howard Cosell. As meticulous as Eddie Robinson was in coaching his team, Collie Nicholson was in tending to its image. He envisioned fame far beyond the circumscribed horizons of Robinson and Jones, and they placed their faith in his audacity. "If Collie told me there's cheese on the moon," the coach once put it, "I'm gonna bring some crackers." Nicholson had already achieved one publicity coup in early 1967, arranging for Grambling's band to perform at halftime of the first Super Bowl. But halftime was when people went to the bathroom or turned down the volume on the TV. Howard Cosell, loved and loathed in equal measure, more famous than ever thanks to his exclusive interviews with Muhammad Ali, got America's attention.

All that Grambling had to do for this one week of October, while Izenberg shot the documentary, was to be Grambling—dominant on the gridiron, humble and worthy off the field. What could make a better setting, a more impressive backdrop, than the wholesome activities of homecoming week? Thousands of alumni were returning to campus like pilgrims to a shrine. Chartered planeloads were arriving from the West Coast. There was the whole panoply of events—the football team and marching band parading through campus, the crowning of the queen and her court, the big dance featuring Gene Chandler, a rhythm-and-blues star ever since "Duke of Earl."

Prez Jones, luxuriating in the serenade on Monday night, gave the appearance of a confident man. If so, he was being either innocently clueless or willfully self-deluding. Because the tremors of an earthquake had been rippling through campus for a week already.

Flyers had started turning up around Grambling from a group identifying itself only as the Informers. The sheets listed some issues that had first been aired the previous spring—curfews for female students, the quality of cafeteria food—but now added to them a set of complaints about academic quality. The library had too few books. The science labs had too little equipment. A national teacher-certification program had placed Grambling on probation. With the first cracks in segregation's wall, a handful of Grambling students had been able to take summer classes at white schools such as Louisiana Tech and Louisiana State and had seen firsthand the intolerable inequities. And the Informers' flyers included one other especially divisive grievance: that Grambling was putting too much emphasis on football.

On the Sunday night of October 22, the Student Government Association showed its weekly movie in a campus auditorium. When the film ended, the Informers stepped onto the stage to introduce themselves. Their leader, Willie Zanders, was the student-body president. One of his comrades, Kenneth Armand, edited both the student newspaper and the yearbook. Two other mainstays were the Brass brothers, Charles and Bennie, James Harris's childhood friends from Monroe, young veterans of the March on Washington; Bennie was already ordained as a minister. About fifteen football players, meanwhile, gathered on the wings of the stage, most watching impassively, but a few glowering.

Zanders and the other Informers went to pains not to depict the athletes as enemies. The protesters and the players were roommates; they were classmates; they were fraternity brothers. Grambling athletes, compared to football stars at big white schools, with their separate dorms and gut classes and secret payments from boosters, lived lives of monkish austerity. The athletic department's annual budget came to a mere $150,000, and the only cash the players received was a $10 monthly stipend for "subsistence," which basically meant laundry money. "We had cheered them on throughout their college career," Zanders later wrote in a memoir of the protests. "We celebrated whenever one of them signed a professional contract and received a new car as a bonus. We marveled at their extraordinary talents and skills. But thousands of other students were not receiving a quality education."

Indeed, the Informers' true adversary, at least the proximate one, was

Prez Jones. The Informers, for the most part, had not grown up on farms with plow mules, unquestioningly grateful for whatever Grambling offered. Zanders had applied to LSU with aspirations of becoming an architect, and had been politicized by its rejection of him, presumably due to his race. Sporting a beard and beret, Armand was the son of a factory worker who was a labor-union activist. Their generation had come of age with Montgomery, Washington, Selma, and, most recently, the violent confrontations between the Ku Klux Klan and the Deacons for Defense in the previously somnolent stretches of northern Louisiana.

In the Informers' eyes, Prez Jones's pretense of fatherly concern for his students masked racial cowardice. His appeals to white politicians were Stepin Fetchit shuffling. While those rednecks got free turkeys from the college farm, Grambling's students paid for turkey necks in their own cafeteria. While Grambling students were forced to use the back door of a clothing store in Ruston called the Vogue, its owner let Jones enter through the front. There was a term of ridicule for local potentates such as Jones in black vernacular: HNIC, "Head Negro In Charge," except, sometimes, to deepen the insult, substituting a different n-word. "I never saw Prez as more than being a caricature," Armand recalled years later, "a caricature of what a college president should be."

After their speeches to the movie audience ended, Zanders and his allies started to walk toward a women's dormitory to spread the message. Several dozen football players wordlessly blocked their way. A long, taut moment passed. Then, again without explanation, the players stepped aside to let the activists pass. Zanders told himself, "Thank God they gave up before we did."

Neither side, in truth, had given up anything yet. No matter how Zanders tried to mollify the football team, the Informers had already made one fateful decision, which put the players and the protesters on a collision course. The best way to attract attention and sympathy to their cause was to hijack homecoming week. Because football, or so it seemed, was the only thing that got the outside world to give a damn about Grambling.

That's My Blood

+ + +

Whistle dangling from his neck, clipboard in his left hand and megaphone in his right, Eddie Robinson prowled the Grambling practice field on the Wednesday of homecoming week. The season, half complete, had reached a critical juncture, and its intensity was even carved into the ground. More than two months of workouts had battered the turf into bare dirt, and after being churned up in recent rains, it had hardened into ruts and pits and cleat marks, like something archaeological.

Robinson paced insistently, broadcasting his impatience with every sharp step, every shake of his head, every burst of instruction. "What do you think we're doing?" he said, voice rising. "Going through the motions?" He looked at the receivers running patterns and barked, "Speed, speed, speed. Hurry, hurry, hurry." He looked at a blocking drill and complained, "We'll get our brains beat out like that." He looked at a defensive lineman who had missed a tackle and cried, "Why don't you go over there and get him? You're too nice, son." Then he climbed into the visitors' bleachers of the adjacent stadium, as if he couldn't bear to be near so many mistakes.

"Last week," he had told the team, "looks like you got soft." It was a conclusion his players could hardly dispute. Unbeaten, emboldened by their upset of Tennessee State, haughty after their demolition of Mississippi Valley, the Tigers had crashed to earth against Jackson State. Harris, coming off two dominant games, threw for just fifty yards on seven completions. The same Grambling defense that had intercepted the great Eldridge Dickey five times surrendered two touchdown passes to Jackson State's freshman quarterback.

The defeat also dimmed the glow of Grambling's moment in civil rights history. The game against Jackson State was the first time black players had ever been permitted onto the gridiron of Mississippi Veterans Memorial Stadium. It had previously been reserved for the all-white teams of Southern Mississippi, Mississippi State, and, most prominently, the University of Mississippi, "Ole Miss," with its Confederate flag and

Rebel mascot. Fittingly, the Grambling–Jackson State game had taken place on the day after another landmark—the conviction by a federal jury of seven white men, including a deputy sheriff and a Ku Klux Klan leader, for the 1964 murders of the civil rights workers James Chaney, Andrew Goodman, and Michael Schwerner.

Now Texas Southern was coming to Grambling with a veteran team on a winning streak and two especially troublesome players. One was Ernie Calloway, a junior nose guard who at 6-5 and 240 boasted the range and speed of an end. Texas Southern's coach, Clifford Paul, took an almost sadistic pleasure in lining up Calloway across from the opposing center; the defender was so fast and so strong, he could shoot through a gap before the bewildered offensive lineman had straightened out of his crouch. Then, on Texas Southern's offense, Grambling had to worry about the wide receiver Ken Burrough, already a star halfway through his sophomore season. At 6-3 and 210, with a sprinter's speed and the soft hands of the quarterback he once had been, Burrough wore white shoes and the number 00. It was partly a tribute to Edwin Starr's hit song "Agent Double-O Soul," and partly a method of making pro scouts pay attention. Opposing coaches already did. Over at Alcorn A&M, Marino Casem had motivated his team to stop Burrough by putting a 00 jersey on a tackling dummy and shooting it full of arrows. Archery contest notwithstanding, Burrough and Texas Southern won the game.

The preparation for Texas Southern, though, was only half of Robinson's job this week. By now, that much was clear. Student protests had simmered along through Monday and Tuesday—more speeches, more leaflets, nothing that Prez Jones didn't think he could outlast or defang. But the demonstrations had burst into fury earlier on this day. For the Informers, the football players were a prize. They were leaders on the campus—heroes, even—and if they joined the movement, then everyone else would follow. And the players, despite all they owed to Grambling, the free education on scholarship and the prospect of a pro contract, could feel the attraction of activism, the magnetic pull. "We had seen the inequality growing up," Harris put it. "We were aware of the difficulties in America. We'd lived with it all our lives."

For his part, even the studiously, scrupulously apolitical Eddie Robinson had been expecting the movement to reach Grambling. He felt its imminence the way some people feel a change in the weather, more by intuition than intellect. His wife, Doris, would recall years later, "You had a feeling things were coming. You didn't know what was coming. And you didn't know how it was coming. But you knew it was coming."

What Coach Robinson and James Harris and the rest almost surely didn't expect was that the object of the protests would be Prez Jones. Not the governor, John McKeithen, who had won election by fighting against integration. Not the twelve white men who comprised the State Board of Education. Not the all-white legislature. Not even the owner of the Vogue. No, the villain was the college president, who was Robinson's colleague, contemporary, collaborator, friend.

Amid the maelstrom, Robinson gave himself one more assignment, and he didn't need to write it on his Ready Sheet as a reminder. It was to keep his players unified, to keep them focused on the game, to keep them out of trouble. He held a team meeting almost every night of this particular week. He never said, in so many words, that he would not permit his players to protest. Instead, he spoke of the importance of obeying the law, leaving unsaid that even in 1967 many of those laws were remnants of the Jim Crow regime. Most often he sounded the note of obligation, telling the team, "Grambling is feeding you. Grambling is sending you to college. Grambling is giving you your opportunity."

Robinson was asking these proud young men to take the risk of being portrayed, as he sometimes was, as an Uncle Tom. Growing up, his sports hero had been Joe Louis, a freedom fighter by inference, and only in the ring; Grambling had engaged in that kind of activism by breaking the color barrier in the Mississippi stadium. Robinson's players, in contrast, admired Jim Brown and Muhammad Ali, who were applying their athletic celebrity to direct political engagement and public dissidence. Robinson was asking Harris and the rest, in essence, to choose. He was asking them, one more time, to trust the system, to take the long view, and to do all of that based on their faith in him.

+ + +

A restless sleeper and early riser, even in less turbulent times, Prez Jones peered out the window of his office shortly after eight on the morning on Wednesday, October 25. He had heard the sound of chanting seconds earlier, and now he could see its source. Dozens of students—students who should have been in class—were pouring into the Square, a landscaped quadrangle outside the Administration Building that was the social crossroads of the Grambling campus.

Then Jones's phone began to ring. There were calls from a science professor, a librarian, a fine arts instructor, all saying and asking the same thing. *What should I do? They started over here.* They were the Informers and a core of about a hundred supporters, and they were bursting into dormitories and classrooms, urging students to walk out and gather in the Square. They took their slogans from Curtis Mayfield and James Brown lyrics—"Keep on pushing," "Get on up"—and some of them wore T-shirts with Malcolm X's credo "By Any Means Necessary."

Jones told his worried staff members, "There is nothing you can do alone," not with the numbers and the mood of the intruders. The pressure had been building for several days already. One female student, refusing to leave her Spanish class, was challenged by a protester, *If a white man raped you, would you just sit there and take it?* By midmorning, hundreds of students filled the Square. Somebody ran extension cords out a dormitory window, supplying power to a loudspeaker and record player. "Hell, no, we won't go," they echoed, turning the mantra of Vietnam draft resisters into a declaration of academic boycott.

As Jones watched the scene through his horn-rim glasses, careful not to betray any outward concern, Bennie Brass began spinning records to draw a crowd. Delles Howell of the football team, approaching the scene out of curiosity, found the spirit almost festive, hard to take too seriously. But as Willie Zanders and other leaders began to pass out copies of two leaflets, each of which had been stealthily printed by the thousand, the magnitude of the mutiny became clear. The first, addressed to "Black Brothers and Sisters," stated, "Our Aim Is Academic Excellence. We Want To Make A Better School. We're Making Our Move. Will You Help Us Make The Administration Make Theirs." The second flyer, labeled, "We Wonder—Is It True?" did not even bother trying to strike a conciliatory tone:

> Is it true that the future of Negro schools is in jeopardy? That the reasons lie in their inability to convince the State Board of Education that Black People are as worthy of Quality Education as the Honkey Taxpayer? Is it true that Grambling has not really progressed past the Elevated High School? . . . Is it true that every "honkey" visitor to campus gets special treatment? . . . Is it true that because of academic unfitness and loss of accreditation Grambling has become a winter and summer resort?

By the end of the day, roughly eight hundred of Grambling's students, some 20 percent of the total, had walked out of their classes. A large number of them carried blankets and pillows into the college's main auditorium to hear speeches and spend the night. Scores of young women concocted makeshift tents from their bedsheets on the manicured lawns of the Square.

And though the protesters permitted Prez Jones to leave his office and go home for the night, he had concluded that this uprising was the real thing, not a fit of undergraduate pique that could be soothed by his charm and sweet talk. He authorized Collie Nicholson to shoot photos of the protesters and release a statement to the local press blaming the events on "Black Power advocates" from the North. Jones and college security officers began placing calls to the parents of the Informers, conveying a message designed to play on the elders' twin fears of their children being expelled from college or arrested by the white police. "I suggest you come and get him and take him home for a few days," went a typical warning. "Otherwise it may be a possibility of him having to go to jail."

In the midst of it all, Jerry Izenberg flew into Shreveport, where Nicholson was waiting at the airport. As the crew's equipment was being unloaded, Nicholson pulled Izenberg aside and said, "I don't know if we can do this show." Izenberg asked how bad the situation was. "I just don't know," Nicholson replied. "We've never had a demonstration before." Izenberg decided to tell his crew nothing and drive into Grambling. No sooner did the ABC group arrive there than the sound man, the only black member of the crew, quit so he could join the protest.

Collie Nicholson was a man who relied on unflappable aplomb, everything just so, from his Stacy Adams shoes to his Dobbs hat, his tie deftly pinned into place so it would remain straight even in a hurricane. He also was a man who had acted on his beliefs, who had broken the color line as a marine journalist and led an NAACP chapter and seen the civil rights volunteer Viola Liuzzo gunned down. And now *he* was the problem? He was the enemy? He was the one having to complain about outside agitators, the euphemism of George Wallace and Bull Connor? All because he wanted Grambling finally to get some credit and some fame? "These kids never lived it," Nicholson said to Izenberg as they drove. Later, at home, he confided to his son, "These crazy kids up there. What are they doing? If they just wait . . ."

When Izenberg entered Jones's home that evening, the Grambling president was on the phone, and based on what the journalist could hear, he surmised that Jones was talking to the police. In all likelihood, it was the commanding officer at the state troopers' barracks in Ruston, someone known and despised around Grambling for persistently calling Jones "Ralph" rather than "President" or even "Mister." The officer apparently was offering a quick, ruthless way of halting the protests: armed police sweeping across the campus. Jones drew upon all the rhetorical tricks he had, the practiced deference and well-oiled guile, but he also dared to show unvarnished emotion, because he was certain that a tragedy loomed.

"Those are not your children out there," he told the commanding officer. "That's my blood. Somewhere in Louisiana, there is some old grandmother that's drying her hands on her apron, saying, 'Ralph, will you take care of my child?' I know y'all got these old mean dogs and those old guns. But if one drop of blood fell, I would not be able to live with myself. So, no, sir, we don't need any help. We'll work it out."

His plea bought a reprieve but not a solution.

+ + +

In a tender yet calculating way, Prez Jones often spoke of his college as "a little out-of-the-way place," "little old Grambling up in the piney woods." His words suggested a campus isolated from worldly things, including political protest. But as he was rapidly learning, the confluence of the civil rights crusade, the anti–Vietnam War movement, and the youth counterculture was sparing few colleges anywhere. For black institutions in particular, the turmoil raised an especially wrenching question. What was the role of these colleges, cautious places created as part of segregation's design, in an era of both increasing integration and mounting black radicalism? Did they still have a reason to exist?

For more than a decade, a number of black colleges—Fisk in Nashville, North Carolina A&T in Greensboro, Howard in Washington, Florida A&M in Tallahassee—had supplied foot soldiers for the sit-ins, boycotts, marches, and freedom rides of the civil rights movement. By the 1966–67 academic year, however, the student protesters' focus had turned inward, from the laws and structures of white dominance to their own black educational institutions, which they now portrayed as cowardly and quiescent. During the year before Grambling's eruption, such demonstrations had swept through Fisk, Howard, Jackson State in Mississippi, and Southern in Baton Rouge.

The most emblematic, and catastrophic, example occurred at Texas Southern University in Houston. For several months in early 1967, students there had been protesting both against racial inequality in Houston and against their own administration's dismantling of a student group affiliated with SNCC, the increasingly militant group led by Stokely Carmichael. The breaking point came on May 16, when police invaded the Texas Southern campus, claiming they had been fired upon from a dormitory. When the subsequent violence ended after five hours, one white police officer was dead, two black college students were wounded, about twenty-five had been beaten by police, and nearly five hundred had been arrested.

At the very time of the Grambling protests in the fall of 1967, Florida A&M experienced a similar confrontation between student protesters and college administrators, this one ignited when the school refused permission for SNCC's Carmichael to speak on campus. "The day is done for the black college," the student newspaper, the *FAMUAN*, proclaimed in an editorial, "whose sole purpose is to produce robots to fit into convenient slots in 'white-middle-class America.'"

In its August 1967 issue, *Ebony* magazine devoted a lengthy article to explaining the "Black College Student Revolt." The essay was most notable for its caustic tone, an assertion of black pride so strident it burgeoned into black self-hate. Student activists "are striving . . . to overthrow the 'plantation milieu' and the 'missionary mores' which continue to grip most Negro colleges under the supervising of an outmoded generation of Negro overseers," declared the author, Howard University sociologist Nathan Hare. "They are no longer willing to cry 'Uncle' to Uncle Sam or Uncle Tom." Black college administrators, Hare went on, dealt with white authorities with a "shuffling 'house nigger' approach" and "prostitute themselves off for 'field nigger' stakes."

If such withering criticism from within the black academic community struck educators of Prez Jones's generation as nearly treasonous, then so did a similarly unexpected indictment from northern white liberals. In early 1967, two Harvard sociologists with active lives as public intellectuals—David Riesman, bestselling coauthor of *The Lonely Crowd* and Christopher Jencks of the *New Republic*—wrote a wide-ranging condemnation of black colleges in the *Harvard Educational Review*. No more than 15 percent of black college students nationally, they stated, scored above average on math and reading standardized tests. State-run colleges such as Grambling and Florida A&M were, in particular, "academic disaster areas." As for the "gray Negroes" who presided over black colleges, "[I]nstead of trying to promote a distinctive set of habits and values in their students, they were, by almost any standard, purveyors of super-American, ultra-bourgeois prejudices and aspirations."

In the face of subsequent outcries by veteran black educators, Riesman and Jencks admitted that they had done very little field research to support their generalizations. They were comparing black colleges and their students to the most elite schools in the nation—Harvard, Oberlin, Cal-Berkeley. Certainly they had no experience of the vise that trapped men such as Prez Jones between the rising expectations of their black students and the demands for order from their white taskmasters in the state capital. Regardless, the Harvard professors' denigration of black colleges inspired follow-up articles in *Time, Newsweek,* and the *New York Times,* transforming controversial premises into conventional wisdom.

Some years earlier, a novelist had more accurately captured the complexity of the black colleges and their leaders. During the 1960 lunch-counter sit-ins in Tallahassee, James Baldwin visited Florida A&M to explore the ideological clash there between activist students and wary administrators. "These men are in an impossible situation," Baldwin wrote of the university's officials, "because their entire usefulness to the state . . . depends on their ability to influence and control their students. But the students do not trust them, which means the death of their influence and their usefulness alike." He continued, "It is easy to judge those Negroes, who, in order to keep their jobs, are willing to do everything in their power to subvert the student movement. But it is more interesting to consider what the present crisis reveals about the system under which they have worked so long."

+ + +

When Prez Jones walked toward his office on the Thursday morning of October 26, he found the main entrance to the Administration Building blocked by about fifty students. So were the other three doors into the building. The Informers and their supporters had implemented their plans so swiftly, with a predawn takeover of the building, that two janitors on the early shift were trapped inside. Something else was stranded, too, in the college's business office: all the printed tickets for the homecoming game against Texas Southern, which was barely forty-eight hours away.

Jones, though, had also come prepared. He was joined outside the building by a contingent of campus police, a group of dormitory counselors, and a set of coaches, including Eddie Robinson. In his suit and his clip-on tie, with an opaque expression on his face, Jones stepped toward a group of protesters, several wearing the sunglasses that had become a kind of Black Power signifier, a couple raising clenched fists. Willie Zanders came forward to face Jones. Until these past few days, Zanders had been a model student; as the student government president during the previous year's homecoming game, he had been deposited by helicopter onto the fifty-yard line on the arm of the queen. Their picture had even appeared in *Jet* magazine.

Now Zanders handed Jones a copy of the protesters' demands, which they called "The Mandates." Perhaps surprised, perhaps contemptuous, Jones let the sheet of paper flutter to the ground. Zanders picked it up and began to recite aloud as the crowd around him hooted and cheered.

Three pages, single-spaced, meticulously outlined with Roman numerals, The Mandates demanded improvements in "academic environment," "political awareness," "democratic rule," and "unsatisfactory conditions." They called for the demotion or dismissal of six staff members, including Collie Nicholson. As for Jones, item I.(7) stipulated, "See that the mandates are carried out. How? It's up to you—or RESIGN."

Jones took a step toward the building entrance. The students barred him with locked arms.

"Ain't nobody gon' turn us around," the students began singing, invoking one of the anthems of the civil rights movement. Then they personalized the verse: "Ain't no president gon' turn us around."

Jones retreated, publicly rebuked. As other employees reported for work, the song resumed. For Ruby Billups, the registrar: "Ain't no registrar gon' turn us around." For Leroy Hawthorne, an assistant football coach turned dean: "Ain't no dean gon' turn us around." For Collie Nicholson: "Ain't no publicity department gon' turn us around."

Later in the day, Jones finally got his chance to be heard at a meeting with leaders of the Informers. "Students have protested at Grambling before," he said, "but have never marched through a building and tried to have students come out of their classes. Nor have they blocked the doors. That is not right. That is wrong. You have blocked the vital services of the college." Part plea, part reprimand, his words swayed none of his student critics.

On the contrary, having succeeded with the class boycott, the Informers turned the pressure on Jones higher by urging students to withdraw from Grambling. "And don't come back," Zanders instructed, "until the place gets straight." Several hundred students had already pulled out by Thursday night. Their parents and siblings, panicked that a police assault on the campus was imminent, hurriedly drove to the campus. The black community of one South Louisiana town hired two buses to evacuate its children from Grambling early the following week.

Jerry Izenberg and his crew, now minus their sound man, dodged and feinted their way amid protesters and campus police, trying to shoot film of football practice and of performances by the college's marching band and gospel choir. Prez Jones gave a preternaturally composed on-camera interview, invoking Booker T. Washington, as if all around him the Tuskegee model of social, academic, and industrial training as the path to racial advancement were not being denounced by Grambling's own students. At one point Izenberg's car was halted by a group of demonstrators, one of them delivering a speech. Desperate to extricate himself, fearful his film's true subject would be discovered, Izenberg said he was shooting news footage about the protests for a Chicago TV station. He ordered the cameraman onto the hood of a car to film the scene, and after a few moments, the protesters let Izenberg pack up and drive away.

The camera, by design, had been empty all along. On his tight budget from ABC, Izenberg could afford only one-tenth the film stock that an hour-long documentary required; there was not a frame to spare.

Meanwhile, though, Grambling's much-anticipated public relations bonanza was, in fact, turning into a public relations disaster. Nicholson's efforts to shape the story favorably—by undercounting the number of protesters and passing on unconfirmed reports of bomb threats by them—worked only with the local white papers in Ruston, Shreveport, and Monroe. *Time,* the *Wall Street Journal,* and the *National Observer* all assigned their own reporters to cover the Grambling protests. Wire-service articles appeared in the *Chicago Tribune, Washington Post,* and *Los Angeles Times.* The movement was being called the "Scholars' Rebellion," and virtually every article contrasted the excellence of Grambling football with the presumed deficiency of its education. Eddie Robinson's great achievement—eighteen Grambling graduates on pro rosters, more than from any college except Notre Dame—was presented instead as evidence of misplaced priorities.

With anyone who would listen, Zanders kept insisting, "I ain't got no problem" with the football players, and simply believed that "everyday people and nonathletes deserve a decent education." Simultaneously, though, rumors were racing through campus that protesters were going to hold a "lie-in" in the stadium on Saturday, blanketing the football field with their prone bodies so the game couldn't be played. Whatever sympathies the players had for the demonstrators' cause, whatever friendships linked them as fellow students, they weren't about to sacrifice their season, and conceivably their pro prospects, out of solidarity.

"We had pretty much lived for that season," Delles Howell put it. "We were lining it up since '65. We had so much unity since the summer, when Shack got everybody to come for practice. We didn't want anything to come between us and our game, our preparation. We couldn't forfeit our season."

Several times during midweek, the tension nearly boiled over. At one point, a dozen football players strode to a portion of the Square where a group of protest leaders were sitting on a low wall, knocking their heels against it in unison. Rightly or wrongly, Kenneth Armand of the Informers assumed the players were a "goon squad," sent on an errand of intimidation by Prez Jones or even Coach Robinson. As the players drew near, one of them, a senior guard named Harold Jones, made eye contact with Armand. They were homeboys from Marrero, a small city across the Mississippi from New Orleans. After that flicker of mutual recognition, the players turned and left.

Toward the end of a football team meeting, a freshman defensive lineman burst into the room looking disheveled—dirt on his T-shirt and in his hair, unable to speak. "Like a tornado had hit him," a teammate recalled. Instantly, the other players concluded that their teammate must have been jumped by the Informers. A group of players dashed out of the room, and the phalanx headed for the encampment of protesters on the Square. "Just show us," the players urged. "Do you remember who did it?" The freshman said nothing. So they implored more. "Just point him out. Who was it?" Again, he stayed silent.

Slowly it dawned on his teammates that the freshman had forgotten about the meeting and tried to cover for his mistake by pretending to have been roughed up. That way, he would be spared Robinson's wrath and punishment—no laundry money for the month, having to run up and down the bleachers during practice. "You made it up," someone said. And once more, the player went strategically mute.

The false alarm rattled the Grambling squad all over again, eroding the composure these young men had been straining to maintain. How close had they come to making a catastrophic mistake, all because of one panicked freshman? So after the team meeting ended and the coaching staff left, Harris convened a players-only session to reaffirm several principles. Stick together as a team. Represent Grambling as best we can. Trust and believe in Coach Robinson. We want to win this championship.

By Thursday night, with the larger conflict nowhere near being resolved, Prez Jones undertook what must have been a dismal task: the black president of a black college calling for troops to suppress black students.

Jones asked for Louisiana's governor, John McKeithen, to deploy the National Guard. Five hundred men had already been mustered at an armory in Ruston. Exactly how McKeithen might use them was a dangerously open question. The governor had been a mercurial political figure—starting out as a piney-woods populist in the style of Huey and Earl Long, winning office in 1964 by courting the George Wallace constituency, and more recently appointing blacks and whites together to a state commission on race relations. Which part of the electorate would McKeithen be playing to when the National Guard marched into Grambling? The part that realized, however sourly, that the Jim Crow days were over? Or the part that wanted those black militants put in their place by bayonet and rifle?

Perched atop the powder keg, Jones attached three conditions to his call for the National Guard. He asked McKeithen to dispatch racially integrated units. He asked for even those units to be augmented by about forty black sheriffs and deputies from around the state. And he asked that under no circumstances would the state police, an entirely white force, be sent into Grambling. A black soldier or a black cop, Jones reasoned, would be far less likely than any white to pull the trigger. Because once the first shot was fired, his life's work, and Eddie Robinson's, would be destroyed.

+ + +

Standing in front of a blackboard, voice firm and eyes smoldering, Eddie Robinson led his players through their last meeting before the homecoming game. It was the Friday afternoon of October 27, and the campus was a study in unresolved conflict. Protest signs shared lawn space with homecoming posters. Alumni in suits and dresses strolled past demonstrators sprawled across building entrances, some of them napping after all-night strategy meetings. With kickoff just twenty hours away, a fundamental standoff remained frozen in place: the Informers would not vacate the occupied buildings and call off the "lie-in" unless Prez Jones promised not to punish them, and Prez Jones said he would make no such decisions until a disciplinary committee composed of his loyalists convened sometime the following week. Hardly anyone except Jones knew that the National Guard was on its way.

The football team was gathered in a meeting room underneath the stadium bleachers, and in this volatile atmosphere it had the sealed-off aura of a fallout shelter. In his coaching, Robinson had always relied on routine, on the dozens upon dozens of repetitions of a given play. During the days of protest, with his players caught in the middle and strained by appeals from each side, Robinson turned routine into a refuge. The more that he insistently went about practices and meetings as scheduled, the less his team would be distracted from the game at hand. But in a quarter century at Grambling, Robinson had never faced this kind of challenge.

His young men sat now at tablet desks in their street clothes, some taking notes, some resting chin in palm, all with eyes obediently forward. Robinson wore a white short-sleeve shirt and a striped tie, and he pointed to a chalk diagram on the board, showing Texas Southern's defensive alignment. It did not take him long to come to the point: Ernie Calloway, nose guard and one-man wrecking crew. With a few new lines on the board, he showed his players Calloway's tendency, which was to rush past the center on Grambling's weak side, the side without the tight end and wingback.

"And this thing falls back to the quarterback," Robinson said, looking at James Harris. "You're gonna have to make the audibles. You're gonna have to change the play at the line." Now the coach swept his eyes across the room. "And everybody's got to be alert. It's like we tell you, men: you got to be intelligent to play our kind of football."

Intelligence was not all he asked. Intelligence could mitigate the threat posed by Calloway, but intelligence needed brute force to defeat it. Robinson told the players he remembered something Frank Leahy, the great Notre Dame coach, had said once at a coaching clinic.

"On the very first play," Robinson said, "in order to be a very good defensive man, when you get down in front of this boy, the first time the ball is snapped, you got to knock hell out of him." Robinson walked from the board right up to the front row of players, inches away, and began sawing the air with his left hand and jabbing with his index finger, one poke

In his pregame ritual, Florida A&M's football coach, Jake Gaither, leads his team in the prayer he composed to the "God of the Rattlers." A minister's son who had aspired to be a lawyer until his father's early death derailed the plan, Gaither brought both faith and eloquence to his gridiron career.

Florida's governor, Claude Kirk, visits Jake Gaither at a Rattler practice during the 1967 season. Part of Gaither's job was managing relations with a series of white governors who generally supported segregation. The patience paid off in 1967, when he won state approval for Florida A&M to play against a white college's team.

With typical intensity, Jake Gaither paces the FAMU sideline, determining strategy.
Kneeling, with his trademark fedora, is defensive coordinator Pete Griffin.
Gaither delegated authority to a highly talented group of assistant coaches, and on
that staff Griffin was first among equals.

Jake and Sadie Gaither pose at home sometime during the 1950s. While this picture was set up for a photographer, their partnership was genuine and lifelong. From her usual seat at midfield, she watched and critiqued every Rattler game.

A Florida A&M publicity shot of Ken Riley in the mid-1960s. Though he played the role here of a traditional drop-back quarterback, Riley was most dangerous as a scrambler who could either throw on the run or carry the ball upfield himself.

A model student as well as a star athlete, Ken Riley shows an unidentified classmate around the Florida A&M campus in this university promotional photo. During most of his Rattler career, Riley had the highest grade-point average of the team, and he was intending to apply for a Rhodes scholarship until the NFL draft intervened. Even so, Riley went on to earn a master's degree.

Green Bay Packers

1265 HIGHLAND AVENUE / GREEN BAY, WISCONSIN 54305 / TICKET OFFICE 494-2355

BUSINESS OFFICE 494-2351
AREA CODE 414

December 30, 1968

Dear Sir:

We are completing information on professional prospects for our 1969 draft which takes place January 28th and 29th, and consider you an excellent prospect. The only way that we can get the complete information on you is by your filling out the enclosed questionnaire.

We realize that you have probably received a number of similar questionnaires to fill out, but this information is very important to us.

The purpose of this letter is to find out directly from you your feelings on professional football as a career. We are particularly interested if you would like to play with the Green Bay Packers, your military status, what position you feel that you could play best in professional football, and whether you would prefer to play in the NFL or in one of the other leagues.

I would appreciate your completing the enclosed questionnaire and returning to our office in the self-addressed stamped envelope.

Thank you and best wishes.

Sincerely,

Vince Lombardi

VL:ljl
Enclosures

1962
1961
1944
1939
1936
1931
1930
1929

MEMBER CLUB NATIONAL CONFERENCE AND NATIONAL FOOTBALL LEAGUE • EIGHT TIMES WORLD CHAMPIONS
TWO TIMES WESTERN DIVISION CHAMPIONS • 1938 - 1960

A letter from legendary Green Bay Packers coach, Vince Lombardi, requesting information from Florida A&M University's star quarterback Ken Riley and expressing interest in him for the upcoming 1969 draft. Ultimately, Riley was selected by the Cincinnati Bengals, whose coach, Paul Brown, had a history of choosing players from black colleges.

In one of many highlights from his fifteen-year pro career with the
Cincinnati Bengals, Ken Riley returns an interception for a touchdown.
Shifted from quarterback to cornerback by the Bengals before his rookie
season, Riley finished his career with sixty-five interceptions, a total that still ranks
fifth in NFL history. His shut-down coverage helped the Bengals reach
the 1982 Super Bowl.

Eighteen-year-old James Harris (center) in late 1964 or early 1965, with his sister, mother, and grandmother around him, signs a letter of intent to attend Grambling College, while football coach Eddie Robinson (far right) looks on.

A Grambling College publicity shot of quarterback James Harris as the Tigers'
starter from 1966 to 1968. The goals of Harris and Coach Robinson were twofold:
to win every college game and to prepare Harris to break the color barrier as the
first black to regularly start at quarterback in the NFL.

James Harris in the NFL as quarterback for the Los Angeles Rams. Between 1974 and 1976, Harris posted a 21-6 record as a starter, leading the Rams to the NFC title game twice and earning MVP of the Pro Bowl.

As the only black quarterback to start in the NFL for many of his pro seasons, Harris was the focus of disproportionate hope and disproportionate hate. This bumper sticker from his fan club attests to what he meant to black Americans—an NFL equivalent to Jackie Robinson.

Eddie Robinson, shown here with an unidentified assistant coach, was a fanatic for detail. He scripted team drills in fifteen-minute intervals, had his team run the same play dozens of times during practice, and spent countless hours reviewing and analyzing game film. He kept projectors both at home and in the office.

In a formal portrait from the mid-1960s, Eddie Robinson, Grambling College's legendary football coach, displays the focused determination that made him such a fierce competitor. He was a consummate sportsman, a mentor who treated his players with respect, but also a perfectionist who hated to lose.

Eddie Robinson at home with his wife, Doris, in the 1960s. He courted her as a teenager, eloped with her soon after college graduation, and for more than half a century made a life with her in Grambling, he as the football coach and she as an English teacher and choir soloist. Grambling's football players often saw them walk the campus hand in hand. Of his life plan, Robinson said, "One job and one wife."

Grambling's Eddie Robinson (center-left, in striped tie) surrounded by teammates and the press on the field of the Cotton Bowl after he broke Bear Bryant's record for most wins with Grambling's defeat of Prairie View. Robinson retired with 408 victories, still the most for a major-college coach.

The official program for the 1967 Orange Blossom Classic football game, when the lives of Grambling's coach, Eddie Robinson; Florida A&M's coach, Jake Gaither; Grambling's quarterback James Harris; and FAMU's quarterback Ken Riley memorably and historically intersected.

for each word. "And let him know one thing, that, boy, you gonna be in trouble this evening. You got a good man in front of you. You got to get in there and deliver the blow. You got to take his head off his shoulder."

Robinson let his players absorb the message for a moment. He told them he knew they had that kind of power. But he reminded them how they had let down against Jackson State, gone weak. Then he returned one final time to his theme, the theme of a man who had been born into nothing and had fought to achieve whatever he has.

"You got to understand this," he said. "You got to beat him. And you got to beat him. And you got to beat him."

When the meeting ended and the players departed, there was still a bit of late-afternoon sun in the October sky. Jerry Izenberg, who had been filming the team meeting, asked Robinson if they could talk as the coach walked for the camera's benefit across the stadium field. For most of the three years Izenberg had been reporting about Grambling, he had found Robinson cautious and guarded, content to let Collie Nicholson serve as buffer. Over the past several days, though, Izenberg had spent hours alone with the coach, hearing stories that went back to Robinson working an ice wagon in Baton Rouge and barnstorming through the hamlets of South Louisiana with his Leland College coach, looking for tall, strong boys to join their football team.

So as he and Robinson walked across the field, Izenberg for the first time felt confident enough to ask a particular question. It was the kind of question that Eddie Robinson, with his fervent patriotism and his Horatio Alger optimism and his willful sublimation of Jim Crow's indignities, had spent a lifetime not answering. The question was, "Do you ever wonder?"

Robinson started his reply with his standard hymn of gratitude, saying, "It isn't sour grapes. I mean, it's all been good to me." Then he paused. Maybe it was the events of the past week. Maybe it was the way the protesters had belittled his life's work—not only winning games, not only producing pro players, but also developing capable young men with college degrees. Maybe it was being called, along with Prez Jones and Collie Nicholson, a "handkerchief head," a "house nigger," an Uncle

Tom. Whatever it was, something compelled him to confess emotions he had swallowed for decades.

"Yeah, I wonder," he told Izenberg. "I wonder, and I'm sure many Negro football coaches wonder, what it would be like to play before eighty thousand people in the stands. And if you had some of the things that some of the other great coaches—Bear [Bryant], Woody [Hayes]—had to work with. If you don't think about those things, you're not real. You got to wonder about it."

+   +   +

At about the same time Izenberg and Robinson were crossing the football field, Willie Zanders walked up to a car parked near the Administration Building. Inside it sat Paul King, the college's business manager. Zanders confided that he had gotten a phone call from King's secretary, Miss Weaver, asking him to please let someone get the homecoming tickets out of the building; they were supposed to go on sale at eight-thirty the next morning.

As much as Zanders appreciated the leverage those captive tickets provided the Informers, he had become friendly with Weaver in his role as student government president. Perhaps, too, he was feeling the indirect pressure of a worried family. His brother, a New Orleans teacher, had driven to Grambling to check on his safety. Even his father, who had left the household when Willie was five, called to warn him, "I heard on TV, the governor's sending the National Guards."

If they indeed came, and if blood were shed, Zanders would bear some personal responsibility. The governor, in fact, had called him several hours earlier, trying to broker a truce. McKeithen's offer called for the protesters to release the buildings and return to classes in exchange for a vague promise that he would make sure college officials considered their demands. Zanders answered with his price tag—amnesty for all protesters—and the conversation ended without agreement. Now, apparently, the governor had decided that talking time was over.

So Zanders, leaning into Paul King's car, offered an olive branch. The student occupiers would allow him into the Administration Building at seven-thirty on Saturday morning to retrieve the tickets. Zanders wanted King to understand that the only reason for the deal was his fondness for Miss Weaver. "If you go in there," Zanders added, "you can't do anything but get the tickets. We're not going to let you do anything else."

Several hours later, with darkness fallen, the traditional homecoming bonfire blazed against the night sky. Instead of evoking festivity, the flames looked from a distance like a building set afire, like the dire rumors come true. Amid the tense, muted celebration, Zanders heard a news bulletin break into a local radio broadcast. Governor McKeithen was calling out the National Guard. One phrase from the newscast especially troubled Zanders: "sweep the campus clean." Then Bennie Brass, listening on a walkie-talkie for any signal of incoming police, heard orders for the Guardsmen to begin taking up positions near the campus.

The Informers called an emergency meeting in the college auditorium. Could they possibly hold on to the occupied building against hundreds of troops? Was the governor serious? Did anyone want to find out the hard way? These young people had believed they could run Grambling better than its president, and now they faced the same anguishing choice that Jones already had: how to simultaneously save face and avoid a bloodbath.

One of the Informers drew a line on the floor. All of the leaders willing to confront the National Guard should step across it, while those opposed should stand still. By literally voting with their feet, the majority would be revealed. A few of the students, weighing their choice, visibly quivered. One activist, a philosophy student, started to recite the speech that Socrates gave before swallowing hemlock. "Shut up, fool," another shouted. "This ain't got nothing to do with Socrates. He ain't here to get killed. It's us."

By a narrow margin, the Informers decided to vacate the occupied buildings immediately. They canceled their plan to lie down on the football field. But they resolved to continue picketing around the campus. And they came up with another scheme involving the homecoming game, a scheme that would not be implemented until almost kickoff.

That's My Blood

+ + +

As the midday sun lifted the chill from the October air, a steady breeze tousled the black and gold streamers tied to goalposts in Grambling's stadium. Cheerleaders sashayed in their pleated skirts and shook their pom-poms like castanets. Dipping and swaying, the Grambling band promenaded onto the field playing a brassy revision of "Ode to Billie Joe," Bobbie Gentry's folk song hit. In its wake, the Tigers charged out of their locker room and across the gridiron. The sellout crowd of twelve thousand cheered, and some fans without tickets looked on from the branches of surrounding trees. Pro scouts squinted into their binoculars.

Saturday afternoon, October 28, was the very picture of Grambling homecoming, except that it was not. Five hundred National Guardsmen, equipped with rifles and bayonets, were lined up along Main Street, the border between the village and the campus. (The integrated units included a black football player from the New Orleans Saints, whose reserve unit had been called up.) Black sheriffs and deputies flanked the stadium entrances. As the Informers had picketed throughout the morning, onlookers rained them with both praise and contempt, every call of "Right on!" being balanced by a shout of "If you don't like it, go home!"

Then, as the stadium clock ticked down the final minutes toward kickoff, dozens of student protesters headed through the gates. The sheriffs and deputies let them pass; the ushers collected their tickets. Instead of taking seats, though, the demonstrators assembled on a slight hill that rose behind one end zone and beneath the scoreboard. In that spot, no spectator would be able to ignore them. The protesters carried copies of The Mandates, along with books and magazines; Zanders was holding one of his political science texts so he could catch up on the assignments he had missed while boycotting classes. This was the Informers' new plan: a "read-in."

The protesters sat in tight rows as the Grambling band arranged itself in a block formation, lifting instruments to mouths, holding sticks near drum skins. With the first notes of the "Star-Spangled Banner," the protesters scrambled to their feet, having expected a different song first. After the National Anthem, it began: Grambling's alma mater. Now Zanders and the rest of the protesters pointedly sat down in silence. And when the last aria to "dear old Grambling" faded, they filled the brief vacuum with their own chant. *Prez told a lie!* This slogan referred to his statement in the local papers that the protesters were just a handful of rabble-rousers. *Prez told a lie!*

With distraction all around and a formidable opponent waiting across the field, Eddie Robinson sent his young men out to save their season. From Grambling's very first offensive play, the difficulty was evident. Texas Southern brought up its three linebackers to join its five defensive linemen, daring Harris to pass. The second Harris dropped back, Calloway surged past the center, trampled the halfback who tried to block him, and leaped onto Harris's helmet and shoulders, collapsing him like a wave crashing down on an unsuspecting swimmer. Several plays later, under pressure again, Harris threw an interception.

As the first quarter wore on, Grambling kept sputtering, with its longest gain a twenty-yard run by the reserve quarterback Wesley Bean on a fake punt. Grambling's offensive coach, Doug Porter, had added screen passes to the game plan to exploit Calloway's furious rush, and Grambling's standard dive play was designed for the fullback to zip past him into open field. On this day, though, none of it was working consistently or well. When Grambling double-teamed Calloway, Texas Southern blitzed its linebackers and moved its ends and tackles toward the middle, outnumbering the Tigers' interior linemen. On one screen, the halfback dropped Harris's pass. Texas Southern recognized another screen, covering the would-be receiver and chasing Harris from hash mark to sideline before he could heave a deliberate incompletion. Grambling's third possession ended when Calloway's second sack forced a punt, and that much futility was more than Robinson could bear.

"Hell, they're not blocking," he said as the offense trudged off the field, getting as close to profanity as his propriety allowed. "He's coming from the inside. We're not getting any blocking. You can't offer any alibi." His anger not yet drained, he called the starting offense around him and told them, "We're whipping ourselves, men." He reminded the linemen about a few familiar blocking techniques and then, with palpable disgust, a distaste for their mere presence, waved them away, ordering, "All of you, get back on the bench."

What saved Grambling, at least initially, was Harris's lifelong friend Delles Howell at cornerback. He had prepared all week to cover Ken Burrough, almost awed by his speed, searching for some advantage. In Texas Southern's pro-style offense, Burrough usually started the game running short patterns, to lure a defender into playing close to the line of scrimmage. Then Burrough would fake short and race long, leaving the hapless defender cross-legged in his slipstream. As Howell studied game films, he noticed that on those shorter square-outs, the lanky Burrough would reduce his stride for a few choppy steps before cutting to the sideline. Howell noticed, too, that Texas Southern's quarterback, David Mays, tossed a soft, catchable ball, sort of like Eldridge Dickey's, the kind of ball that gave a defensive back the extra half second to close in.

So on Texas Southern's first series, Howell laid back, about eight yards off the line of scrimmage. Sure enough, Mays hit Burrough on a five-yard square-out. The next time, Burrough pushed ten yards forward as Howell backpedaled, giving the impression he would concede the modest completion. Instead, as soon as he saw those choppy steps, Howell ran forward at full speed, taking aim at the bull's-eye of Burrough's 00. Mays sent the pass high, and even at six-foot-three Burrough had to leap for it. Howell drove his shoulder pads through the receiver's calves, and Burrough pinwheeled backward, his helmet slamming against the turf. A few minutes later, Howell caught sight of the Texas Southern trainers helping Burrough take off his pads. "Playing Grambling," the star receiver would recall years later, "was like going to Vietnam."

With his main weapon disarmed, Mays switched strategy. Rather than throw to a backup receiver going against Grambling's top pass defenders, Howell and safety Robert Atkins, he passed against the supposedly lesser pair on the opposite side, cornerback Hilton Crawford and safety Roger Williams. Gifted as Mays was, though, he was still a freshman, playing in the biggest game of his brief career, with a hostile crowd in the stands. Grambling added to the pressure by rotating seven different players through its defensive line, keeping fresh legs and fresh lungs in the pass rush. No way was Robinson's defense going to let another freshman quarterback embarrass them the way Jackson State's had the previous week. Midway through the second quarter, Mays made his first big mistake, floating a sideline pass that Grambling intercepted, giving the Tigers possession at midfield.

Two feeble running plays brought Grambling to a third and seven. Harris went to his staple, a square-out to Charlie Joiner, for a first down at the Texas Southern thirty-one. Texas Southern stayed with what had been working: eight men crowding the line, snorting in their impatience for the snap, and just two cornerbacks and a safety covering the receivers. Harris answered with a formation that had succeeded against Tennessee State, splitting out both ends and using Essex Johnson as a flanker. That meant one-on-one coverage, and Harris believed Joiner could beat any double team anyway. Harris dropped back just five yards, giving Calloway less time to reach him, while Joiner ran straight up the left hash mark. Once he had the defender retreating, fearful of a long pass, Joiner curled to his right, facing Harris. He caught a dart of a pass, pivoted forward, and ran laterally toward the right sideline. The other defensive backs had been following Johnson on his crossing pattern, right to left, and could only grab air, sliding like pedestrians on an ice patch as Joiner scooted past them, toward the end zone.

Grambling went into the locker room at halftime ahead 6–0 but hushed with disappointment and worry. As the players dropped onto the bare wooden benches, Robinson delivered a mixture of urgency and lamentation. "We told you before you went out there," he began in the tone of a chastising father, "you're going to have to suck up your guts and play ball." Then he intoned one of his favorite aphorisms: "You got to put strength on strength and let weakness go to hell." Then he said, mindful of Ernie Calloway, "You got to chop him, man. It's football." And finally, in that spartan room beneath the bleachers, he shifted his voice to a quieter tone and delivered his equivalent of an alma mater: "All we asking you is to give what you got and do what we know how to do. Now let's get after them."

Harris and Howell and Joiner and the rest did not shout or stomp. They clomped out of the room in wordless resolution. Robinson had not said it, of course, but there was a reason besides Calloway for the lackluster first half. The last week had been a campus civil war, with dorm floors and fraternities and clubs all divided. Protest or not? Boycott or not? Drop out or not? Amid the maelstrom, the players were not some protected caste of jocks, musclebound mercenaries removed from the real world. "Sometimes people didn't understand," Harris observed years later, "that *we* were students and we had our own feelings about the unfairness."

From their hillside during halftime, the protesters booed the introduction of the homecoming queen. Willie Zanders took a special satisfaction at seeing her unescorted, since he, the student government president, would normally have filled that role. Suddenly, with the ceremony over, several members of the queen's court strolled in their dresses and hairdos to join the demonstrators. *Prez told a lie!* they resumed chanting, *Prez told a lie!* Zanders swore that, from this distance, he could make out Jones in the bleachers, weeping.

Back on the field to start the third quarter, Harris put together a drive—two sweeps for twenty yards, a square-out for fifteen, a fullback dive for two or three. Then Texas Southern sacked him again. Lining up for the next play, smelling weakness in the Grambling blockers, one of Texas Southern's linemen jumped offside. Some back-and-forth shoving broke out, and in the midst of it, Grambling's center, Thomas Ross, surrendered to the frustration of his long afternoon with Ernie Calloway. He whacked Calloway with a forearm, and Calloway smartly backed away and lifted his arms for the referee, as if showing a cop he had no gun.

Who, me? What'd I ever do wrong? The referee whistled Grambling for a penalty, stifling the drive, and ejected Ross from the game.

When Ross reached the Grambling bench, Robinson was waiting, waiting with a wrath that seemed to betray the pressure he had endured all week. It was not his way, except in humor, to criticize a player's character rather than his performance. So maybe, as he lit into Ross, he was talking both to him and through him, all the way to those students on the hillside behind the end zone.

"You have satisfied yourself," Robinson said, each sentence a staccato burst. "You have satisfied yourself. You got him back. But we told you about stability and self-control. Now you think about us. We don't have a center, and we got to play the rest of the game. But you satisfied yourself. You jumped on him." Robinson indicated the other players, standing on the sideline or sitting on the bench. "Look at what you did. Look at the people you let down." He drew breath, then spat out one last word. "Disgraceful."

With an untested freshman now at center, Grambling limped along on offense. But again, the defense compensated. The more Grambling's defensive linemen attacked, trapping him in the pocket, the more David Mays hurried his throws. After being picked off three times in the first half, he tossed five more interceptions in the second. Roger Williams returned one of them forty-six yards for a touchdown late in the third quarter. Trailing 13–0, Mays grew even more desperate. Early in the fourth quarter, another interception and return by Grambling put the ball on the Texas Southern thirty.

For the next three plays, the Tigers looked like their normal efficient, effective selves. And those three were enough: a twenty-yard pass from Harris to Essex Johnson on a crossing pattern, a seven-yard throw to halfback Willie Armstrong on an audible by Harris, and then a two-yard touchdown run by Henry Jones, the fullback. After a game of fitful offense, like an engine misfiring, the Grambling line had finally shoved Calloway and company backward.

Leading 20–0 now, Grambling's defense relaxed enough to allow

Texas Southern two meaningless touchdowns, the second of them with just forty-three seconds remaining. It was not the easiest victory of the season, and it certainly wasn't the prettiest, with the Tigers being outgained 322 yards to 154, fumbling 4 times, and taking 105 yards in penalties. But amid an atmosphere of unprecedented tension, the most turbulent week in the college's history, Eddie Robinson's team had maintained enough of its concentration to convincingly defeat a highly ranked foe.

As the players jogged off the field, cheerleaders at their side, the protesters filed from the hillside back to their dorms. Some, like Zanders, had pointedly ignored the game. Others had not been able to resist watching and rooting. Most of them, like most of the football players, were planning to hear Gene Chandler at the homecoming show that night. As the stadium emptied, a checkerboard of white rectangles covered the demonstrators' hillside. They were copies of The Mandates.

+ + +

After a full day of quiet on the campus on Sunday, October 29, Governor McKeithen withdrew the National Guard from Grambling. In their separate ways, Prez Jones and Willie Zanders had helped spare their college the kind of bloodshed that had befallen Texas Southern the previous spring. Jerry Izenberg and his crew flew back to New York with the footage for a documentary he had already titled *100 Yards to Glory.*

The conflict at Grambling, however, wore on and in some ways grew uglier. On the Monday after homecoming week, Jones convened his handpicked disciplinary committee, including Eddie Robinson, and it voted to expel twenty-nine protest leaders, including Zanders. The ousted students, in turn, retained one of North Louisiana's lonely white liberals, a civil rights attorney from Monroe named Paul Kidd, to take their case. In mid-November Kidd won an injunction from the US District Court to forestall the expulsions pending a state hearing and a federal trial. The demonstrators' initial, principled nonviolence, though, gave way to vandalism and harassment—bomb scares anonymously called in, windows broken and plates shattered in the cafeteria, fires set in several dormitories. No longer did their cause look quite so pure.

Nor did Prez Jones emerge with his reputation unscathed. On the first Sunday in November, he was sitting in his usual pew as a deacon of Rocky Valley Baptist Church when the pastor, Rev. Mose Pleasure, launched into a sermon titled "You Can't Do Right Doing Wrong." Already intending to leave the Grambling pulpit, Rev. Pleasure spoke without regard to consequences. "It should be clear that it does not take an evil man possessed with such power to create a monstrously evil system," he preached. "It would only take a man who has little preparation for the use of such power, or a weak man, or a man with any of a hundred shortcomings."

So Eddie Robinson still had the task of keeping his team unified and focused, keeping up with classwork and winning on the field. The Tigers got a huge break when previously winless Wiley College upset Jackson State, putting Grambling back atop the Southwestern Athletic Conference. On the consecutive Saturdays of November 4 and 11, the Tigers routed Arkansas AM&N by 39–13 and Wiley by 70–12, with Harris throwing four touchdown passes in the latter game. They were 7-1 heading into the regular-season finale against Southern University, one win away from the undisputed conference title.

Even before that game, though, Robinson's team collected a more valuable prize. It was a bid to play Florida A&M in the Orange Blossom Classic on December 2 at the Orange Bowl in Miami. For black college football, as James Harris put it, "that game was our Super Bowl."

8

BORROWED TIME

Florida A&M vs. Southern, November 11, 1967

Jake Gaither headed into Florida A&M's game against Southern University on the Saturday night of November 11 with several goals and a single fear. His Rattlers had clobbered hapless North Carolina A&T by 63–6 the previous week to raise their record to 5-1, and now Gaither intended to push the team back into the national rankings by beating a far more formidable foe. Southern filled the bill with a 5-3 record and half a dozen pro prospects. Gaither also relished the chance to humble the Florida players on Southern's team, including both quarterbacks and the top receiver, to make them regret having spurned his offer of a football scholarship and turned down the coach nobody was supposed to turn down. Gaither had drummed on the theme of disloyalty all week during practice, saying of those ingrates, "Let 'em know what it feels like to be hit by a Rattler.

Make 'em wish they'd never been born." And, of course, Gaither wanted to win because he always wanted to win.

The counterweight, though, was that fear, the fear of injury to a key player. Gaither spoke in the euphemism of wanting his team to "stay healthy," as if stating the concern overtly would hex it. As deep as the talent ran on the A&M squad, as fully as Gaither used his roster in the waves of Blood, Sweat, and Tears, he was loath to lose a starter at this pivotal point in the season. In consecutive weeks after the Southern game, the Rattlers would face opponents of both ceremonial and competitive importance. First, on November 18, was A&M's cross-state rival Bethune-Cookman in what would be the final home game of the Rattler season. Next, on November 25, was Texas Southern in the inaugural Tampa Classic, the test run for a future game against a white school. Finally, on December 2, was Grambling in the Orange Blossom Classic. The Classic promised to be a genuine championship game, pitting the two greatest teams and two most legendary coaches in black college football against each other for only the third time. Gaither fretted over the possibility of going against Eddie Robinson shorthanded.

With four minutes left in the first half against Southern, all seemed pretty much on track. Ken Riley had already thrown two touchdown passes to John Eason, though his two interceptions had helped Southern tie the game at 13–13. Despite a lot of vicious hits by the Southern defenders—clothesline tackles on receivers, chop blocks aimed at ankles and knees—none of the Rattlers had been hurt.

Now, with the ball on A&M's fourteen-yard line, Riley faced a third down with eleven yards to go as he tried to put the Rattlers back into the lead before halftime. He dropped back, looking far downfield for Eason, his favorite target. Southern's defensive linemen closed in, squeezing the pocket, leaving Riley no time and no room to plant his feet and pass. He squirted several yards straight ahead until his path was closed off by a tangle of rushers and blockers on the turf. A Southern defender's hand reached out from the knot of limbs and grabbed one of Riley's ankles. Riley spun away, jumped several yards to his left, then skipped backward to avoid another tackler, sucking in his stomach to evade outstretched arms. For all his dazzling choreography, though, he was still near the line of scrimmage, well short of a first down. So he shifted into some forward gear and dashed for the near sideline, racing along it upfield past the twenty, then the twenty-five. It was quintessential Ken Riley, the athletic ad-lib that transformed futility into promise, replacing an imminent punt with a new set of downs.

Except that as Riley was darting up the sideline, one of Southern's defensive tackles, Alden Roche, was tracking him, cutting diagonally toward him, moving 250 pounds with surprising speed and frightening momentum. Riley was looking upfield, oblivious to the pursuit, when Roche caught up to him at the twenty-seven. Roche threw a forearm around Riley's neck and helmet, twisting him off his feet and then driving him into the ground. Riley lay on his right side, motionless, his arms crossed atop his chest, a protective gesture made a few seconds too late.

As the sold-out crowd went silent, Riley gradually staggered to his feet and plodded woozily to the Rattler bench. Here was Jake Gaither's direst premonition incarnate. All season, the coach's plan had been to open up his offense, and Riley's strong arm and scrambler's feet were essential ingredients. He had been peaking these past few weeks, since displacing Elroy Morand as the starter, throwing for 3 touchdowns and 242 yards against North Carolina A&T. In the days leading up to the Southern game, Gaither had stated plainly, "We'll need our best and it looks like Riley is it." Now the best sat on the sideline with his helmet off, his condition uncertain, the team trainer on the way to examine him.

Morand, meanwhile, took over as quarterback. With a deft mix of plays—halfback runs off-tackle, a quarterback sneak, a long rope of a pass on a bootleg—he moved the Rattlers deep into Southern territory. Then, on a third and five from the twenty-three, Morand rolled out to his left, not a pass rusher within ten yards of him, and lofted an arching spiral toward Eason in the end zone. At the last second, a defensive back named Mel Blount, one of those Southern players coveted by the pros, cut several yards in front of Eason. Blount was tall for a defensive back, six-foot-three, and at the height of his jump he stretched his left arm skyward. It tipped the ball down into his right hand. Without breaking stride, he raced toward the far sideline and then cut upfield.

Back in the Southern end zone, an official had thrown a penalty flag. It was interference against Southern; the other defensive back covering Eason had shoved him to the ground while the ball was still in the air. Nobody except that official, though, seemed to realize that a penalty had been called. Blount was already running up the sideline right in front of the Florida A&M bench. Four or five Rattlers were bearing down on him. One of them, a tackle named Gerald Henderson, grabbed Blount's jersey collar, knocking him out of bounds. Henderson, thrown off balance, barreled uncontrollably toward a graying man in a white short-sleeve shirt and a stingy-brim hat: Jake Gaither.

Gaither could see the oncoming collision but he could not make his legs move. He stood rooted to his spot, unable to slide sideways out of danger. The assistant coaches, the people on the Rattler sideline who had known Gaither longest, cringed. They knew what was happening. This immobility was one of the lingering vestiges of the surgery that had saved Gaither from brain cancer. All these years later, he still suffered bouts of dizziness, still walked with a trace of uncertainty, still struggled to keep his car straight on the road. One time, while Gaither was driving his staff to an away game, Costa Kittles had to grab the steering wheel to keep the car from plunging into a ditch. As for Gaither's ability to move laterally, one day in practice John Eason had been running a pass route when he found himself closing in on the coach. Their eyes briefly met, and Eason could see something like panic on Gaither's face as his brain could not order his legs to flee to safety. Now the same thing was happening. Henderson smashed into Gaither at the waist, and the coach's body folded over as if he had been walloped with a baseball bat. He crumpled and his legs twisted. Several players who had been trailing Blount stumbled over the pile of Gaither and Henderson.

Instantly, a couple of coaches began sorting through the body parts to extricate Gaither and help him to his feet. Some players ran over to

Hollis Jones, a reserve lineman who had been standing near Gaither before the crash. "Why didn't you jump in front of him, Bubba?" they shouted. Gaither shook off the assisting hands, steadied himself on his feet. He was doing what he had always taught his players to do. *Shake it off, play through the pain, don't let the other guy know he hurt you.*

But he did know that he was hurt. He could feel something very wrong with his right leg, down around the shin. He asked George Thompson, the Rattlers' trainer, to rub on analgesic balm. Thompson said no, heat was the wrong thing, balm would cause swelling. Instead, Thompson wrapped Gaither's leg. Out on the field, the interference penalty gave A&M a first down on the Southern one-yard line, and Morand scored on the next play, giving the Rattlers a 20–13 lead.

For the rest of the game, Gaither moved more by hopping than walking. Somehow, both at halftime and game's end, he hobbled unaided into the locker room. He drove home, where he and Sadie hosted their usual postgame party. But at one point in the merriment, Gaither slipped away from the platters of chicken and the clinking highball glasses and the hearty chatter to confide to George Thompson, "Baby, you were right."

The game had ended well, even impressively. After consecutive touchdowns by Southern put it ahead 25–20, Florida A&M roared back with sixteen fourth-quarter points—a safety and touchdown runs by both Morand and Riley. Riley's injury, it turned out, had been minor. He ended up playing much of the second half and finished the game with ninety yards and two touchdowns passing and another forty-six yards rushing. The quarterback, like the rest of his teammates, went to sleep on Saturday night assuming that Jake Gaither was fine.

Gaither, after all, was the man who had survived brain cancer; he was, as assistant coach Hansel Tookes put it, "one tough old rascal." In more ways than one, Gaither considered himself fortunate to be alive, every day a day of borrowed time, time from God. His twin brother, Alphonso, had died at a year old. One of his sisters, Eliza, had passed at age four. His oldest brother, Cicero, had been stabbed to death, at just thirty-five years old, by a customer of his Pittsburgh tavern. Having made it into his sixties, Gaither was much too grateful to complain.

About five o'clock on Sunday morning after the game, however, he awakened moaning and writhing with pain. He was in such agony that Sadie worried he was having a recurrence of the brain cancer. She took him straight to the hospital on A&M's campus. When the Rattlers assembled that afternoon for "skull practice," reviewing films of the last game and studying strategy for the next, Jake Gaither did not stand at the blackboard. He was nowhere in the classroom. He was nowhere in the building.

Gaither lay prone and bedbound in the university hospital, where X-rays had revealed a complex fracture of the tibia. The injury that Gaither had dreaded most, one to Ken Riley, had set into motion the sequence of plays that led to the injury Gaither had never imagined, one to himself.

+   +   +

Jake Gaither's hospital room filled quickly with telegrams, fruit baskets, flowers, get-well cards, even a teddy bear from George Halas, the owner and head coach of the Chicago Bears. Gaither's most famous player, the world-record sprinter Bob Hayes, took a leave from his NFL team, the Dallas Cowboys, to fly to Tallahassee. Hayes had always called Sadie and Jake Gaither "Ma" and "Pa," and they gave him a key to their house and a bed in their guest room. The coach had used his political connections to obtain a pardon for Hayes from a youthful robbery conviction and to cobble together money for him to compete in international track meets. When a few A&M players once complained that Gaither favored Hayes, that Hayes got all the publicity, that they wanted their share of the limelight, Gaither replied, "You only have to do one thing. Outrun him."

Now "Bullet Bob" Hayes, the prodigy of pro football, All-Pro in his first two seasons, repaid the coach's solicitude. He smiled and chatted at Gaither's bedside, pointed to his bandaged leg for the benefit of photographers, and delivered a scroll with autographs of all the Cowboy players. Gaither, supine in his hospital gown, gazed up glowingly from his pillow.

He was convincing himself, and anyone else who would listen, that he had suffered only a "minor injury." He talked to a local newspaper reporter less about his leg than his pride in the Rattlers for their come-from-behind win over Southern. "It takes a team with class to do that," he said, "and this one has it." As for his physical condition, Gaither dispensed with the topic in a defiant tone, announcing, "I plan to get out of here sometime this week, if I have to go in a wheelchair."

The only place he rolled, as it turned out, was into the operating room. On November 15, the Wednesday after the Southern game, surgeons sliced open Gaither's shin, cleaned out torn cartilage, and inserted pins to reconnect the shattered pieces of his tibia. Then the doctors delivered their prognosis: two weeks of bed rest, followed by two weeks on crutches, with a cast from thigh to foot for a total of six weeks. At that rate, Gaither might be able to return to the sidelines with his crutches for the Orange Blossom Classic, just maybe.

Idleness and uncertainty began to chafe at him. He could occupy his mind for only so long with issues of *Sports Illustrated, Time,* and *Life.* He sought comfort in religion, reading the Bible, telling visitors that God has His reasons. "We're an earthly people," Gaither said, quoting one of his minister father's favorite sayings, "and the man above will decide for us."

Faith, though, did not calm him for long. Gaither incessantly scripted plays on a notepad. He phoned his assistant coaches every ten minutes, or so it seemed to them, with nagging questions. *Have your boys got their assignments? Do your boys know what to do? Can your boys do the cross-block?* The frustration of enforced inertia had transformed Gaither from a head coach who trusted his assistants, who willingly delegated authority to them, who always said he didn't want a yes-man, to a busybody consumed by worry and doubt. When Bobby Lang, the defensive-line coach, visited Gaither in the hospital, he came away thinking of him as "an animal stuck in its cage."

Nobody was immune to Gaither's agitation. Every time he awakened from sleep or a nap, he expected Sadie to be waiting at his bedside, regardless of her duties as an English instructor. "Baby, where were you?" he would ask when she did arrive. And she would answer, dipping into her own dwindling supply of patience, "You forgot, Jakey. I had a class." Gaither would summon his top assistant coach, Pete Griffin, after practice, and ask, "How'd it go today?" Griffin, knowing full well that Gaither was pestering everybody else for reports, replied, "You probably know already."

For the most part, Gaither did not want his players to visit, to see him so diminished. He made an exception only for his quarterbacks, Ken Riley and Elroy Morand. They were his surrogates on the field; they were the instruments of his ambitions. He tried to set an almost convivial tone, asking Riley, "Baby, how are you doin'?" Riley replied, "No, Coach, how are *you* doin'?" Gaither ruffed up his voice into an agreeable growl and said, "Oh, I'm all right."

Leaving the hospital room, the quarterbacks were less than convinced. Unnerved was more like it, shaken. Riley thought of the sight of Gaither at summer practice in his T-shirt and football pants, with his enormous calves visible above the sweat socks. How could anything break one of those legs? Morand spoke like someone who had suddenly discovered the concept of mortality. "You never felt he would get hurt," he said of Gaither. "It was amazing to find out he *could* get hurt."

The November days crept by without Gaither getting any closer to being discharged, as he had so confidently predicted. He struggled to master his crutches, to make his way spasmodically up and down the ward's corridor. This was the football season in which he'd had to prove himself all over again; this was the season in which he'd had to show he wasn't obsolete; this was the season in which he'd had to silence those emerging doubters. And he had done all of those things. His team was 6-1 after the Southern game. It had avenged its 1966 losses to both Southern and South Carolina State. Gaither had revised his offense so effectively that the quarterback tandem of Riley and Morand was on track to set Rattler records for passing yardage and touchdowns. Yet now, with the season rising to its crescendo, Jake Gaither was a sixty-four-year-old man with a broken leg, consigned to the periphery of his life's work. "My team needs me," he said plaintively one day to his secretary, Lillian Hagins. "How could this happen to me?"

+ + +

With Jake Gaither miserably convalescing, there was no question who would take over as interim head coach: Pete Griffin. Anytime in the past when Gaither had missed practice because of an appointment or illness, Griffin had overseen the drills. During the week before the annual Orange Blossom Classic, when Gaither was often in Miami drumming up publicity for the game, Griffin had habitually prepared the team. He ran such rigorous sessions, in fact, that Gaither told a standard joke about returning to the practice field the following day to "find half the team broken."

The bond between Gaither and Griffin traced back to 1938, when Gaither was an assistant coach and Griffin the starting center on the A&M team that won the black national championship. Several years later, Gaither helped entice Griffin back from Ohio, his home state, where he was studying for his master's degree, to join the Rattler staff. The two men shared the same mixture of athleticism and erudition, composed the same kind of eloquent letters, shared the same passion for black history, experienced the same heartache at not being able to have children (though Griffin and his wife did adopt a daughter). Griffin sounded like no one so much as Gaither when he wrote in one essay, as if to obliquely answer both white bigots and black militants, "Blacks helped to literally build America. Therefore we Blacks should take pride in exclaiming, 'This, too, is my country.'"

In the spirit of Gaither's motto—"A-gile, Mo-bile, and Hos-tile"—Griffin exuded a physical presence, maintaining a boot-camp physique well into middle age, setting an example for his players that couldn't be missed. As A&M's track coach, Griffin first recognized Bob Hayes's potential as a sprinter. And Griffin's intensive training regimen, which emphasized distance runs as well as focused bursts of speed, transformed Hayes from being only the third-best hundred-yard-dash man at A&M to capturing the gold medal in the Tokyo Olympics as the "world's fastest human."

Despite all their similarities, all their mutual trust, Griffin differed from Gaither in one fundamental way. He preferred being the sidekick to being the star, being the second banana to being Mr. Showtime. Off the football field, he devoted himself to solitary pursuits—gardening, poetry, calisthenics. His own wife, Charlotte, said of him, "He's not a talker." When Griffin did start conversations, the subject often arose from his private interests. He talked about the *Rubáiyát of Omar Khayyám,* for instance, with Darryl Tookes, the artistically inclined son of Hansel Tookes, another assistant coach.

When it came to the inspirational aspect of coaching, Griffin had always readily conceded it to Jake Gaither, the master manipulator with his prayers, his tears, his invocation of past triumphs, his slowly ascending way of declaring that somebody has got to pay. Gaither, after all, had aspired as a young man to become a minister or a lawyer, professions that celebrated oratory. He addressed his football team as if he were swaying the jury or coaxing a sinner down the aisle to accept the Lord. As for Pete Griffin, one of the Rattlers' offensive linemen, Zeke Sims, once overheard him say, "I don't like being up there talking." Griffin was more strategist than motivator, perpetually equipped with clipboard and pen, a onetime chemistry teacher working the playbook's X's and O's like the valences of the periodic table. It was one thing to replace Gaither for a day or two or three, knowing he would be returning on schedule. It was another thing entirely, one Griffin had never anticipated, to be head coach for the foreseeable future.

Griffin met with Gaither at the hospital after each day's practice and spoke often by phone. The other assistant coaches did their part to fill the gap left by Gaither's injury. Costa Kittles, who coached the quarterbacks, screened game films on his living-room wall night after night, eventually falling asleep with a legal pad full of diagrammed plays in his lap. Hansel Tookes, who coached the offensive line, also scouted the upcoming opponents. So adept at statistics that he occasionally taught the course at FAMU, he could expertly analyze a team's tendencies and probabilities. Many evenings, Tookes walked across the wide backyard between his home and Griffin's to discuss his findings with the emergency head coach.

The players instinctively understood their responsibility, almost a kind of moral obligation, something filial. "You get it done," Gaither often told his young men. "That's your job. That's why I got you here. Don't give no excuse. Everybody's got one of them." Ken Riley had never forgotten that day the previous spring when he blew off practice to check out girls on The Set, and Gaither had rolled up in his Lincoln. *Baby, you supposed to be the leader. You supposed to be my coach on the field. If you're lying to me, baby, who can I trust?* With three pivotal games left, three games that would define the season, Riley had three more opportunities to demonstrate just what kind of player he was, to prove he was worthy of that trust.

Against Bethune-Cookman on November 18, Riley threw for 193 yards and a touchdown and Morand for 141 yards and 2 touchdowns as A&M won 30–6. A week later, the Rattlers soundly beat a 6-2 Texas Southern team by 30–7. Morand passed for 3 touchdowns and Riley ran for another one. Very clearly, Griffin was sticking with Gaither's plan for an aggressive, passing offense. The result was a regular-season record of 8-1, A&M's best since 1964.

With their achievements, the Rattlers also chipped away at the edifice of segregation. The game against Texas Southern, the Tampa Classic, had drawn nearly twenty-three thousand spectators, proving A&M's box-office appeal with a nonconference, black opponent. That kind of turnout promised even greater numbers for a history-making contest against a white school. Two of the Rattler seniors, tight end John Eason and defensive back Major Hazelton, were selected for postseason all-star games, recognition rarely accorded to players from small black colleges.

Named to the North-South Shrine game in Miami, Hazelton would
be playing alongside stars from the very schools in the Southeastern,
Southwest, and Atlantic Coast Conferences that had refused to recruit
black players like him. Eason would be participating in the Blue-Gray
game, titled with the Civil War in mind, held in the Alabama capital
of Montgomery, the city of Martin Luther King's bus boycott and of
George Wallace proclaiming, "Segregation now, segregation tomorrow,
segregation forever!" Paradoxically, or perhaps subversively, Eason would
be wearing a uniform in the color of the Confederate Army.

In the last weeks of November, Jake Gaither managed to visit the
Rattlers' practice field once or twice, conveyed across campus on a golf
cart. The players heard and clung to rumors that Gaither would coach
the Orange Blossom Classic from his wheelchair. But on Thanksgiving Day, Gaither could not deliver his traditional speech to the team, a
cherished ritual in which he expounded about Pilgrims and Indians and
America and gratitude. For him to miss it was a disturbing sign.

Then, on November 30, the day before the Rattlers were to travel to
Miami and two days before the Orange Blossom Classic itself, the *Tallahassee Democrat* confirmed the worst in its headline: "Gaither Won't
Go To The Classic." In the article, Gaither tried to make light of the
disappointment, laying blame on those darn doctors. "They tricked me,"
he said. "They told me if I could move up and down that hallway on
crutches, I could go with my team to Miami. Well, I've been moving
around, but now they won't let me go."

If those words were meant to provide some levity to his young men,
some relief and reassurance, they had the opposite effect. "Everybody was
concerned about the leadership without Coach Gaither," Otis Collier, a
defensive back, remembered decades later. "We were concerned that if we
needed some direction, we were used to getting it from him. He could
always add that little something we were missing. We had that you-don't-
want-to-let-him-down mentality."

John Eason felt the same kind of apprehension, almost a sense of
foreboding. "You look at going into the championship game without

your head coach," he recalled. "The kids are used to listening to one guy all the time. One guy to make changes. One guy to tell them what to do. One guy, when there's trouble on the field, for them to go to. And then he's not there."

Denied by God or nature or fate any children of his own, Jake Gaither had succeeded all too well in serving as the father figure to hundreds, perhaps upward of a thousand, of the players he had coached over a four-decade career. Among them all, few were more tightly bound to Gaither than Ken Riley. He had grown up without his father at home, with the paternal role being taken by grandfathers and uncles. Then, at FAMU, Gaither had become that patriarch who was ever present, who taught and who cared. For Gaither, in turn, Riley embodied the ideal son—a gentleman, an accomplished student, a tenacious competitor on the field.

Riley had never had a choice or a voice in the type of relationship he had with his father. Circumstance had simply presented it to him in childhood. But he was twenty now, grown up, fully aware of the sudden absence of Jake Gaither, the surrogate father for him and for everyone else on the team. Riley was old enough, too, to do something about it, to try to repay Gaither for all that the coach had given. The conference title didn't matter the most. The national rankings didn't matter the most. "It was all," Riley said, "about winning the Orange Blossom Classic."

9

JUNETEENTH IN DECEMBER

Grambling vs. Florida A&M, December 2, 1967

n the afternoon before the Orange Blossom Classic, as the Grambling Tigers ran wind sprints in their sweat suits on a practice field in Miami, two buses glided to a halt across the street. Out of them poured a hundred of the Florida A&M Rattlers, clad in full uniforms of white, orange, and green. For just a moment, Eddie Robinson and his players assumed there must have been a mistake, and somebody in charge had double-booked the gridiron at Dade North Junior College.

Then the Rattlers formed a line and began to trot around the perimeter of the field, circling it twice and chanting as they went, "It's so hard to be a Rattler." Robinson watched and seethed. This was no innocent error; this was a provocation. The A&M team, in fact, had driven twelve miles out of its way, twelve miles in the wrong direction from its own practice field in Miami Beach, just to bluster and gloat.

Once their audacious performance was complete, the Rattlers climbed aboard their buses and drove away. Meanwhile, a fuming Eddie Robinson gathered his players around him. Woofing at the line of scrimmage was one thing, an accepted part of the game; disrupting an entire practice was something else again, a breach of sporting protocol. Robinson might have expected this kind of stunt from a coach such as John Merritt, but never from Jake Gaither, a class act.

"They think they already got this game won," Robinson said, nearly screaming. "Our pride has been challenged. They have disrespected us. We need to let them know we are Grambling." Then, alluding to a well-known symbol used by the protest movement against the Vietnam War, he vowed, "The peace dove flies out the window tomorrow!"

Within twenty minutes or so, the Florida A&M team debarked its buses again, this time for its real practice at Flamingo Park. The Rattlers ran through their drills to the befuddlement of the park's usual contingent of Jewish retirees and Holocaust survivors, as well as the more assessing eyes of pro scouts in their Ray·Bans and stingy-brim hats. The receivers made a show of catching passes behind the back, and the runners swiveled like pinball flippers, dodging imaginary defenders, smiling for a local television station's cameras. Ken Riley calmly and methodically went through his throws, looking serene as always in the face of challenge.

Jake Gaither's team, after all, considered the Orange Blossom Classic the equivalent of a home game. The Rattlers played in it every year and attracted a noisily partisan crowd. Sovereignty had been the whole point of the display at Dade North: to remind the Grambling players that they were strangers, newcomers, country cornflakes in the big city. And the psych-out had indeed delivered its desired effect. "We were a bunch of kids from the hills and swamps," Delles Howell would recall years later. Until this day, December 1, 1967, almost none of them had flown in a plane, seen the ocean, or stayed in a hotel, much less a luxurious and integrated one such as the Cadillac with its limousines and bellhops and poolside cabanas. What little they knew about this beachfront resort strip came from Jackie Gleason's variety show on television, which was broadcast each week, as the announcer brassily put it, "from Miami Beach, the sun and fun capital of the world."

Some of the Grambling players had heard that you had a better chance of surviving a plane crash if you sat in the back, so there had been an elbowing rush for the rear rows that morning at the airport in Monroe. An apprehensive silence filled the cabin every time turbulence shook the plane. An awestruck quiet settled in the team bus as it wound from the Miami airport to the beachfront Cadillac.

Before the trip, Robinson had prepared his young men for their role as Grambling's ambassadors with a refresher course on etiquette from Mildred Moss, the professor from the Social Usage class. He had Collie Nicholson conduct practice interviews with fake microphones for top players such as James Harris. He scripted the entire two-day schedule in Miami down to fifteen-minute intervals. He warned the players against taking home any unofficial souvenirs—a monogrammed hotel towel, for instance.

Despite all the planning and instruction, there were bewildering moments. During a banquet at the Algiers Hotel the night before the Classic, several players dashed panic-stricken to Robinson, brandishing plates of prime rib. On the rare occasions when they had eaten steak in the college cafeteria, it had arrived well done, no ifs, ands, or buts. Baffled by the restaurant's options, a few players had unintentionally ordered their meat rare. Aghast when the entrées arrived looking raw, they pleaded to Robinson, "Coach, I can't eat this. This got blood in it." The coach had to reassure them the food was safe.

A resort hotel and a swanky restaurant, though, accounted for only part of the Tigers' culture shock. The Orange Blossom Classic routinely drew upward of forty thousand spectators to the Orange Bowl stadium, as many people as Grambling played for in all its home games combined. Just as worrisome, Grambling had shown an atypical tendency to slack off in postseason games, most recently in its 20–7 loss to North Dakota State in the 1965 Pecan Bowl. The Grambling season always reached its emotional peak in the upstate-downstate match against Southern in late November, and most years the Thanksgiving holiday fell five days later. At that point, many players left campus early for home or stayed there a few extra days, ditching practices for the bowl game.

As a corrective, James Harris had taken it upon himself this year to address the team in the wake of the Southern game. No extra days at home with Mom and Pop. No missing class, even if you still had your three permissible cut days. No skipping practice. Way too much was at stake, and those stakes had been building ever since Harris's high school days in Monroe. There was a reason he had not taken a scholarship to Michigan State and switched position to tight end. There was a reason he had returned to Grambling after nearly transferring during his frustrating freshman year. There was a reason he had persuaded all the key players to spend this past summer on campus for his unofficial preseason practices. What was it he had said to Delles Howell after they nearly died in that car accident? *This is a message. We've been spared. If we didn't die, I know the Lord got something for us to do in September.* That something would culminate in the Orange Blossom Classic.

Grambling and Florida A&M as teams, like Eddie Robinson and Jake Gaither as head coaches, were respectful but fervid rivals. Their fierce passion had been whetted all the more by enforced distance. Playing in different leagues, they rarely got the opportunity to settle matters directly. Without any black football on television, and little of it in the main newspapers and magazines, Grambling players kept track of their A&M antagonists in the pages of *Jet* and *Ebony,* in the columns by Rick Roberts and Bill Nunn in the *Pittsburgh Courier.* Over in Tallahassee, the Rattlers tuned in the sports broadcasts on WLAC, the rhythm-and-blues station in Nashville, whose clear-channel signal at night sometimes reached the Caribbean.

So what, exactly, was the competition like between Jake Gaither and Eddie Robinson, Florida A&M and Grambling? The Yankees and the

Dodgers in the World Series? Sugar Ray Robinson and Jake LaMotta? No, those confrontations occurred frequently. More than anyone, perhaps, the titans of black college football resembled Duke Ellington and Count Basie and their bands. Gaither and his Rattlers were Ellington—urban, sophisticated, innovative. Robinson and his Tigers were Basie—from somewhere out in "the territory," swinging the hell out of the basic riffs. And in all their decades of traversing the country—indeed, the world— Ellington and Basie had brought their bands in the studio together just once for the cutting contest to end all cutting contests, a session in 1961 that yielded a record led off by a piece aptly titled "Battle Royal."

Up until 1967, in the quarter century that Gaither and Robinson had coached their teams, Grambling and Florida A&M had squared off only twice, each time memorably. In 1955, both teams had entered the Orange Blossom Classic unbeaten, with the Rattlers having outscored opponents 348–66 and the Tigers having done so by 302–33. A&M featured Willie Galimore in its backfield, while Grambling built its defense around Willie Davis. The Tigers won 28–21, giving Robinson his first black national title and sending Davis into the NFL and stardom. Nine years passed before Jake Gaither got the chance for payback. In the 1964 Classic, his Rattlers thrashed a 9-1 Grambling team by 42–15, administering the worst beating Robinson had taken in nearly a decade. The seniors on the 1967 Grambling team had been freshmen then, and some of them remembered the sight of Bob Hayes outracing the safety Goldie Sellers on a punt return. After the play, Robinson, indignant, had marched up to Sellers to demand, "Why you stop running?" Still winded, Sellers panted out a reference to the Olympics: "Coach, they didn't catch him in Tokyo, and I can't catch him here."

For public consumption, in the days leading up to the 1967 rematch, Eddie Robinson adopted his well-rehearsed alter ego, the doubt-riddled naysayer whom Collie Nicholson had jokingly dubbed "Glum Eddie." "We have one big problem—A&M," Robinson grumbled to a *Miami News* columnist. He lamented that the Rattlers outweighed Grambling across the front line. Presented with proof that the Tigers actually held a twenty-pound advantage on average, Robinson groused, "I coach 'em. I don't know how big they are. You can't win the Kentucky Derby with a jackass."

James Harris meanwhile had been reading up on Ken Riley, John Eason, and Major Hazelton. Before the Grambling team left Louisiana, he had gone with Delles Howell and Eddie Robinson Jr. to watch the brittle sixteen-millimeter film of the 1955 Orange Blossom Classic. Grambling's offensive-line coach, Melvin Lee, had been the center in the game. Harris wanted the same thing the 1955 Tigers had: the championship.

"When we played Florida A&M, we had some unfinished business," Harris would later recall. "We had to beat them to be considered the best team. We wanted to win this game in the worst kind of way. This was for bragging rights. The other thing you played for was that Grambling players in the NFL bragged about us against [players from] other schools. You played for their reputation, too, for all those ex-players in the NFL."

Florida A&M, despite its swagger, was clearly feeling some pressure of its own. After all the times in his pep talks when Jake Gaither had tactically pretended to be elderly and infirm—all those teary, melodramatic speeches about "I don't know how much longer I'll be around"—for this Orange Blossom Classic his mortality was no longer a fabrication. He was old. He was crippled, at least temporarily. He was not with his team for one of the most important games of his career. Idled back in Tallahassee, Gaither could only complain about his doctors to the *Miami Herald,* "They are trying to make an invalid out of me."

Nobody else on the Rattlers readily emerged as the inspirer in chief. Private by nature, Pete Griffin steered clear of any pregame interviews, leaving that duty in the hands of Eddie Jackson, the young sports information director. Ken Riley and Monster Sims, the most catalytic players on offense and defense for FAMU, were not locker room–exhortation types. Riley liked to say that he talked trash by the way he played on the field. But sometimes a team needed more than leadership by example. It needed a sermon or a dare or a cry for blood.

The most volatile of the assistant coaches, Costa Kittles, tried to supply it, and the Rattlers' haughty intrusion into Grambling's practice was probably his brainstorm. Yet those antics had betrayed doubt more than they had brandished confidence. They were a case of trying too hard to fill the vacuum left by Gaither's absence. When A&M played on the road, Gaither had always reserved the right to take back the wheel of his Lincoln from whichever coach or trainer was driving so he could cruise the last few miles onto the opposing campus, horn blaring, assurance incarnate. In trying to project the same aura without Gaither in command, the Rattlers had overreached.

Instead of being intimidated by Florida A&M, Grambling was incensed. Robinson's main concern was keeping his players composed at the bowl banquet on December 1 and the scholarship-award breakfast on game day, December 2, when the two teams would be seated mere feet apart. "You don't have to talk back," he advised about A&M's taunts. "Take it out on the field."

The coolest, most analytical heads on each side belonged to the coaches who had done the scouting. Hansel Tookes, a self-described "snoop," had watched Grambling defeat Southern University. Doug Porter of Grambling had seen A&M's game against Southern, sitting in the press box with his binoculars and stopwatch and charts. These two men looked for answers to many of the same questions. What are our opponent's basic formations? Do they run any trick plays? What are their tendencies in certain situations—position on the field, down and yards to go?

Grambling offered few surprises, even to a team it played as rarely as FAMU. The Eddie Robinson playbook had not changed since he had installed the wing-T almost a decade earlier. The one new element was the current set of personnel, especially Harris at quarterback and Charlie Joiner at split end. Tookes had come away from his scouting trip with a slew of empirical data and one visceral hunch: you had to keep the ball away from Harris, you had to keep the Grambling offense off the field.

Bobby Lang, the Rattlers' offensive-line coach, knew all he needed to know from the heights and weights listed on the Grambling roster. His blockers were not going to be able to outmuscle the Tigers' defensive linemen, most of them topping 250. Lang had been training his men to get off the snap fast and drive their shoulders low on the defenders' legs. Grambling's size, though, also conferred one advantage on FAMU. With the Rattlers' superior speed and rigorous conditioning program, based on three-a-day practices under the Florida summer sun, they might be able to wear out the Tiger defense by the fourth quarter. Twenty extra pounds per man across the front line didn't matter as much if they were cramping up and gasping for air, bent over double with exhaustion before each new play.

Doug Porter, scouting the Rattlers, had taken note of their speed. Although Morand and Riley had combined to throw for more yards and almost as many touchdowns as James Harris, Porter did not fear A&M's passing. He worried about the way Riley "could hurt you with his feet." On the defensive side, he paid particular attention to Major Hazelton, a cornerback who had set FAMU's career record with seventeen interceptions and tackled as fiercely as a linebacker. "You have to always know where he is," Porter advised Robinson.

Robinson, in turn, translated the scouting report into a game plan. To control Riley's scrambling, all the defensive linemen and linebackers had to stick to their designated lanes for rushing, never let him break to the sideline. They had to hold their position even when a play seemed to be flowing away from them, lest Riley or halfback Hubert Ginn slash back, using the defenders' momentum against them. "Stay at home," Robinson said. "Play your technique. Don't go chasin' ghosts." As for Major Hazelton, he tended to creep up close to the line of scrimmage so he could pounce on opposing runners. Grambling might be able to sucker him with play-action passes. Or the Tigers could simply match Charlie Joiner against him, daring Hazelton to stop him all night. "Put strength on strength," Robinson often said, and that theorem had a corollary: "Put speed on speed."

As furious as the athletic rivalry ran between Grambling and Florida

A&M, two teams that expected victory every game, they had become allies in meeting a different challenge. For Gaither and Robinson and all of their players, the Orange Blossom Classic offered a chance to prove to the wider world—the white world—the excellence of black college football. They knew full well that most of the sports fans in America would spend December 2 focusing on the Alabama-Auburn and Army-Navy games. The sports pages during game week had been filled with articles about the Heisman Trophy—won by a white quarterback, Gary Beban of UCLA—and the announcement of the Associated Press All-America team. More than a third of its twenty-three players were from all-white college teams in the South and Texas. Even the small-college polls had ignored Grambling and FAMU, listing them merely as "Honorable Mention" in the final rankings of the 1967 season.

New Mexico Highlands, Waynesburg, Eastern Kentucky—how many players had those schools, all ranked in AP's small-college Top Ten, ever sent to the pros? As of the 1967 season, Grambling had twenty alumni in the pros and Florida A&M had ten. The most farsighted pro football executives—George Halas of the Chicago Bears, Paul Brown of the Cleveland Browns, Sid Gillman of the Los Angeles Rams and then the San Diego Chargers—had been scouting prospects at the Orange Blossom Classic since the 1950s. Other pro teams relied on black scouts specializing in black colleges. Bill Nunn, who moonlighted for the Pittsburgh Steelers while writing for the *Pittsburgh Courier,* would even attend dances to see which of the big linemen were lightest on their feet. Several pro teams hired Bernie Rosen, the sports director of a Miami television station, to freelance for them shooting film of pregame practices.

So if the people in the know, the people paid to make clinical judgments of talent, flocked to the Orange Blossom Classic, why did it still feel like the Gramblings and the FAMUs of the football world were playing "behind God's back"? Collie Nicholson, who had spent much of his life crashing through racial barriers, wrote and syndicated an article to newspapers nationwide in the week leading up to the game with this blunt assessment:

Grambling College was completely ignored by the wire service polls this fall, but don't be surprised if the Tigers have the last laugh.

While Coach Eddie Robinson and his talented giants were being snubbed by pollsters, pro scouts were beating daily paths to the North Louisiana campus to watch likely leaders in the pro rookie class of 1968.

Robinson himself spoke in an uncommonly bold way. Miami's press corps provided one of those moments, as on Howard Cosell's radio show in 1964, as with Jerry Izenberg walking the gridiron in Grambling, when a particular question poked through Robinson's uncomplaining facade and liberated the righteous aggrievement behind it. "The boys they pick on these college All-Americas," he said in one interview, "are no better than the boys you see each day—boys playing for you. It's just unfortunate. The top writers, the large crowds don't see the Negro colleges play."

Adding to Robinson's ire, the former NFL head coach Buddy Parker had recently been quoted disparaging the intelligence of black players, particularly for offense. Their "animalistic" quality, Parker conceded, did qualify them for defense. When Tommy Fitzgerald of the *Miami News* asked Robinson for his response, the Grambling coach got "a little frothy." Robinson knew that Parker's calumny was widely shared in pro sports, to say nothing of America as a whole. He knew that it stood in the path of James Harris playing quarterback in the NFL. So Robinson addressed the point, preemptively and directly, in a pregame interview with the *Miami Herald.* "If a Negro athlete can come on and win for a pro team, he'll play," Robinson declared. "I just hope he's from Grambling."

+   +   +

The calendar of black America circa 1967, a calendar of which most American whites remained ignorant or oblivious, included several racially specific holidays. There was Watch Night, each December 31, when black churches held worship services to commemorate the way their forebears had stayed up all night awaiting the issuance of the Emancipation Proclamation on January 1, 1863. There was Juneteenth, celebrated every June 19, in honor of the day the Union Army liberated slaves in Texas. There was Kwanzaa, a seven-day festival of African heritage beginning on December 26, which had been created by the black nationalist intellectual Maulana Karenga in 1966. And there was the Orange Blossom Classic.

The Orange Blossom Classic, in fact, had become both the most important annual sporting event and the largest annual gathering of any kind for black Americans. For most of the past twenty years, more than forty thousand spectators had attended the game itself, while tens of thousands more had thronged the parade route of the Florida A&M marching band. Black tourists flocked to the hotels, restaurants, and clubs of the Overtown and Liberty City neighborhoods. For most whites, it all might as well have been nonexistent.

As football game and communal celebration, the Orange Blossom Classic had arisen as a black answer to invisibility, the kind of invisibility Ralph Ellison had famously rendered in his novel. It demonstrated what was life-affirming and self-sustaining in black life, especially black college life, on its own terms. When Miami in 1937 opened the Orange Bowl stadium, a public facility built with public funds, it excluded blacks from all but one roped-off section of the eastern end zone. No integrated football team was permitted onto the gridiron until the Nebraska Cornhuskers played Duke in the 1955 Orange Bowl. Blacks were barred from participating in any of the pageants and events related to the bowl game, much as they were barred from patronizing the resort hotels in Miami Beach. The black maids and janitors and cooks and bellhops who composed the human infrastructure of those establishments needed to obtain identification cards from the police. Even the black performers who drew the crowds—Sammy Davis Jr., Nat King Cole, Ella Fitzgerald—were forbidden to stay in the hotels where they entertained.

So during the 1930s, Miami blacks began their own competitor to the Orange Bowl festivities, which they called the Coconut Festival. It had its own beauty queen, its own parade, and its own football game, played in Dorsey Park, a segregated square block named for Miami's first black millionaire. The Coconut Festival game, though, lacked much football pizzazz. That was where J.R.E. Lee Jr., the son of Florida A&M's president, came in.

Even before Lee, black colleges had sought to create their own version of the season-ending bowl games. Beginning in the 1920s, Lincoln and Howard played annually in the self-proclaimed Football Classic of the Year, and Tuskegee met Wilberforce yearly at Soldier Field in the Midwest Chicago Football Classic. Inspired by these examples, Lee conceived of a "Black Rose Bowl," naming it the Orange Blossom Classic. In the first game, in 1933, A&M beat Howard 9–6 before two thousand spectators at a black ballpark in Jacksonville. For the next thirteen years, the contest migrated among Jacksonville, Orlando, and Tampa, an itinerant attraction that gradually built its audience and reputation. Then, in 1947, Lee linked its fortunes to the Coconut Festival's and settled it in Miami.

Miami had the largest stadium in Florida. Miami had the greatest concentration of media anywhere in the state. And Miami, as it entered the postwar boom, was beginning to shake off its rigid segregation, owing largely to the influx of Jews from the North, most of them either tacitly or actively supportive of civil rights. The very first Classic game in Miami made racial history. For the first time, black fans were permitted to sit in the main stands of the Orange Bowl. (In a perhaps unwitting reference to the Civil War, blacks sat on the northern side of the stadium, whites on the southern.) When a Rattler receiver named Nathaniel "Traz" Powell caught a forty-five-yard pass to break a 0–0 tie with Hampton Institute, he became the first black to score a touchdown on the Orange Bowl's previously whites-only gridiron. Powell had grown up in Miami as the son of a laundress and a laborer at the city incinerator. For years to come, blacks around the state would speak about his touchdown as if he'd been Rosa Parks refusing to surrender her seat.

Firmly established by the 1950s as the de facto black national championship, the Orange Blossom Classic far outdrew the University of Miami's football games and, later, those of the new NFL franchise the Miami Dolphins. One year, the comic Nipsy Russell joined the Rattlers on their sideline; another time it was Sammy Davis Jr. All week long, the streets of Overtown and Liberty City were "crowded like the state fair, music pouring out of doorways," as one participant remembered. At the Zebra Lounge and the Hampton House, in the Harlem Square Club and the Rockland Palace, all along the stretch of Northwest Second Street called the Great Black Way, stars of jazz, soul, and rhythm and blues headlined. Women spent a year's savings on their Orange Blossom dresses, and beauty salons stayed open all night to handle the female demand. When the parties ended near daybreak, people went their tipsy way for chicken and waffles before a sunrise snooze.

On the surface, Orange Blossom Classic week in 1967 gleamed with the familiar dazzle. Percy Sledge and Johnny Taylor, two of soul music's biggest stars, were playing the black clubs. The Double Deck Club offered an "Orange Blossom Revue." Exotic Fashions Beauty & Wig Salon promoted an "Orange Bowl [*sic*] Classic Special" of "Free Eye Brow Arch with Any Hairdo." As for the game itself, the sports columnist of the *Miami Times,* the city's weekly black newspaper, exulted, "The selection of Grambling adds Super Bowl status to the classic."

In many ways, the Orange Blossom Classic in 1967 also embodied the recent progress in race relations. The Grambling and Florida A&M teams were both staying in integrated hotels in Miami Beach. The Ballantine brewing company was sponsoring a tape-delayed broadcast of the game on television stations in Atlanta, Philadelphia, Washington, DC, and New York, with Buddy Young, the first black executive in the NFL's front office, providing the on-air commentary. The local publicity for the game was being handled by Julian Cole, a transplanted northern Jew who counted the ritziest Miami Beach hotels among his clients.

The Orange Blossom Classic's souvenir program featured advertisements from major national companies—Humble Oil, Prudential Insurance, RC Cola. Coca-Cola sponsored a float carrying the Grambling College queen and her court in the pregame parade. The celebrities in attendance included the first wave of black executives hired by corporations in search of black consumers. Pepsi-Cola, the leader in the field, dispatched Charles Dryden, a bona fide war hero as one of the Tuskegee Airmen, now its vice president for special markets. Greyhound sent Joe Black, the former Brooklyn Dodger pitcher who had been newly appointed the bus company's vice president of special markets. F. W. Woolworth, a company trying to repair a reputation damaged by its segregated lunch counters in southern cities, assigned Aubrey Lewis, a former Notre Dame football star and FBI agent it had recently hired as an executive recruiter. At a breakfast on the morning of the Classic game, Woolworth's presented a scholarship to Ken Riley as the Rattler with the highest grade point average.

Doors were opening in realms beyond sports. In late November, Miami had elected Althalie Range as the first black ever on the City Commission. Her victory came amid a groundbreaking political year for blacks throughout America, with Carl Stokes and Richard Hatcher winning the mayoralties of Cleveland and Gary, respectively. Sidney Poitier's film *To Sir, with Love* and the Sam & Dave song "Soul Man" were crossover hits. Miami's chapter of the civil rights group CORE, essentially a coalition of black Christians and white Jews, had succeeded in desegregating buses, beaches, golf courses, lunch counters, virtually every public institution except schools.

Yet the vigor of the Classic's weeklong festival, the vigor of Overtown and Liberty City, had depended paradoxically on Jim Crow. Segregation had necessarily funneled all the skill, vibrancy, inventiveness, and spending power of Miami's blacks into their own neighborhoods. All the excellence, just like all the poverty and despair, had nowhere else to go. To strive for racial equality, as the Orange Blossom Classic did in its way, was simultaneously and unintentionally to diffuse that concentration of black talent. And to raise the expectation of full and complete equality, as the civil rights movement and the Johnson presidency had done, was to invite disappointment and even rage when the promise remained unkept.

In the name of urban renewal, the federal government had run Interstate 95 straight through Overtown, gutting the historic and cherished neighborhood. In 1967, for the first time, the Orange Blossom Classic parade had to be moved into Liberty City. At the same time, Miami was cutting funding to its antipoverty programs, as if centuries of structural, official inequality had been magically rectified in just a couple of years. After the city's antipoverty agency could not even meet its November payroll, hundreds of blacks marched through downtown in protest.

None of the discontent was unique to Miami. In the week leading up to the Orange Blossom Classic, Martin Luther King announced plans for a "Poor People's Campaign"—a march on Washington to demand an "Economic Bill of Rights." Seven months earlier, in a speech titled "A Time to Break Silence," King had publicly assailed his most powerful ally, President Johnson, on the Vietnam War, likening it to racial segregation and even the Holocaust as examples of injustice. Days before the Classic, two more examples of the war's political impact appeared. Robert McNamara, one of the architects of American involvement in Vietnam, resigned as secretary of defense, and Eugene McCarthy, a senator from Minnesota, declared that he would challenge Johnson for the Democratic Party's nomination for president. In the sporting world, a twenty-four-year-old sociology professor named Harry Edwards announced a plan for black athletes to boycott the US team in the 1968 Olympics.

All the turbulence found its way to the heart of the Orange Blossom Classic, and specifically to the Florida A&M Marching 100. The band's director, William Patrick Foster—an innovator and autocrat known variously as "the Maestro," "the Legend," and "the Law"—had decided that the Marching 100's halftime show would be "Kaleidoscope of Music," one of its staples. "Kaleidoscope" typified Foster's mixture of tradition and modernism, featuring soul hits from Stevie Wonder ("Uptight") and James

Brown ("Cold Sweat") along with a medley of patriotic marches. In previous years, it had hardly mattered to the student musicians that they would be playing the "Marine Hymn," "Anchors Aweigh," and "Stars and Stripes Forever." It had hardly mattered that a narrator would proclaim over the stadium loudspeakers:

> Duty, honor, country: these three words build courage when courage seems to fail; give faith to those who guard this beloved land, an ideal so noble that it arouses a sense of pride and yet humility; an expression of the ethics of the American man at arms. I therefore believe it is my duty to my country to love it.

No, for a long time nothing had seemed controversial or objectionable in the flag-waving ritual. The ROTC, after all, had long been a fixture in the Florida A&M curriculum. Since its desegregation twenty years earlier, the American military had offered a proven route for blacks into the middle class. Its bases were comparative oases of equality in the Deep South. In Little Rock, Arkansas, and Oxford, Mississippi, federal troops famously had protected the black students who integrated previously all-white schools against virulent resistance. Men of William Foster and Jake Gaither's generation had embraced the ethos of Double Victory, seeing black valor in combat abroad as the ultimate argument for black civil rights at home.

During the rehearsals in Tallahassee for the 1967 Classic, however, the old bromides provoked a revolt. Foster's musicians had come of age amid the atrocities of the civil rights era—fire hoses, police dogs, churches bombed, marchers beaten, Medgar Evers and James Meredith shot, Chaney and Goodman and Schwerner murdered. All of that had happened during the students' years of high school and college. Now Martin Luther King had come out against the Vietnam War, calling the peasants and Communist guerrillas there "our brothers." And Stokely Carmichael, who had spoken near the A&M campus earlier this month, had told them America was a sham.

The most politicized members of the band met secretly after rehearsals and poured out their anger. *Why do we have to do this? . . . We're tired of proving ourselves to America. . . . To us, it's a lie. . . . We're playing this music that we don't believe in.* Double Victory meant nothing if America itself was immoral. Possibly inspired by the talk of an Olympics boycott, some musicians floated the idea of refusing to perform at the Classic unless the patriotic medley was replaced.

Word of the mutiny soon reached Foster. He called a band meeting shortly before the group's departure to Miami. There, in a manner befitting one of his honorifics, he laid down the law: *This is my band.* Faced with the prospective consequences of disobedience—being kicked out of the band, losing their music scholarships, letting down the parents who had sacrificed so much, and just plain missing the star turn of performing at the Classic—the rebels relented. But as they practiced those military marches, the activists resented every sprightly note they struck and every ebullient step they took.

The band's first performance in Miami was a parade through downtown on December 1, the day before the Liberty City parade and the game itself. The downtown show was, in its way, a sop to the custom, if no longer the law, of segregation. White shoppers and office workers could enjoy the famous band along the commercial corridor of Flagler Street, rather than having to venture into the alien terrain of Overtown or Liberty City. This year, though, after the band finished its route down Flagler, dozens of black teenagers swept through the crowd, snatching purses, grabbing items off store shelves, roughing up passersby. By the time a detachment of motorcycle police arrived, most of the young looters were gone, and a restive crowd of several hundred blacks was forming in a nearby park.

In a country that had seen Newark and Detroit burn just five months earlier, this brief spasm of looting barely registered with the national media. Within Miami, though, and particularly within black Miami, it struck a sobering note during a celebratory week. In 1967, in America, the Orange Blossom Classic was no longer able to be an unalloyed holiday.

+ + +

Two hours after sunset on a balmy Saturday night, as tens of thousands of spectators poured into the Orange Bowl seats, the Florida A&M Rattlers gathered in their locker room in the stadium's southwestern corner. Clad in a coat and tie, clutching a pipe, wearing his ever-present horn-rim glasses, Pete Griffin cut an oddly professorial figure in this motivational moment. On a wooden bench nearby him lay an unusual piece of football equipment: a tape recorder.

Then George Thompson, who doubled as trainer and technician for A&M, cued a reel of tape he had brought from Tallahassee. As the tape advanced, a voice emerged from the recorder, a voice everyone in the locker room recognized as Jake Gaither's. It intoned the prayer he had uttered on the first morning of practice in August, and before every game of the season, the stations on the path to this championship match.

> Dear God of the Rattlers, a sweet and just God, the only God we know. We submit ourselves humbly today for Your blessing. You have been so good to us, much better than we deserve. We ask You for the ability to do our best, so that every one of these kids gets every full measure. Let them block, let them tackle, let them run like they've never run before. Grant us the wisdom to know what plays to call and the strength to follow them through. Help us, Lord Jesus, to transfer your strength and wisdom to the game of life. This is my prayer.

The taped message was also the answer to his team's unspoken prayer. Jake Gaither on a strip of brown tape, Jake Gaither through a tinny speaker, was not Jake Gaither in his orotund and corporeal presence, but that disembodied voice was far better than Jake Gaither entirely absent, Jake Gaither marooned in a hospital hundreds of miles away. When it came to the technical aspects of football, the pregame strategy and midgame adjustments, the players trusted Griffin and the other assistants. By December they had been through thousands of repetitions of their primary plays and formations and assignments. What only Gaither could provide his young men, though, was the ineffable, incalculable commodity of inspiration.

Three minutes into the first quarter, taking over on their own fifteen-yard line for their first offensive series, the Rattlers set about proving they still had it. Ken Riley, starting at quarterback, knew his mandate from the game plan: run the Grambling linemen up and down the field, run them from sideline to sideline, run them till they droop with fatigue, and then run them some more. Riley knew, too, what to look for as he surveyed the Tigers on defense now. Were they crowding the line to stop A&M's rushing attack? Yes, they were. Were the defensive ends pinching toward the middle, impatient for a sack? Yes, they were.

So after a couple of short runs and a Grambling penalty gave the Rattlers a first down on the twenty-five, Riley put what he knew to use, ordering a sweep called the Toss-8. He lined up the team in an I formation rather than the usual T. Instead of splitting out the speedy flanker, Eugene Milton, Riley tucked him at the base of the I as a tailback. Riley took the snap, pitched back the ball to Milton, and then watched as he sprinted to the right. Within seconds, Milton had outrun the Grambling linemen and turned the corner to dash upfield along the sideline. Thirty-nine yards later, at the Grambling thirty-six-yard line, he was finally wrestled down.

A short run and another Grambling penalty put the ball on the fifteen. From there, Riley rolled out to his right, his favored side for passing, forcing Grambling's defensive backs to stay downfield with the Rattler receivers. With the defensive backs' speed neutralized, all Riley had to do was beat the slower linemen and linebackers to the sideline, just as Milton had done, and then throw in a few stutter steps and hip jukes to leave a late-arriving safety clawing at empty space. Riley finally went down at the one. On the next play, as the Rattler linemen drove Grambling's front five backward, halfback Preston Johnson scored.

Nine plays, eighty-five yards, 7–0 Florida A&M, 9:20 still left in the first quarter: this was the football version of a preemptive strike. The very things that Eddie Robinson had most wanted to avoid had happened, and they had happened in a hurry. His team, one built to take and hold leads, was trailing. His defense, one drilled to contain the Rattlers' speed, was instead chasing and panting. And he had no way of knowing the fuel for his opponents' fire: that tape-recorded oration from Jake Gaither.

In the wake of Preston Johnson's touchdown, the A&M defense forced Grambling again to punt from deep in its own territory. All year, punting had bedeviled the Tigers. The center was a converted tackle, still shaky on long snaps. The kicker was a reserve quarterback, Wesley Bean, too eager to improvise a run or pass instead of just booting the ball, as he was supposed to. Eddie Robinson, who couldn't resist coaching every position during practice, often ran out of time and attention for the punting unit. Besides, Grambling expected to pummel opponents, to physically whip them, not to eke out victories in a field-position chess game.

Based on Hansel Tookes's scouting report on Grambling, Pete Griffin recognized punting as a weak spot to be exploited. So as the Tigers lined up at their twenty, with Bean waiting for the snap back at the five, Griffin ordered a ten-man rush, forgoing the chance of a decent punt return in favor of gambling on a punt block. The snap fluttered to Bean, a little bit high, and he bobbled the ball. By the time he righted it, a linebacker named Melvin Rogers had burst through a gap in the Grambling line. Bean dodged him, retreated into the end zone, broke momentarily free, and ran up to the five-yard line. By then, Rogers was bearing down on him again. Instead of kicking, Bean threw. It was a foolish choice, since Grambling already had linemen downfield, guaranteeing a penalty. And it was a faulty choice, since the ball went straight into the hands of defensive back Otis Collier at the Grambling twenty-eight.

On first down, Riley zipped a pass to John Eason, taking the Rattlers to the five-yard line. Three runs pushed it to the one. Jake Gaither had always advocated for overkill—*Kill a mosquito with an ax, run over a pig with a bus*—and in that spirit Griffin shunned a field goal and kept his offense on the field for fourth and goal from the one. A touchdown would put the Rattlers ahead 14–0 in the first quarter; it would force Grambling away from its patient and conservative offense.

Riley assembled the Rattlers in a wing-T formation, with the best blockers loaded on the right side. As he took the snap, the whole A&M team flowed in that direction, and Riley expected Grambling to flow along with it. Which was why, instead of handing off, he kept the ball and squeezed straight ahead, searching for a seam in the Grambling line. But the Rattler blockers, outweighed and outmanned in the middle, could not budge the Grambling defenders. In the scrum of stiffened chests and churning legs, amid the spit and grunts and crash of helmets, a freshman reserve who had been inserted on the goal-line defense, Scott Lewis, reached from the bottom of the pile to grab hold of Riley's ankle. Riley twisted and writhed, turning his torso sideways, and tried to fling his right arm, with the football in it, over the goal line.

One of the officials, standing in the back of the end zone, raised his arms to signal a touchdown. Then, as he ran closer to the pile, he waved off his own call. Two Grambling linemen, Robert Smith and Edward Watson, were battering at Riley's chest and shoulders, while down below Lewis kept clinging to that ankle, tenacious as a terrier with a pants leg in its jaws. The head linesman, the official closest to the fray, whistled the play dead.

No touchdown, Grambling ball, a collective groan of deflation along the A&M sideline: the God of the Rattlers was evidently more the capricious than the benevolent kind.

The only advantage for FAMU was that Grambling was pinned down inches from its own goal line. The position especially suited Griffin's defensive scheme. He massed all his men to stop the running game—six linemen up front, two linebackers just a step behind them, all three defensive backs within seven yards of the line of scrimmage. He was daring James Harris to pass. More to the point, he was daring Eddie Robinson to break his habit. So far, Harris had completed a couple of passes to Charlie Joiner, but nothing very damaging. With the ball on the Grambling one, Robinson refused to risk another, and soon Bean was back to punt again. He followed orders this time, but A&M took over possession in Tiger territory, presented with a second chance to score a second touchdown.

On the sideline during the Grambling series, Ken Riley, his helmet tilted back, had stood next to Costa Kittles, the backfield coach. Taking off the helmet would have meant conceding the next offensive series to Elroy Morand. Loyal soldier though he was, Riley wanted every play on this night. He could even persuade himself it was better that the Rattlers hadn't scored last time. Getting in front by too much too soon made a team complacent. *You think it's gonna be a cakewalk. But things change.* The helmet on his head was Riley's wordless way of saying to Kittles and Griffin what every kid who ever played organized football had sometime said: *Coach, put me in.*

Instead, according to the season-long system, Morand trotted onto the field for his fair share of snaps. From the Grambling thirty-eight he dropped back, well protected in the pocket, and lofted a pass toward John Eason on a square-out near the left sideline. Delles Howell, playing cornerback on that side, watched the pass making its feathery way through the night air, watched the laces on each revolution of the soft spiral, and darted in front of Eason. Maybe Morand had not even realized he was throwing at Grambling's best pass defender; Howell was wearing a benchwarmer's number 25, instead of his usual 20, because his jersey had been lost on the trip to Miami and Grambling couldn't afford extras. He snatched the pass at Grambling's twenty-six and carried it to A&M's thirty-one, a forty-three-yard reversal of fortune.

Now James Harris and Eddie Robinson had their turn in the battle of wits with Pete Griffin. Harris called a formation with Charlie Joiner as a tight end. He suspected, correctly, that FAMU would still commit two of its three defensive backs to covering Joiner. That tactic would give Grambling's other receivers a one-on-one matchup, often against a slower linebacker. Throughout the game, in the huddle or on the sideline, whenever he had the chance, Harris had been debriefing his receivers, gathering intelligence. What he had heard, especially from

Essex Johnson, was that the A&M pass defenders were now giving some cushion.

A screen pass from Harris to Willie Armstrong took Grambling just inside the ten-yard line. Again, Harris had Joiner line up tight, and he split out Essex Johnson wide to the right as a flanker. Harris saw what he had been anticipating: single coverage. He remembered what Robinson always said: "Our guy's supposed to beat their guy. That's why we practice so much." Johnson broke from the line, then slanted left, toward the goalposts. He was past the nearest linebacker before the defender even noticed, and several yards in front of the safety. Johnson caught the pass in stride, already in the end zone, and spiked it for emphasis. Less than a minute into the second quarter, Grambling had evened the score and responded in kind to the Rattlers' mind games.

Florida A&M spent the rest of the quarter grinding its way back into a small lead. Grambling, deep in its own territory, botched a reverse, and linebacker Leroy Jackson tackled Willie Armstrong in the end zone for a safety. After receiving Grambling's subsequent free kick, the Rattlers marched with Morand down to the Tiger five-yard line. The drive stalled there and Horace Lovett kicked a field goal.

It looked then, with barely two minutes remaining in the half and Grambling starting at its own twenty-one, like A&M would take a 12–7 lead into the locker room. A five-point margin, less than one touchdown, hardly qualified as dominant, but after Riley's failed quarterback sneak and Morand's interception, a lead was a lead. Most important, Griffin's defensive plan had worked. Grambling was abandoning its running game, passing sixteen times already, and had only seven points from a thirty-one-yard drive to show for the aerial assault.

Then, five more times, Harris passed. He completed nearly all. The last throw, fifty-six yards to Robert Atkins, put Grambling on the A&M two. From there, Henry Jones blasted into the end zone on a fullback dive. The scoreboard told the tale: 14–12 Tigers at the half. What the scoreboard didn't tell was the playing time. During the second quarter, the game clock had broken. For the moment, that snafu seemed more annoying than important. Surely, in the stadium that a pro team called home, somebody would know how to fix something as essential as the scoreboard clock.

+ + +

After thirty minutes of football, Grambling and Florida A&M were no longer strangers. They had poked and prodded each other, searching for weaknesses. They had tested out plans and strategies. They had learned in football's bruising form of empirical research what worked and what didn't. In the separate locker rooms, at opposite corners of the Orange Bowl, they had quickly filled chalkboards with the X's and O's of refinements for the second half, the adaptations that would separate winner from loser in a championship game of equals.

Florida A&M, having kicked off to start the game, got the ball first after halftime. The Rattlers had already tried out two surprises—the disruption of Grambling's practice and Jake Gaither's recorded prayer—and for all that cunning were still trailing by two points. Huddling the Rattlers around him, Riley set into motion the next trick. He ran Hubert Ginn on several sweeps around the right end, the same side A&M had exploited all night, starting with Eugene Milton's long gain three minutes into the game. Ginn's rushes took A&M to midfield with a first down. More important, on those plays Riley recognized that Grambling's linemen and linebackers, particularly those to his left, were running laterally to catch Ginn rather than holding their position. They were doing exactly what Eddie Robinson had warned them not to: chasing ghosts.

Riley called the next play, "Quarterback Throwback." It was one Grambling would not have seen in scouting because FAMU rarely used it. It was one the Rattlers had practiced only a few times all season, most recently the day before, in Flamingo Park. And it would have looked, to the untutored eye, like a bunch of sandlot goofing-around. Taking the snap, Riley pitched the ball back to Ginn, who lunged toward right end. Obligingly, most of the Grambling defenders slid in that same direction. As they did, Riley dashed upfield on the left side, easily bypassing the defensive end and outside linebacker. Stopping in place, then swiveling left, Ginn lobbed him the ball, and Riley brought it deep into Grambling territory for a thirty-one-yard gain. Several plays later, Robert Lampkin bolted in from the three-yard line for the go-ahead touchdown: 19–14 Rattlers.

Now it was Eddie Robinson's turn to implement midcourse corrections. After weathering twenty-one passes from James Harris in the first half, Florida A&M returned to its normal defense, with five linemen and four defensive backs, allowing double coverage on both wide receivers. Robinson had been expecting it. He relished it. As he had once told an audience at a coaching clinic, "Your offense must dare the defense. Dare them to come up on the run because we have the action pass. Dare them to set back for the pass because we have the run. Dare them to stalk outside for the sweep because we have the fullback up the middle."

Robinson replaced Robert Atkins, his best receiver at tight end, with Billy Ray Newsome, a crushing blocker. He assigned both the center and his best guard—Henry Davis, nickname "Hatchet Man"—to double-team Monster Sims, the toughest Rattler lineman. And he instructed Harris to do what the coach most loved to do: call the dives and counters that everybody knew Grambling relied on, and execute them with so much precision and muscle that nobody could stop them.

On Grambling's first possession of the second half, a block by Hatchet Man sprung a freshman halfback, Virgil Robinson, for a thirty-six-yard touchdown run. On the Tigers' next series, three rushes by Essex Johnson accounted for sixty-three yards of a seventy-six-yard drive, including another touchdown.

Entering the fourth quarter, Grambling led 28–19. Its defense stifled Elroy Morand, now taking his turn at quarterback, and forced a FAMU punt. As the Tigers took over at their own nineteen, they needed just one more score to put the game out of reach. A Harris pass to Joiner and two runs gave Grambling a first down at its thirty-nine. The Rattler defense had been on the field almost nonstop for the past twelve minutes of game time. It was taking a beating; it was getting worn down.

Juneteenth in December

The Grambling huddle, meanwhile, bubbled with a confidence bordering on arrogance. Already envisioning the award for most valuable player, Johnson chided Harris about an errant pass when the wingback had been wide open.

"Man," he said, drawing the syllable out for mock-irritated effect, "you don't want me to be MVP."

Harris reminded Johnson that the award came with a fancy wristwatch, too. "You might as well look at it," the quarterback said. "I already got it."

+   +   +

From Eddie Robinson's youth as a boxer, he understood in a visceral way the concept of a knockout punch. Being on the receiving end of one, in fact, had laid to rest his aspirations for the ring. He knew what he needed now, as Florida A&M's defense struggled, trying like a battered fighter to clutch and clench and hang on until the bell. Robinson ordered the play he hoped would end the game. It was the same play that had gone for a touchdown earlier in the second half, a fake reverse with Virgil Robinson running the ball.

Harris handed off to Robinson, and the halfback scooted parallel to the line of scrimmage, heading for the right sideline. Essex Johnson, who had lined up on the right flank, ran in the opposite direction, placing his waiting hands just above his waist, pretending he was going to get the ball from Robinson. Bewildered by all the motion and misdirection, the Rattler defenders scrambled out of position. Everything, for Grambling, was going exactly right.

Until Robinson, a freshman who had played only sparingly during the season, behaved like the greenhorn he was. As he pantomimed the handoff to Johnson, he bobbled the ball. Then he dropped it to the turf. When it bounced back up to him, a moment of sheer luck, he saw Monster Sims and company closing in. Instead of just falling to the ground and conceding a short loss, he panicked, reversing field and surrendering ground by the chunk. With the entire A&M defense by then in pursuit, he was tripped up back at the twenty, having lost nineteen yards.

On second and twenty-nine, conventional football logic dictated a safe play that could burn some time off the clock. Instead, Eddie Robinson went again for the kill, this time by air. He restored Robert Atkins to the lineup and ordered a long pass, the kind that always made him say, with an appreciative sigh in his voice, *I love to see that scoreboard light up.* At the snap, Atkins ran past A&M's linebackers, then slanted right toward the sideline, two defensive backs on his heels. Harris lofted a pass of such perfect trajectory that it could land only in one spot: the inches between Atkins's outstretched arms and the sideline. A trailing defender would have no chance. Atkins clutched the pass, kept his feet in bounds, and put Grambling back on its forty-four, now needing only five yards for a first down.

After all his years of tutelage from Eddie Robinson, all his games as the coach's proxy on the field, Harris knew what came next. He called for the staple of Grambling's passing game, a square-out to Charlie Joiner. Inexplicably, the Rattler defense chose this time to cover Joiner with only one man, Major Hazelton. Six yards downfield, Joiner cut sharply to the left sideline, and Harris put the pass right in his hands. But then Joiner did something in defiance of his normal football wisdom. Instead of either stepping out of bounds with the first down secured or shoving forward against Hazelton for another yard or two, he pivoted, dipped backward, and tried to circle away for a long gain. Hazelton lunged, snagging Joiner at the ankle, and upended him one yard shy of the first down.

After Grambling punted, putting FAMU on its own twenty-one, Ken Riley returned as quarterback. A Grambling penalty, a pass to John Eason, and a short run put the Rattlers on their own forty-one with a second and nine. Riley took the snap and rolled out to his left. In the Grambling secondary, Delles Howell read the clue. Riley threw right-handed and favored that side; if he was rolling out to the left, it had to mean a run. All game, Howell had been telling himself, *Don't lose your coverage when he's scrambling. Let the front seven contain him.* This time, though, he outthought the rule. As Howell surged forward toward Riley with several lanky strides, the Rattlers' split end, Melvin Jones, the quarterback's roommate, raced straight past the defensive back into open field. A second later, Riley was cocking his arm, and then the ball was in the air. Howell tried to untangle his legs and twisted to stretch his right arm to swat down the pass. It sailed safely above him. Howell was left to slap his thighs in disgust and watch Jones sprint all the way to the end zone. There he spiked the ball two-handed, as if to one-up Essex Johnson, as if to tell all of Grambling, *This thing isn't over.*

The A&M fans, standing and roaring on the touchdown, began to settle back into their seats. The next play, the extra-point kick, should have been routine, all but automatic. It would be valuable, too, putting the Rattlers only two points behind and so capable of winning the game with a field goal. But a Grambling defender broke into the backfield and dove forward, forcing Horace Lovett to shank the kick wide of the goalposts, leaving the score 28–25 Grambling. The rusher's momentum also landed him on the ankle and foot of Lovett's kicking leg. Lovett crumpled into a heap. Riley, the holder on the extra point, shouted for a roughing penalty to be called, miming an official tossing the flag. None came. He was left to help Lovett limp to the sideline.

More than halfway through the fourth quarter, separated by only three points, Grambling and Florida A&M shifted into a game of chicken. Pete Griffin restored the aggressive defense he had employed in the first half, packing eight men on or near the line of scrimmage. With their running game shackled, Eddie Robinson and James Harris threw without hesitation. On the first series after A&M's touchdown, Harris barely missed a third-down pass to Joiner at the Rattler twenty-eight. Getting the ball back after forcing an A&M punt, Grambling moved from its own thirty-three to the Rattler forty-eight on several running plays. There the Tigers faced third and six with barely four minutes remaining. With a first down, they would be able to consume probably three of those minutes, all but ensuring victory.

Harris set Grambling in the formation that had worked so well on its first touchdown. Joiner lined up tight, occupying two defensive backs. Essex Johnson split out wide to the right, drawing single coverage. With the snap, Joiner stayed on the line, joining in the wall of blockers protecting Harris. Johnson meanwhile ran fifteen yards downfield before cutting hard to the right sideline. He already had a step on the cornerback, Nathaniel James, and plenty of open field ahead of him. Harris laid the ball right into the receiver's hands, and Johnson turned upfield toward the goal line. Except that in the split second of glancing ahead, he had taken his eyes off the ball, and now he was bobbling it, trying to secure it, an amateur juggler losing control of his trick. As Johnson's momentum carried him across the sideline, the ball fell to the ground. There would be no more woofing about who was going to win the MVP. Grambling had enough to worry about just winning the game.

For now, the Tigers had to punt, and punting had been a misadventure all night long. Wesley Bean had thrown an interception in the first quarter. Then, early in the fourth, the center had sailed the snap far over Bean's head, and it skittered all the way into Grambling's end zone for an apparent safety. The down was replayed—and the A&M score wiped off the board—only because Grambling had drawn an illegal procedure penalty for a false start before the snap. And when it took a bad mistake to rescue his team from a worse one, that was the kind of football that made Eddie Robinson spiral his voice up into its exasperated range and utter the closest words he had to a profanity: "Damn it all to hell."

This time Bean did his part more than well, angling a punt out of bounds at the A&M eleven-yard line. Over all his years at Grambling, Robinson had hewed to a defensive philosophy he distilled in print as "intimidation of the offense with CONSTANT PRESSURE." Even when guarding a narrow lead, there was no falling back into a prevent defense, no trying not to lose. This whole game against FAMU, Robinson had been rotating players through the defensive line, making sure nobody got winded, replenishing the pass rush with full lungs and rested legs. After being stung in the first half by the Rattlers' outside speed, especially Riley's, he had moved his defensive ends several extra yards wide. They formed the outermost bars of the quarterback's cage.

There was a saying among the Rattler players and coaches: *The fourth quarter is ours.* They had proven it twice already this season, against Alabama A&M and Southern. That kind of confidence suited Ken Riley in particular. Screaming, shouting, bragging, boasting, getting up in somebody's face—that had never been his way. Riley didn't begrudge his teammates their chosen methods, but he had always harbored an unspoken warning: *Don't leave it in the locker room.* Now, fewer than four minutes left, nearly ninety yards to go, a championship hanging in the balance, he was where he wanted to be: on the field, running the show, ready for every obstacle.

And of obstacles, he faced many. Riley did not know exactly how much time he had left, because the stadium clock had never been repaired. He could ask the official keeping time on the field, but chasing him down would waste precious seconds. With Lovett injured, Riley did not dare settle for a field goal. Who would kick it?

There was one more problem. The Rattlers didn't have a hurry-up offense. While Jake Gaither had put heightened emphasis on the passing game in this season, he had never gotten around to installing a two-minute drill—a set of throws designed to gain yards fast and get out of bounds often to stop the clock. With just a handful of exceptions, Riley had only the standard repertoire of rollouts and play-action passes. Those plays depended on tricking a defense with fake runs, luring defensive backs out of position, the way Delles Howell had been enticed on the touchdown pass to Melvin Jones. With so little time remaining, though, Grambling knew full well that A&M could not keep the ball on the ground, not for eighty-nine yards. Even if Riley gave an Oscar performance, nobody on the Tigers' side was going to be fooled.

+ + +

So deep in Rattler territory, Riley had to choose between two risks. Try to pass the ball against a withering rush and risk a sack that would leave

A&M in an even more precarious position. Or try to run the ball and risk squandering valuable seconds unsorting the pile after the tackle and lining up for the next play. Riley went with the second option, calling for an off-tackle run by Preston Johnson. In the tension of the moment, though, Johnson never grabbed the handoff, and there stood Riley alone, with the ball and no blockers, in the Rattler backfield. Instantly, he squirted up the center of the field, turning what looked like a certain loss into a five-yard gain. On second and five Johnson redeemed himself, running a sweep around left end for seven more yards and a first down.

Now, with the comparative cushion of being at the twenty-three, Riley called for "Quarterback Throwback," the razzle-dazzle play that had fooled Grambling earlier in the half. Riley pitched back to Hubert Ginn, who started dashing right on a sweep. Riley circled out of the backfield to the left and saw exactly the result he wanted. One of the fastest runners on a team of champion sprinters, one of the most elusive college quarterbacks in the entire nation, he was being covered by a defensive end fifty pounds heavier. Within seconds, Riley had bolted nearly ten yards beyond the Grambling defender, Clarence Powell, and was waiting for the pass that would win the game.

When Grambling had lined up for the play, though, Robinson had put in a defensive stunt. He inserted Billy Ray Newsome, normally an end on both offense and defense, at defensive tackle, where he would be too quick even for FAMU's nimble linemen. Sure enough, Newsome burst straight into the Rattler backfield and zeroed in on Ginn. By the time the A&M halfback was setting up to throw the pass, Newsome was draped over him. The ball floated and wobbled and began falling to earth ten yards short of Riley. It took all of the quarterback's speed to reverse course and bat down the pass before Powell could intercept it and essentially end the game.

With the reprieve, Riley tossed a swing pass to Ginn for a first down at A&M's thirty-nine. Ginn then ran for two yards. The play ended in a gang tackle, the opportunity for the Grambling defenders to hold on a few extra seconds to a Rattler calf or ankle, to take their sweet time peeling themselves off the pile—nothing illegal about it, just part of shrinking the clock. Riley signaled a time-out, the first of A&M's three. He spoke on the sideline to Costa Kittles and Pete Griffin, and they decided on a play. Then, when Riley lined up the Rattlers for second and eight at their forty-one, and with barely two minutes remaining, he overruled the coaches with an audible. It was called the 400.

Riley split out John Eason at left end. He saw Grambling crowding the line to rush. He saw the cornerbacks waiting seven or eight yards off the line, making sure no pass got behind them. And he saw the entire middle of the Grambling secondary vacant, empty as a pasture. Riley looked over to the wide receiver on his right. Then he looked over to his left, as if just going through a routine set of checks. Then, preparing to call the signals, he tapped the left side of his helmet. Eason, head tilted sideways so he could see the quarterback, watched and understood.

At the snap, Eason slanted into the middle, into all that open space. Riley took a single step back from center, jumped up above the blockers and pass rushers, and flung him the ball. Eason grabbed it at midfield, shook off a horse-collar tackle by Delles Howell at the Grambling forty-five, and was finally wrestled down at the thirty-seven. Better yet for FAMU, the officials stopped the clock as they moved the chains. It was like an extra time-out.

Along the Grambling sidelines, James Harris drew deep, anxious breaths. He could only hope that A&M didn't score. Or if it did, that it scored quickly. *So there'll be some clock left for us.* On the field, even surrounded by the din of A&M fans, Robert Atkins heard his inner voice all too clearly. *If they score, we won't have time. Don't let me be the person who makes the mistake.* After all the times over all the years when Atkins and Harris and Howell and Joiner and all the rest had griped about the way Eddie Robinson practiced—*Why we runnin' the same plays over and over?*—they now realized what all those reps had been for. They had been to instill the discipline, the technique, and the confidence not to unravel with the national title at stake, in front of a hostile crowd, under the spell of Ken Riley's sorcery.

On first down, Grambling responded. As Riley rolled to the right, cornerback Hilton Crawford knifed inside of a block by Preston Johnson and snagged Riley by the sleeve, twirling him down at the Grambling forty-eight for a loss of eleven yards. With fewer than two minutes remaining, the Rattlers took their second time-out. On the next play, second and twenty-one, Riley rolled toward the left and found himself in trouble again. Walter Breaux, a Grambling tackle, was charging straight at him. Riley spun around to evade him and ran toward the right side, his stronger side. Robert Jones, another Grambling lineman, dove at Riley's legs and barely missed. Then Scott Lewis, the same player who had foiled the quarterback sneak in the first quarter, moved in for the tackle. Riley scampered around him, a little bit of revenge.

Yet after all of Riley's efforts, he was still deep in his own backfield and pinned along the right sideline. He pumped his arm as if to pass, freezing Grambling's linebackers and defensive backs in place. Then he streaked upfield, inches within the sideline. Every few strides, he pumped again. He pumped even after he crossed the line of scrimmage and could not have passed, and his feint kept working on the Grambling defenders. Meanwhile, A&M's center, a lanky freshman named Willy Miller, took off into the Grambling secondary, looking for someone to flatten. That someone turned out to be defensive end Clarence Powell, who had dropped into pass coverage and was waiting for Riley at the Grambling thirty-eight. At that yard line, A&M would have faced third and nine. Instead, Miller chopped down Powell, and Riley made it all the way to the thirty. From there, on third and two, Robert Lampkin ran for six yards and a first down. The officials moved the chains, and the clock briefly stopped again.

At that moment, Horace Lovett's missed extra point returned to haunt A&M. With that one more point, the Rattlers would have been trailing 28–26 and capable of winning with a field goal. Without that point, the best they could do was tie. There was no overtime, no sudden death in college football; even bowl games were allowed to end in ties. Every football fan in America had grumbled the previous fall when

Notre Dame and Michigan State, ranked first and second, respectively, in the nation, played to a 10–10 standoff in what had been touted as the "Game of the Century." The decision by Notre Dame's coach, Ara Parseghian, to safely run out the clock had inspired the sardonic slogan "Tie one for the Gipper." No Jake Gaither team was going to settle for avoiding defeat. The game would end the way somehow it had to end, something preordained about it: one loser, one winner, one champion, no doubt.

First and ten from the Grambling twenty-five: Riley rolled out to his left and threw hastily under the oncoming rush. A Grambling safety, Roger Williams, dove to nearly intercept at the two-yard line.

Second and ten: Riley rolled to the right, and Grambling linemen poured through the A&M line to pin him against the sideline. Even under their pressure, Riley spotted John Eason, who had slipped behind two defensive backs and was skating along the back line of the end zone. Leaping as he threw, Riley lofted the ball over the defenders. Eason jumped and extended his arms, only to watch the pass fly inches above his fingers.

Third and ten: Twenty-five yards from their goal line, with nothing to fear from a run, Grambling's linemen outnumbered and overwhelmed the FAMU pass blockers, and Clarence Powell smacked down Riley back at the thirty-eight. With about thirty seconds remaining in the game, Riley took A&M's final time-out. He was facing fourth down and twenty-three yards to go. Realistically, without any more time-outs, he had to score on this play.

In the huddle, Riley made the call: 35 Slant Pass. The play gave him four options. His top choice would be Eugene Milton crossing from right to left about fifteen yards downfield; with Grambling so concerned about guarding the edges against Riley's scrambling, the crossing routes had been open all night. Both John Eason and Melvin Jones would run square-outs into opposite corners of the end zone. Even if neither man got open, they would pull lots of coverage away from Milton. As a very last resort, Riley could dump off a pass to Hubert Ginn in the flat, and pretty much pray that Ginn would not only get the first down but also get out of bounds to stop the clock.

Riley took the snap and rolled from the center of the field toward the right hash mark, searching for an open man. What he saw instead undermined the whole plan. Grambling, renowned for its aggressive man-to-man pass coverage, had shifted into a zone. The middle linebacker, George Muse, was dropping back into the central area where Riley had hoped to find Milton unguarded. The safeties, Robert Atkins and Roger Williams, were patrolling the deep field, one responsible for each side, in a scheme called the "cover-two." *Keep everything in front. Keep everything in the middle.* That was the rule. That was the law.

At the hash mark, Grambling's Walter Breaux and Ernest Sterling, nearly six hundred pounds of problem, thundered toward Riley, who darted toward the right sideline to escape. Football in his arm, arm at his side, he kept looking, looking, looking. Then he saw something, maybe Eason. Riley planted his feet and pulled back his arm to throw. Just then, a defensive lineman named John Mendenhall, a freshman who had been part of Eddie Robinson's rotation this night, slammed the quarterback to the ground.

While Riley lay prone, Mendenhall sprang to his feet and hurled his right arm skyward in triumph. After the last seconds ticked off the official's watch and he whistled the game to its close, Sterling knelt and pounded his fist against the ground, a gesture not of frustration but of exultation. James Harris threw his arms around Charlie Joiner. The Grambling players lifted Eddie Robinson onto their shoulders. Then, without any protesters around to ruin the spirit, they sang the college alma mater.

Heads bowed, feet dragging, arms limp, the A&M players and coaches staggered toward the locker room. From a telephone somewhere within the Orange Bowl, Pete Griffin called Jake Gaither with the news. John Eason, silently disconsolate, tormented himself with the thought that he should have caught that end-zone pass for the winning touchdown. With his adrenaline spent, Ken Riley began to ache from the beating he had absorbed. On the morning after the game, a young FAMU secretary named Castell Bryant watched the Rattler players boarding the team bus for the long, somber trek back to Tallahassee. "Guys, you let 'em kill me last night," she heard Riley say to a few of A&M's offensive linemen. "Wait till we get back in the dorm."

+   +   +

In its immediate aftermath, the 1967 Orange Blossom Classic was extolled by many sportswriters as the greatest game in series history. The final statistics attested to a closely fought contest. FAMU had compiled 396 yards of total offense, slightly more than Grambling's 382. James Harris had thrown for 174 yards, and Ken Riley had nearly matched him, with 110 yards passing and 62 more rushing.

Even in defeat, even in absentia, Jake Gaither had answered his doubters with an 8-2 season, as his Rattlers proved that he remained at the peak of his talents. Harris and Eason shared the award for Most Valuable Player, raising the profile of each with pro football scouts. When Grambling's players returned to Monroe, they assembled for a team portrait outside their airplane. Not only were they national black champions, their pose seemed to say, but these "kids from the hills and swamps," as Delles Howell had called them, now carried themselves like city slickers.

The only discordant note to emerge from the game was the attendance: 37,631, the lowest in years, nearly 10,000 beneath the Classic's peak. Yet even that news strangely heartened John A. Diaz, a columnist for the *Miami Times*, the city's weekly black newspaper. He wrote under the heading "Let's Keep Pace with Changing Times":

> Times have changed. . . . There was a time when Negroes were not permitted to purchase tickets at box offices patronized by whites; when Negroes were not admitted to the Orange Bowl's New Year game; when at the Orange Blossom Classic game Negroes and whites were

segregated. That's all over now. It therefore seems that the time has arrived for an interracial Orange Blossom Classic game.

Long before Diaz wrote those words, Jake Gaither had been making very similar plans. The only question was when they would come to
fruition.

10

HISTORY IN THE AIR

Florida A&M vs. University of Tampa, November 29, 1969

Half an hour before kickoff, a blond-haired, blue-eyed boy, five-foot-three and skinny as a fence post in the way only a twelve-year-old can be, walked with his father through an entry gate at Tampa Stadium. They knew they were lucky to be there at all. A day or two earlier, during his Thanksgiving vacation from seventh grade, the boy had said to his father, "I really want to go to this game." Even at his young age, Jim Gardner understood that there was something special about the University of Tampa, his hometown team, his favorite, playing against Florida A&M. It was a white school versus a black school, and such a contest had never taken place in the South. Jim remembered how, nearly four years earlier, he had sat with his father and watched the five black players of Texas Western defeat all-white Kentucky for the 1966 NCAA basketball title. He remembered how his father had said, "This is historic."

So Jim wanted to see history made again. The problem was that so did a great many other people. Days before the November 29 game, all forty-seven thousand tickets in Tampa Stadium had sold out. FAMU alumni were coming by the carload from as far away as New Jersey; ticket agents in Miami and Daytona Beach had been selling seats in blocks of fifteen or twenty. Not wanting to disappoint his son, Melvin Gardner drove with him on the afternoon of game day to the stadium's main box office. There, the clerk explained, not surprisingly, that every ticket was long gone.

Melvin turned to Jim and said, "I have an idea." They walked around to the east side of the stadium, the visiting team's side, which was less accessible from the highway. A secondary box office sat just outside the stadium fence. Improbably, incredibly, the clerk had a pair of seats—on the forty-five-yard line, no less. Maybe someone had returned them moments earlier. Maybe some VIP had decided not to use them. Who knew? Who cared?

Four or five hours later, Jim and his father returned for the game. As they walked from their car, they passed through hundreds of fans prowling for spare tickets. This game was so big it had scalpers, a word never before associated with sports in Tampa. The Gardners went through the gate, wound through the concession booths, and climbed the steps to their seats, about halfway up the 102 rows of the concrete grandstand. As they sat down on the aluminum bleachers, something occurred to them. They were on the Florida A&M side. They were surrounded by black people. Among nearly twenty-four thousand Rattler faithful, the Gardners were, as far as they could tell, the only two whites. Melvin said to Jim in an almost jaunty tone, "This is going to be an adventure."

+ + +

The struggle to achieve this game had begun with Jake Gaither's backstage maneuverings two years earlier, during the 1967 football season, when he persuaded the state Board of Regents to grant stealthy, unwritten approval for A&M to play against a white school. The opportunity might have gone unfulfilled and the racial barriers unbroken, however, without a young man named Fran Curci having been hired in 1968 as Tampa's football coach.

Though he had spent most of his life in Florida, Curci was an outsider to the South's racial code, a transplanted northern Catholic. His hairdresser father had moved the family from Pittsburgh to Miami in 1945 so he could open his own shop, and young Fran was shocked to see black women forced to forgo empty seats on the segregated city buses he rode to school. After starring at quarterback for the University of Miami, still all-white then in the late 1950s, Curci played on integrated teams in the military and during his brief AFL career. There he roomed with Abner Haynes, a black running back who had been on the first integrated college team in Texas.

When Curci returned to Miami in 1962 as an assistant coach to Andy Gustafson, he saw firsthand the resistance to integration at a southern school. Despite a personal request from the university's president, Henry King Stanford, Gustafson refused to recruit black players. Three years later his successor, Charlie Tate, finally broke the barrier, signing a wide receiver, Ray Bellamy, who beyond being a sports star was both an honor student and class president in high school. Even so, as Bellamy began his freshman season at Miami in 1967, he received "Dear Nigger" letters from strangers and endured racial slurs from teammates. Police arrested him for sitting in a car near the campus with a white female classmate, and it required President Stanford's intervention to secure Bellamy's release. When Miami traveled to Alabama the following season for a game against Auburn, Bellamy received death threats. An FBI agent guarded his hotel room the night before the game.

For Curci, such incidents were not revelations but confirmations—of what was poisonous about racism and of what had to change in sports. "I had those feelings before those things happened," he put it years later. "That's who I was."

What Curci lacked, as an assistant coach, was the power to hasten the pace of change, to determine it. But during the 1967 season, as Miami was heading to a 7-4 finish and a bowl game, halfway across the state the University of Tampa was sliding to a 2-8 record and firing its head coach, Sam Bailey. When Tampa offered Curci the top job, he issued two conditions. He must be permitted to recruit black players. And he must report only to the university's president, David Delo. A Lutheran minister's son from the Midwest, Delo readily granted Curci's terms. Besides sharing a belief in integration with his new coach, the president went on to develop a self-interested gratitude when Curci deployed football players to guard campus buildings, and by their brawny presence intimidate demonstrators, during antiwar protests at the university.

The first player Curci recruited for Tampa was Leon McQuay, a running back from Blake High, one of the city's two all-black secondary schools. While playing there under head coach Abe Brown, a FAMU alumnus, McQuay received the offer of a football scholarship by mail from Jake Gaither, a man he had never met. By visiting McQuay's family nearly every day, winning over his mother, Curci stole away the prized recruit. He proceeded to sign three other black players by the start of the 1969 season. He also instantly transformed Tampa's on-field performance. After a 2-8 season in Bailey's final year, Tampa went 7-3 in 1968 under Curci. Even though it competed in the small-college ranks, Tampa beat the major colleges Tulane and Mississippi State.

Near the end of the 1968 season, Curci went to watch FAMU play Texas Southern in Tampa. That game, the second version of the newly created Tampa Classic, drew more than twenty thousand spectators, a decent enough turnout but hardly one worthy of the lofty title. Curci already knew Gaither from coaching clinics, so he approached him with a proposition: "Why don't we play each other?" He had no idea of Gaither's confidential deal with the Board of Regents. Gaither, for his part, said nothing about it to Curci, pretending instead to take the idea under advisement. Some weeks later, perhaps after confirming the plan with the regents, he called back Curci to schedule the game.

Whatever idealism Curci attached to the interracial game was well seasoned with practicality. Only twenty-nine years old, ambitious and impatient, Curci wanted big-time ink for himself and his team. He wanted sellout crowds instead of a half-empty stadium. Taking on a black team, particularly one coached by the legendary Gaither, promised to draw plenty of attention. And Curci was brash enough to brush off the more negative kind of attention, all those folks around Tampa declaring, "You can't have a white school play a black school. You can't have the fans sit together. There'll be a riot."

Such concerns were not unfounded. Tampa had exploded into two days of rioting in June 1967, the start of what became known across the nation as "the Long, Hot Summer." After a white police officer shot to death a black teenager suspected of burglary, a wave of arson and looting swept through the black business district. The violence was severe enough to be investigated by the Kerner Commission, a panel appointed by President Johnson and led by Illinois governor Otto Kerner to examine the causes of 1967's wave of urban turmoil. In issuing its alarming overall conclusion—"Our nation is moving toward two societies, one white and one black, separate and unequal"—the commission specifically identified wide racial disparities in education, economics, and political power in Tampa. Indeed, the assassination of Martin Luther King Jr. in April 1968 nearly rekindled the flames. As it was, violence erupted elsewhere in Florida, including on the A&M campus in Tallahassee. Jake Gaither had to plead with Governor Claude Kirk not to allow state troopers to respond with live ammunition.

By the time Curci and Gaither were proposing their 1969 game, the racial and political climate of the entire nation had grown even more volatile. With King slain, Robert Kennedy assassinated, the 1968 Democratic National Convention racked by police attacks on protesters and journalists, and the entire South won by either Richard Nixon or George Wallace in that fall's presidential election, the hopefulness of the civil rights movement just a few years earlier had been replaced by bitterness, trauma, and cynicism.

In spite of that forbidding climate, or perhaps as their blow against it, Curci and Gaither agreed to proceed with the interracial game. If Gaither felt relieved and thankful to finally have a white partner, he hid it well.

"Fran, this is my game," he insisted to the Tampa coach. "Make sure you know it's my game."

"But it's my stadium," Curci replied.

Beneath the coaches' joking camaraderie, the potential for friction at the event loomed. Each school was going to sell one side of the stadium to its own supporters, ensuring a stark racial divide in the stands. Each school was even going to print its own program. Only on the field itself were the races assured of mixing. And nobody knew what kind of effect a hard tackle or a late hit down there might have on a packed, passionate crowd.

+ + +

Jim Gardner, that especially interested boy in the stadium stands, was the child of an actress mother from Chicago and a doctor father from Philadelphia. Yet he had spent nearly all of his young life in Tampa. With the influence of parents on one side and of place on the other, his boyhood offered a kind of moral test, a short course in how a white person should respond to privilege predicated on race.

Dr. Gardner had moved his family to Tampa when Jim was two years old to join a psychiatric practice there. Thanks to the doctor's income, the family could afford to live in a large home with its own pool in the tony neighborhood of Davis Island. Jim was able to attend a private school that adopted the British model to the point of, for instance, calling sixth grade "form six." The Gardners also employed a middle-aged black woman from a public housing project, Geneva Bonney, to clean their home and cook their meals.

Jim received clear instruction from his parents never to call Bonney a "maid," a term they considered demeaning. She was the "housekeeper." Under whatever title, she prepared French toast and fried chicken and negotiated between the pack rat tendencies of Melvin and the neatnik inclination of his wife, Radiance. Bonney also felt comfortable enough to pass judgment on all the prospective boyfriends of Jim's older sister Bobbi.

And Bonney taught him, without consciously teaching, about civil rights. The lesson was implicit in the way she rooted for the Los Angeles Dodgers, all because of Jackie Robinson. It was implicit when she taught Jim the gospel songs of dignity and endurance "Take My Hand, Precious Lord" and "His Eye Is on the Sparrow." It became manifest when Jim and his younger sister Elizabeth went for a sleepover to Bonney's home, meeting her husband, who did construction labor, and playing with black kids in the neighborhood.

As Jim grew, his conscience kept grating against the unquestioned norms of Tampa. When he visited school friends, he noticed how their maids (and that was the word always used) referred to them as "Master" or "Young Master." He listened in silent discomfort every time his junior high football coach extolled Bear Bryant, the coach of Alabama's all-white teams. With integration beginning in a hesitant, begrudging way, Jim once heard a teammate casually say of an opposing school's team, "They've got a really fast nigger."

Worst of all, perhaps, was the day when his little sister was in first grade and complained that Geneva Bonney had burned the breakfast pancakes. "I will not eat these Negro-colored pancakes," Elizabeth announced, not fully aware of the subtext of her words. Jim realized then and there that all the noxious attitudes of the South could infect even an open-minded household. They were in the air. You breathed them. You had to choose to be different. Enlightenment wouldn't happen by itself.

So Jim woke himself up early every weekday to watch the *CBS Morning News* before school. He read the issues of *Time* and *Life* that accumulated in his father's waiting room. He followed his parents' discussions about the Vietnam War. On that terrible night in April 1968, he listened in as his mother tried to console Geneva Bonney on the phone. "They shot King, they shot King," she wailed as Jim made himself proximate to her grief.

For all those reasons, Jim Gardner paid special attention when the Tampa-FAMU game was announced. Though he knew Bonney was mostly a baseball fan, he made sure to tell her he was hoping to see the game with his father. Even more than Melvin Gardner, a middle-aged man, fully formed in his ways, twelve-year-old Jim was part of a new generation, with its values still capable of being shaped. He was the very person whom Jake Gaither was hoping to reach. And, even before kick-off, Gaither had.

+ + +

Purely as a football game, the contest between Tampa and Florida A&M was alluring. Tampa entered the game with eight consecutive victories, an 8-1 record, and a seventh-place ranking in the small-college polls. The Spartans averaged more than 400 yards of offense per game. Leon McQuay had already rushed for nearly 900, and quarterback Jim Del Gaizo had thrown for almost 1,900 as well as 17 touchdowns.

For their part, the Rattlers were 6-1 and coming off a 60–15 demolition of their intrastate rival Bethune-Cookman. While Jake Gaither had lost to graduation the mainstays of his 1967 squad—Ken Riley, John Eason, Monster Sims, Major Hazelton—he still had Hubert Ginn in the backfield and Otis Collier on defense. His quarterback, Steve Scruggs, was originally from St. Petersburg, right across the bay from Tampa, and had a particular incentive to impress the hometown crowd.

"This game is going to make Pearl Harbor look like a lawn party," crowed Tampa's defensive-line coach, Rich Gillis. Somewhat more plausibly, Curci likened the game to "the Ohio State–Michigan situation." Leon McQuay went through practice wearing a "Beat FAMU" sticker on his helmet.

Gaither eagerly put McQuay's perfidy to use as a motivational tool. "He turned me down," Gaither told his players. "He could have been a Rattler, but he turned me down. He could have been one of us, but he turned me down. He decided he would rather be a Spartan than a Rattler. I want you to remember that every time McQuay gets the ball. Remember he could have been a Rattler, he could have been here on this field today. So when he gets the ball, this is what I want you to do. I want you to hit him high. I want you to hit him low. And then I want you to *stretch* him."

Despite all the signs of parity between the teams, the wire-service poll rated FAMU only sixteenth in the nation, and the pregame betting line had Tampa as a seven-point favorite. The Spartans had routed a major-college team, Tulsa, earlier in the season, while the Rattlers had played only other small black colleges. The track record of black colleges against white ones also fed a prejudiced skepticism. Grambling had lost 20–7 in 1965 to North Dakota State in a small-college bowl game (though Grambling did beat Sacramento State 34–7 in 1968). Tennessee State had been defeated by San Diego State 16–8 to start the 1967 season. As the conventional line of white reasoning went, black schools could put out good players, since blacks were "natural" athletes. But black teams couldn't beat white ones, and that meant there must be something deficient about black colleges and black coaches.

Gaither knew all about the double standard. Even with 201 victories in his career, even with an 83 percent winning record, even with six black national championships and twenty-two conference championships, even with decades of instructing the top white college coaches at his clinics, even with his award as small-college coach of the year in 1962—despite all that, as A&M's spokesman and publicist Eddie Jackson put it, "An invisible asterisk hung over his incredible career."

No major college, no integrated college, had ever offered Gaither a job. Neither had any pro team, not even when the *Washington Post's* influential sports columnist Shirley Povich had floated the idea after the 1967 season. As for integration on the field, the South still largely resisted. Florida and Florida State had finally signed one black player apiece in 1969. But the looming showdown between top-ranked Texas and number-two Arkansas, the de facto championship game for the major colleges, involved two all-white teams.

Gaither was aware that his own time was draining away. He experienced such physical weakness at points during the 1969 season that he couldn't get out of his car at the end of a workday and had to be helped into his home. He felt emotionally alienated by the rise of politically dissident black athletes, as exemplified by John Carlos and Tommie Smith, who had bowed their heads and given clenched-fist salutes from the medal stand at the 1968 Olympics. The coming of everything from marijuana to dashikis to beards as the counterculture rolled across black campuses left Gaither decrying what he called "the new breed" more vociferously than ever before. The chance to make history with this interracial game was the major reason, almost the sole reason, why Jake Gaither had not given up and retired already.

In the days leading up to the FAMU-Tampa game, neither head coach spoke publicly about its larger import. They echoed the line that it was "just another game." For his part, Gaither worried that stressing the social and political consequences might overwhelm the emotions of his players and distract them from the immediate imperative of winning. It fell to Fred Girard, a sportswriter for the *St. Petersburg Times,* a courageous newspaper throughout the civil rights era, to candidly lay out the stakes:

> Although neither coach wants to admit it, the game could be an influence on the way the wire services—and the nation—regard Negro college football. If Tampa . . . should whip A&M by a large margin, there will be a lot of I-told-you-so's. "A&M may have looked good before," they will say, "but they weren't playing anybody."
>
> Or, if the Rattlers win or at least make it close, the wire services would have no choice but to admit that football in the black colleges is on a par with football anywhere else, and treat those colleges accordingly.

+ + +

Up in the east stands of the stadium as kickoff approached, Jim Gardner started cheering for Tampa. A Florida A&M fan, seated a few rows below him to the right, glanced up at the boy and genially chuckled as he called back, "I think you're on the wrong side."

Down on the field, meanwhile, the opposing coaches met for a pre-game handshake—a ritual of good sportsmanship and on this night a good deal more.

"This is bigger than I thought it would be," said Curci, indicating the capacity crowd.

"Not me," Gaither answered.

Up in the press box, at the same time, a special guest of Gaither's found a seat: Eddie Robinson. Grambling and FAMU were already scheduled to meet one week later in the Orange Blossom Classic in a rematch of the spellbinding 1967 game. But Gaither's invitation to Robinson had not been purely a courtesy. With everything involved in the game against Tampa, with history itself in the air, Jake Gaither wanted and needed Eddie Robinson to bear witness.

+   +   +

Over the next sixty minutes of playing time, the game surpassed all expectations for drama and intensity. FAMU and Tampa battled through three ties and four lead changes. They amassed more than 1,100 yards of total offense, with the Rattlers rushing for 321 and Tampa passing for 423. The outcome was not settled until the final 26 seconds.

In the first half, the teams' offensive units had taken turns sweeping down the field, marching end zone to end zone with the irresistible regularity of the tides. The half ended with the score tied 14–14. When Curci had tried to bring his team back onto the field for the second half, he ran straight into one of FAMU's favorite tricks—the bandmaster, William Foster, keeping the Marching 100 on the field performing for five or ten minutes beyond the official intermission time, the better to idle and frustrate an opponent. Sure enough, A&M seized the advantage in the third quarter, putting up two touchdowns for a 28–14 lead. Less than a minute after the second of those FAMU scores, Leon McQuay ran for a

Tampa touchdown. Then, after the Spartans intercepted a Rattler pass, Jim Del Gaizo threw sixty-four yards for the tying touchdown. Midway through the fourth quarter, it was 28 all.

Steve Scruggs responded by passing and scrambling to move A&M down the field. When Tampa's defense stiffened at the ten-yard line, Horace Lovett kicked a twenty-seven-yard field goal for a three-point lead with barely two minutes remaining. But Tampa had jumped off-side on the play, which presented Jake Gaither with both a choice and a dilemma. Football logic dictated that a coach never take his team's points off the scoreboard. Tampa's offensive firepower, though, made A&M's three-point lead look flimsy. So Gaither accepted the offside penalty, which wiped out the field goal but gave the Rattlers a first down at the Tampa five-yard line. Three plays later, rewarding the coach's risk, Hubert Ginn swept around left end for the go-ahead touchdown.

Then Lovett missed the crucial extra point, just as he had against Grambling in the Orange Blossom Classic two years earlier. Tampa re-mained in position not merely to tie but to win. Starting on the Spartan twenty-seven with 1:58 remaining, Del Gaizo completed four passes to bring Tampa to the Rattler fourteen. With fifty-eight seconds remaining, he had plenty of time.

On first and second downs, A&M defensive backs broke up Del Gaizo's passes. On third down, he fired incomplete. Finally, on fourth down, with 46,477 spectators standing, with the Rattler side howling to disrupt the offense and the Tampa side futilely trying to give Del Gaizo quiet to call signals, the quarterback dropped back and spotted one of his running backs, Paul Orndorff, wide open on the left side of the end zone. As the ball sailed toward Orndorff, A&M's best cornerback, Leroy Charlton, flew toward it. He leaped, stretched, and grazed the pass with his fingers, just enough to tip it away. The Rattlers took over possession and ran out the clock to win 34–28.

Fran Curci dashed from the Tampa side toward the FAMU bench, meeting Jake Gaither at midfield. As the entire stadium watched, the white coach hugged the black one. "Jake, congratulations," Curci said. "You had the better team. And you outcoached me."

Up in the stands, where Jim Gardner had shouted himself hoarse, a black man nearby offered his hand and said with both pride and kindness, "I hope you see that the better team won." No one around Jim and his father left their spots. Still standing in place from watching the last frenetic plays, they gazed down to the field, where the Rattler players were carrying Jake Gaither in triumph. The fans kept standing as the Marching 100 assembled in formation, and when the band started to play one of A&M's anthems, the Rattler congregation joined in song.

I'm so glad I'm from FAMU
I'm so glad I'm from FAMU
I'm so glad I'm from FAMU
Singing glory hallelujah
I'm from FAMU

Dr. Gardner, shrugging amiably, looked at his son and said, "What the hell." They both began to sing along.

+ + +

After Jake Gaither congratulated his team, and after the players showered and dressed, he told them that the next game, the Orange Blossom Classic rematch against Grambling, would be his last. As they boarded the bus, he made an offer none of them had ever heard before from their coach: no practice on Monday. Carlmon Jones, a tackle, led an immediate mutiny. The team didn't want a day off. Gaither asked if everyone agreed. The shouts of "yes" rang through the bus.

Gaither stuck around the locker room to accept congratulations from friends, alumni, visitors, passersby. When he was finished and he and his wife, Sadie, started walking to their car, she noticed a group of white men up ahead, blocking their path. She whispered to Jake that maybe they'd better find another way out. He kept walking toward the men. As he reached them, one of the white men extended his hand and shook Gaither's. The rest soon followed. This apparent mob, this visible echo of so many white mobs, of so much bloodshed and bigotry, turned out to be members of Tampa's football booster club. Like their coach, Fran Curci, they wanted, in spite of defeat, to pay tribute to a great man.

In the next day's edition of the *St. Petersburg Times,* which Gaither read after a sleepless night, Fred Girard wrote of the game, "They carried Jake Gaither off the football field at Tampa Stadium last night and 63 years of prejudice, confusion and misinformation left with him." Victorious and vindicated, Gaither finally felt liberated to admit how much the game had meant to him, a man who had studied black history so deeply. He later told a journalist:

> That game has to be the most important game of my life, for that proves a game of that type—with tension and competitiveness—could be played between whites and blacks in the Deep South without any undue racial violence, without the fans, the players, or the community becoming upset, with good sportsmanship by both teams and the public. I wanted to prove to myself that it could be done in Florida—the deepest state in the Deep South. And we did it.

The most resonant words may have been uttered by Eddie Robinson, Jake Gaither's rival and ally, before the game was even over. Up in the Tampa Stadium press box at halftime, a reporter for the *Tampa Tribune* had asked the Grambling coach for his thoughts. "We're at the place where we can do just about anything we want to do these days," Robinson replied. "There are still rednecks who'd object, but there are enough people who are concerned about seeing good football to make it possible for us, too. They know we have to live together now."

Epilogue ▶

THEIR LIVES, THEIR LEGACY

James Harris, Ken Riley, Eddie Robinson,
Jake Gaither, 1968–2013

n the morning of January 28, 1969, James Harris walked into Collie Nicholson's office to wait for word from the NFL draft. In those days before cell phones and e-mail and websites, Nicholson had the best means of quick, accurate information: personal connections. As the day wore on, and as Harris shuttled between the office and his classes, the phone rang only once with news for a Grambling player: Charlie Joiner had been taken by the Houston Oilers in the fourth round. By nightfall, the first seven rounds had been completed, and six quarterbacks had been chosen, none of them James Harris.

He had been expecting, and dreading, that kind of snub. Even after being chosen the small-college player of the year by the Pigskin Club of Washington, even after being named quarterback on the *Pittsburgh Cou-*

rier's Black All-America team, Harris had not been invited to any of the postseason all-star games that served as NFL auditions—not the North-South game, the Blue-Gray, the East-West, the Hula Bowl, the Senior Bowl. Weeks before draft day, he had seen some of his Grambling team-mates driving new cars, evidently with cash advances from their agents. Nobody had offered him a car. He had only hoped to get enough of a signing bonus to buy his mother a washing machine. Now even that modest goal looked impossible.

So Harris drove home that night to Monroe, much as he had driven home three years earlier as a freshman frustrated at losing playing time after an injury. He knew perfectly well why he hadn't been drafted. Both he and Eddie Robinson had made it clear to anyone from the NFL who had asked that, no, James Harris was not willing to change position. James Harris was going to make it—or not—as a quarterback. He was Shack, after all, nicknamed by his minister father for the Bible's Meshach, one of those three Jews in ancient Babylon who refused to bow to an alien god. Now the league, and the nation, had responded.

Robinson called Harris at home and persuaded him to come back to campus. There were ten more rounds in the draft. There was still a chance. The next morning, the Buffalo Bills selected Harris in the eighth round, the 192nd player picked. The Bills already had two veteran quar-terbacks, Jack Kemp and Tom Flores. Harris told Robinson he wasn't going to a team, indeed a league, where he'd have no chance. So Robin-son walked with Harris over to the football bleachers, empty now in the off-season, and started to talk.

"The decision is yours," he said. "I just want to say this to you. If you choose to go to the NFL, and don't make it, don't come back and tell me it was because of you being black. And if you choose to go, don't expect it to be fair. You got to be better. You got to go out there and prepare yourself better. You got to throw more balls every day. You can't miss a day. You got to be the first one to practice and the last one to leave." Then he paused and leveled his voice. "I know you're good enough to make it."

Every night from the Bills' training camp, Harris phoned Robinson for reassurance. Every morning he waited for a knock on the door to inform him that he'd been cut. When the knock came, though, it was for his roommate. Some days on the practice field, Harris didn't get in for a single play. Still, he was included along with the six other quarterbacks in camp in throwing drills. Eventually, given the opportunity, he led scoring drives in scrimmages and an exhibition game. Meanwhile, injuries slowed both Kemp and Flores, and Harris grew more familiar and comfortable with the Bills offense.

And so, on the first Sunday of the regular season, James Harris started at quarterback, the first black ever to start at quarterback on opening day, the first of many firsts to come in his NFL career. The reality of breaking ground, however, was harsh. Playing against the defending Super Bowl champion Jets, Harris injured a groin muscle during the first half. In the huddle, some of his white teammates asked what he was saying. When one missed a block, he blamed it on not hearing the play call because of Harris's "diction." Harris had to admit to himself he had no experience looking at white folks, talking to white folks, much less issuing orders, as a quarterback must. His rookie season ended with a knee injury in the sixth game.

The football world around him provided incessant reminders of the odds against him. His roommate, Marlin Briscoe, had been a starting quarterback for the Denver Broncos for part of the 1968 season, throwing fourteen touchdown passes—and then they'd benched him and traded him to Buffalo, which turned him into a flanker. Eldridge Dickey, Harris's college rival at Tennessee State, had been taken in the first round of the 1968 draft by the Oakland Raiders and unceremoniously shifted to receiver. Onree Jackson of Alabama A&M, picked in the fifth round in 1969 by the Boston Patriots, was cut before training camp. Then there were the letters, letters with drawings of nooses and watermelons, letters that came by the basketful.

Now that you pickaninnies no longer dance for us on streetcorners, it is only right that you do so in stadiums. We all love to watch you jigs do your jigs. We like to watch you spike the ball (or as our children call it—"niggering" the ball). . . . We will all be at the Raiders Game to watch you do your act for us "boy." [Signed] White America.

At the start of Harris's third year, the Bills put a white rookie from San Diego State, Dennis Shaw, ahead of him at quarterback. Even after Harris won several games in relief of Shaw, the Bills cut Harris before the next season. He called Robinson, and Robinson called several pro teams, and none of them called back with an offer. So Harris drove to Washington to resume on a full-time basis what had been his off-season job at the federal Commerce Department—placing black students in internships with major corporations. As for being a pro quarterback, he told himself, "It's over."

About a month later, during the fall of 1972, Robinson's efforts finally paid off. The former Grambling star Tank Younger, a scout for the Los Angeles Rams, arranged a tryout for Harris. Though he had not thrown a pass for weeks, Harris did well enough to land a spot on the Rams' practice squad. The next year, he made the roster as a backup, consigned to mopping-up duty at the end of routs.

But several games into the 1974 season, Harris earned the starting job. He won seven of the next nine games, leading the NFC in passing efficiency and taking a 10-4 Rams team all the way to the NFC championship game, which Los Angeles lost to Minnesota. After barely missing a chance at the Super Bowl, Harris was selected for the Pro Bowl, where he was chosen the MVP. In 1975, with Harris now the team captain, the Rams went 12-2, though they lost again in the NFC title game with Harris injured. Despite injuries, he led NFC passers again in 1976.

All the wins, all the touchdown passes, Pro Bowl star, team captain, consecutive trips to the conference championship game—for virtually any other quarterback, credentials like those would have guaranteed job security. Instead, by trade and draft, the Rams brought in a sequence of white challengers to Harris: Ron Jaworski, Pat Haden, Joe Namath, Vince Ferragamo. Maxine Waters, a Los Angeles politician later to serve in Congress, took the issue of Harris's treatment to the City Council. The *Los Angeles Times* devoted a multipart series to exploring the racial context of the Rams' quarterback controversy. The Rams bluntly settled matters before the 1977 season by trading Harris to the San Diego Chargers, where he then spent five years as a backup to Dan Fouts.

From 1969 until 1977, except for six games that Joe Gilliam Jr. started for the Pittsburgh Steelers in 1974 before being suspiciously demoted, Harris was the only black first-string quarterback in the entire league, the focus of all the hope, all the pressure, all the hate. He made history and he also suffered for history. On a Saturday night before a home game with the Rams, when the team was staying at the Beverly Hilton, security officers told Harris that the hotel had received death threats against him. Guards protected his room that night and the Rams' bench during the game. Less lethally, but just as corrosively, Harris spent his whole career with the knowledge that one mistake could cost him his starting job. "The thing that I regret to this day," he said in 2012, "is that I personally know I didn't play my best football in the NFL. Because of that thing I was mentally dealing with."

What he clung to during the lonely and difficult years were Eddie Robinson's words to him in the Grambling bleachers. He also had a scrapbook from his high school and college years in which his mother had written her own enduring admonition: "Study hard, play hard, stay humble & God will carry you through. Don't forget to pray that God will crown your head with wisdom and understanding." Those pillars of support help explain why Harris survived in the same crucible that drove other black quarterbacks of his generation—Briscoe, Dickey, Gilliam— into bitterness, despondence, and drug addiction.

After retiring from the field in 1981, Harris became one of the earliest and most successful black front-office executives in the NFL, helping to assemble a Super Bowl championship team for the Baltimore Ravens in 2000 and a Super Bowl contender with the Jacksonville Jaguars in 2007. Most recently, as a senior personnel executive with the Detroit Lions, he has been an essential part in transforming a franchise that had been a winless doormat in 2008 into a playoff team three years later.

By his example, Harris opened the door for every black quarterback to follow, from Warren Moon to Donovan McNabb to Steve McNair to Cam Newton and Robert Griffin III. The most significant of Harris's football progeny, Doug Williams, had grown up in Louisiana admiring Harris and gone to Grambling because of it. Williams finished fourth in the 1977 Heisman Trophy balloting, the best result ever by an HBCU player, and was selected in the first round of the NFL draft by the Tampa Bay Buccaneers. In 1988, playing for the Washington Redskins, Williams became the first black quarterback to start and to win a Super Bowl game.

"I just pull for them," Harris said of black quarterbacks. "Because of my experience, I automatically become a fan. People say to me sometimes, 'It wasn't possible without you.' And I'm appreciative of that. But I don't talk about it. During the season, I'm always involved in what I'm doing. And most of the players now—I'm in football, I scout them—don't even know of my contribution."

+ + +

Ken Riley gave up the opportunity for a Rhodes scholarship to enter the NFL draft in 1969. He was chosen by the Cincinnati Bengals in the sixth round and shifted to the position of defensive back by the team's renowned coach, Paul Brown. The decision, in this instance, turned out to be prescient. During fifteen seasons as a cornerback, Riley snared sixty-five interceptions and was named All-Pro four times. He helped the Bengals record nine winning seasons, make the playoffs five times, and reach the 1982 Super Bowl. (Cincinnati lost to the San Francisco 49ers.) After the 1976 season, Riley and James Harris renewed acquaintance as two honorees of the NFL Players Association, Riley for leading the AFC in interceptions and Harris for leading the NFC in passing efficiency. Even now, long past his retirement in 1983, Riley ranks fifth in NFL history in interceptions.

After leaving the playing field, Riley coached defensive backs for the Green Bay Packers for two years. Then, in 1986, Jake Gaither asked Riley to return to Florida A&M as head football coach. In eight seasons with the Rattlers, he won two conference titles and posted a 48-39-2 record. Riley subsequently became FAMU's athletic director, serving from 1994 to 2003. In retirement from A&M, Riley moved back to his hometown of Bartow, Florida, where he works as a school administrator. He says that his proudest achievement is that every member of his family—himself, his wife, Barbara, their three children—has earned a master's degree.

In a startling oversight, Riley has not been voted into the Pro Football Hall of Fame, even though he compiled more interceptions than many of the defensive backs who have been inducted. "For all intents and purposes," as the football website Bleacher Report stated, "Riley was and remains one of the most underrated defensive players in the history of the NFL." The site ranked Riley high on its list of the "50 Most Glaring Pro Football Hall of Fame Omissions."

While Riley played in a relatively small media market, that fact alone can hardly explain the NFL's failure to honor him. The inescapable conclusion is that, even in his pro football home, Riley has suffered for his principled refusal during his career to be extravagant in word or gesture. He never talked trash or indulged in end-zone dances or awarded himself a memorable nickname. Precisely those gambits created far greater recognition (and endorsement deals) for such Bengal players over the years as running back Ickey Woods, whose "Ickey Shuffle" remains a YouTube sensation, and receiver Chad "Ochocinco" Johnson. "I've always been a modest low-key type of guy," Riley put it. "I've always thought your work would speak for you."

At this point, his only hope for that work to be deservedly recognized would be for Riley to be inducted under the Hall of Fame's category for "senior selections," those players whose careers have been over for at least twenty-five years. Riley, as yet unrecognized, retired thirty years ago.

+ + +

On a September night in 1968, Eddie Robinson led his Grambling Tigers onto the field of Yankee Stadium in New York to face Morgan State.

Virtually every seat in the house was filled, sixty-four thousand strong. This was a singular event, not only as Grambling's first trip ever north of the Mason-Dixon Line, but also as a benefit game named for the civil rights leader Whitney Young and raising money for college scholarships. Even though Grambling uncharacteristically lost by 9–7, the inaugural Whitney Young Classic set into motion two elements of Robinson's lasting impact.

Thanks to Robinson's coaching skill and Collie Nicholson's marketing wizardry, Grambling grew into a national, even international, attraction in subsequent years, playing games as far afield as Los Angeles, Hawaii, and Japan. A weekly television show of Grambling football highlights, modeled on Notre Dame's Sunday-morning show, was broadcast throughout the United States. Robinson even appeared in an Oldsmobile commercial and on a collectors'-edition bottle of Coca-Cola.

More broadly for black college football, the success of the Yankee Stadium game inspired a number of annual classics played in major cities with stadiums to match. The Bayou Classic, pitting Grambling against Southern University, often drew seventy thousand spectators at the Superdome in New Orleans. Atlanta, Chicago, Dallas, Indianapolis, and Orlando, among other metropolises, played host to annual games featuring such top black college teams as Florida A&M and Tennessee State. These classics also served as celebrations of African-American college culture—marching bands, step shows, Greek-letter societies.

As part of his commitment to racial equality, Robinson began recruiting white players to Grambling, starting with quarterback Jim Gregory in 1968. Gregory's experience there became the basis for a 1981 television movie, *Grambling's White Tiger*.

Robinson went on to coach at Grambling for a total of fifty-five years, sending more than two hundred players into the pros. He became the winningest coach in college football history in 1985, when he surpassed Bear Bryant of Alabama in recording his 324th victory. Robinson broke the 400-win mark in 1995 as Grambling defeated Mississippi Valley State, and received a congratulatory phone call from President Clinton. The Grambling coach retired in 1997 with a career record of 408 wins, 165 losses, and 15 ties. What cannot be tabulated is the number of substantial, productive citizens whom Robinson developed in his years at Grambling—from ministers to insurance agents to real estate brokers—by emphasizing scholarship, religious commitment, and personal integrity as relentlessly as he emphasized the correct way to run the 126 Counter.

Robinson was inducted into the College Football Hall of Fame in 1997. The Eddie Robinson Award, established by the Football Writers Association of America, honors the year's top coach in major-college football. Grambling's stadium has been named for Robinson, and a museum about his life and Grambling football opened in 2010 on the college campus. After Robinson died on April 3, 2007, at age eighty-eight, his funeral drew thousands of mourners to Grambling's gymnasium, was carried live over Louisiana television stations, and was covered by major national newspapers. Among those who offered eulogies was the civil rights activist and presidential candidate Rev. Jesse Jackson, who had played quarterback during his college days at North Carolina A&T.

"What's unique about football, and it's the American story," Jackson said, "is that whenever the playing field is even, and the rules are public, and the goals are clear, we can make it. That's what football says."

Eddie Robinson had always seen Grambling as a complete and fulfilling place, and he did not require the approval of the white world to validate it or him. He did, however, expect to be judged on his record. And in spite of all that Robinson accomplished, he was never offered a head coaching position by any major college or professional team. A fervent and eloquent patriot, Robinson once pointed out that the first time in his life when he was introduced as an American, rather than as a black, was during Grambling's trip to Japan in 1976, not in his own nation.

+ + +

Jake Gaither retired as football coach at Florida A&M after defeating Grambling 23–19 in the 1969 Orange Blossom Classic, though he remained athletic director until 1973. He finished his coaching career with a record of 203 wins, 36 losses, and 4 ties for an .844 winning percentage. To this day, he ranks ninth in winning percentage in college football history. Forty-two of his players went on to the AFL or NFL. Some of Gaither's greatest accomplishments, though, were felt off the field. In a survey of ninety-six former Rattler players by John Eason as part of his doctoral dissertation, eighty-six graduated from college. Of those, sixty earned advanced degrees.

Only in retirement, however, did Gaither receive the national accolades that had been denied him for so long—the Amos Alonzo Stagg Award from the American Football Coaches Association and the Walter Camp Football Foundation Man of the Year Award. He was inducted into the College Football Hall of Fame in 1975. Three years later, the Alonzo S. "Jake" Gaither Award was established to honor the best football player each year from the historically black colleges and universities, a kind of HBCU equivalent to the Heisman Trophy.

In the decades since, Gaither's role as an innovator has been largely forgotten. His strategy of recruiting players for speed and of using speed at every possible position is now the norm of major college teams, particularly in the dominant Southeastern Conference, and in the NFL. The system of splitting offensive linemen widely apart to put stress on a defense—popularized in the past decade by Coach Mike Leach of Texas Tech, who was erroneously credited with being the first to devise the formation—owes a large, unacknowledged debt of gratitude to Gaither.

With Gaither's career as both coach and administrator concluded, and with no children to survive him, he did take steps to secure his reputation. He left his collected papers, including the texts of his eloquent speeches about black history, some showing his handwritten editing marks, to the Black Archives at Florida A&M. As part of an oral history program undertaken in 1976 by the white women of the Junior League of Tallahassee—a most unlikely interlocutor for an African-American football coach—Gaither spoke more candidly than ever before about his experiences with racism, going all the way back to the coaching clinic at Duke that he had been barred from attending, even as a janitor.

Gaither died on February 18, 1994, at age ninety-one. His widow, Sadie Robinson Gaither, died in 1997, when she was ninety-two. Their home in Tallahassee, as of this author's last visit there several years ago, still contains a bounty of photographs and memorabilia, begging for a museum exhibition. A statue of Jake Gaither and his coaching staff stands outside the gymnasium that bears his name on the Florida A&M campus.

+ + +

Shortly after the 1967 football season ended, many of the politically engaged members of the South Carolina State team joined in protests against a segregated bowling alley near the campus in Orangeburg. On the night of February 8, 1968, an all-white force of state troopers opened fire on the student demonstrators, killing three and wounding twenty-eight. Among the dead was one football player, Samuel Hammond. Several other players were injured by gunfire, one of them temporarily paralyzed. The episode soon became known as "the Orangeburg Massacre," and it grimly anticipated the lethal attacks by troops on student protesters at Kent State and Jackson State Universities in 1970.

In the aftermath of the Orangeburg Massacre, Willis Ham, a starter on the South Carolina State football team, joined three classmates in running forty-two miles from the college campus to the State House in Columbia to draw attention to the injustice. Their effort went for naught. The state troopers who fired on the demonstrators were acquitted of all charges. Cleveland Sellers, the SNCC activist who had organized the student protests in Orangeburg, was the only person ever arrested in relation to the violence there, and served seven months in prison on charges of rioting. He is now the president of Voorhees College in South Carolina.

"[T]here was no play as vicious as that play," a former player who was shot and wounded in the Orangeburg Massacre, Harold Riley, recalled years later. "To see people crying and dying, you know, that kind of stuff. You don't die on the football field. You miss a play, you get up and you run another one. This play here was a play you never forget."

+ + +

On January 21, 2001, the US Senate confirmed Rod Paige as secretary of education. During his term in office, he was entrusted with applying and enforcing the landmark No Child Left Behind law on racial inequality in public education. Along with Colin Powell and Condoleezza Rice, Paige was one of three African Americans to serve in the cabinet of President George W. Bush.

As it happens, Paige is also a former football coach at two black colleges, Jackson State and Texas Southern. (His 1967 team at Jackson State handed Grambling its only loss.) The fact that he was deemed worthy of a cabinet position raises the pungent question of whether he would have been considered similarly qualified to be head coach for a major college or pro team.

The NFL, which has made diversity a priority, has had as many as eight black head coaches for its thirty-two teams in some recent seasons— including Mike Tomlin of the Pittsburgh Steelers, who won the 2009 Super Bowl. As of the 2012 season, there also are six African-American general managers in the NFL, among them Jerry Reese of the New York Giants, who assembled the teams that won the 2008 and 2012 Super Bowls, and Ozzie Newsome of the 2013 champs, the Baltimore Ravens.

Yet college football, in an era when a black coach can be a cabinet secretary and black coaches or general managers have been part of seven consecutive Super Bowl games, severely lags. As of 2012, there are only 15 African-American head coaches among the 120 major-college football teams, even as nearly half of the players are black. The outstanding black football players of the South—the kind who made Grambling, Florida A&M, Tennessee State, Southern, and South Carolina State powerhouses in the Jim Crow era—now star for white coaches on such formerly segregated teams as Alabama, LSU, Florida, Florida State, Texas, and Georgia. This form of expedient integration has proven a profoundly mixed blessing, as black athletes are too often exploited for their football talent and allowed to falter in the classroom. A study of the seventy major-college teams competing in bowl games after the 2012 season found that at more than half of those schools, black players had a graduation rate at least twenty points below that of white players.

In spite of all the advances since the 1967 season, then, the struggle that Jake Gaither and Eddie Robinson undertook for racial equality in sports, and through sports in American society at large, remains unfinished. Their luminous legacy is yet to be completely fulfilled.

Acknowledgments ▶

By the time I began work on this book in July 2006, Jake Gaither was dead and Eddie Robinson was in the late stages of Alzheimer's disease. Without them, I depended enormously on five individuals who took the risk of trusting me—a northern white who had never been a sports journalist—with the sacred task of writing about football and civil rights in the black colleges of the South.

So, first and foremost, I offer my immeasurable gratitude to James Harris and Ken Riley, two men of intellect, sensitivity, and dignity; to Doris Robinson and Eddie Robinson Jr., the keeper of Coach Robinson's flame; and to Eddie Jackson, who rose from sports information director to vice president at Florida A&M and is an estimable author himself. All of these people not only were generous with their own time, insights, and memories but also helped open doors for me with many other sources.

While my bibliography lists all the persons whom I interviewed, I feel compelled to single out some of them again here. From the Grambling Tigers: Delles Howell, Doug Porter, Melvin Lee, Doug Williams, and Ralph Cheffin. From the Florida A&M Rattlers: John Eason, Bobby Lang, Zeke Sims, and Otis Collier.

Several current and former administrators at Florida A&M provided essential help with the history of sports and civil rights there, and for that assistance I thank James Ammons, Sharon Saunders, Alvin Rollins, Murell Dawson, Vaughn Wilson, and Roosevelt Wilson. Miriam Gan-Spalding of the Florida State Archives was endlessly responsive to my requests for primary-source materials.

On the Grambling side, Wilbert Ellis, Raynauld Higgins, Roger Tilley, and Sailor Jackson gave me access to vital materials in the Louisiana State Archives and the Eddie G. Robinson Museum. Ron Pennington, a former Grambling player, personally salvaged many of the 1967 game films when they were about to be discarded and made them available to me.

As someone who is a self-taught historian, I am humbled by the generous assistance shown to me by such professionals as Mildred Gallot and Paul Gelpi. Barbara Rust made my research at the National Archives as efficient and fruitful as possible. Michael Hurd, author of the definitive history of black college football, gave me the benefit of his deep knowledge of the subject.

I am also indebted to those journalists who have thoughtfully covered black athletes and coaches and put them in the context of the civil rights struggle. My work was enriched by theirs: Jerry Izenberg, William Rhoden, Skip Bayless, Mitch Albom, Bill Nunn, and Marion Jackson.

Alex Gecan traversed the Southeast on research assignments from me, and Peter Edelman masterfully pulled material off online databases and library shelves. Tim Spayd and Craig Hettich at Columbia Journalism School made digital copies of game films on many occasions. David

Miller of the Columbia staff rescued some essential primary-source materials I had misplaced.

During the years I worked on this book, I confronted both medical and legal obstacles. For guiding me through them, and as a result helping me stay focused on the work, I am enduringly grateful to Dr. Mindy Weiss, Dr. Patrick Walsh, Wendy Parmet, Elysa Greenblatt, Woody Greenhaus, Linda Zhou, Nicole Fitzgerald, and Rosa Wilson.

For sundry other kindnesses, I thank Natasha Simon of *Sports Illustrated,* Casey Woods, Sonny Rawls, Sandy Padwe, Vin Cannamela of ESPN, Trei Oliver, Lori Mason, Emmett Bashful, Oree Banks, Joe Gilliam Sr., Fran Curci, Kevin Byrne of the Baltimore Ravens, Ashley Till and Breon Phillips at South Carolina State University, Mark Wellman, Joyce Evans, Julian Zelizer, Nick Kotz, Jimmy Nicholson, Jamaal LaFrance of the San Diego Chargers, Jason Wahlers of the Tampa Bay Buccaneers, Cristine Ergunay, Dave Lawrence, Kendall Jones, Yvon Morris and Wallace Dooley at Tennessee State University, James Thweatt and John Howser at Vanderbilt University, Rodney Bush at Texas Southern University, Larry Wahl of the Orange Bowl Committee, and Ken Mack and Lon Samuelson at CBS Sports.

No writer could ask for a better "kitchen cabinet" of fellow authors than I have in Michael Shapiro and Kevin Coyne, who read and critiqued the first draft of this book. Farrell Evans and Michael Jacobs, two other cherished friends in the writing life, brought their editorial talents to assaying the subsequent, almost-final version. Pat Toomay gave me the benefits of his experiences as both an author and a collegiate and professional football player. Jim Lefebvre, a friend since college and a first-rank sports historian, helped me in the revision process of several chapters. As has been the case since 1990, my own writing has been improved by the experience of teaching and editing my students at Columbia Journalism School. As much as they have to live up to my standards, I have to live up to theirs.

With this book, I celebrate a longevity with my agent, Barney Karpfinger, and my editor, Alice Mayhew, that is sadly rare in publishing these days. It is a pleasure and an honor to have been with Barney for twenty-seven years and seven books, and with Alice for twenty years and four books. Their loyalty, their taste, their enthusiasm—all have nourished and sustained me. Jonathan Cox, the newest in a long line of talented protégés of Alice's, gave a superb line edit to the manuscript. I am especially pleased to be in the Simon & Schuster family of authors at a time when Jonathan Karp, a man of talent and vision, has become the publisher. For the time and attention they have put into this book, I thank Jackie Seow, Michael Accordino, Aline Pace, Katie Rizzo, Julia Prosser, Maureen Cole, Rachelle Andujar, Elisa Rivlin, and the entire team at Simon & Schuster.

This book opens with an epigraph from the late August Wilson, who was an inspiration, a mentor, and a friend to me. I wrote about the proudly black world of Grambling and Florida A&M with August always in mind and with a photograph of him hanging above my computer. August, I hope I did you proud.

My children, Aaron and Sarah, shared the challenge and the exhilaration of my work on this book. They fill me with joy and with pride. Plus, they're Giants fans, so what's not to like?

Finally, all my love and gratitude to Christia Chana Blomquist, my soul mate, my *bashert*. (And also, one heck of an editor—a truly intimidating figure with red pen in hand!) It took more than thirty years, but at last we came together. I guess it was the fourth-quarter rally of my life, and I thank God for it every day.

S.G.F., November 16, 2012

1967 Regular-Season Records ▶

Florida A&M

Florida A&M 43	Allen University 0
Florida A&M 25	South Carolina State 0
Florida A&M 45	Alabama A&M 36
Florida A&M 44	Morris Brown 0
Tennessee State 32	Florida A&M 8
Florida A&M 63	North Carolina A&T 6
Florida A&M 36	Southern University 25
Florida A&M 30	Bethune-Cookman 6
Florida A&M 30	Texas Southern 7

Grambling

Grambling 13	Alcorn A&M 7
Grambling 13	Prairie View A&M 10
Grambling 26	Tennessee State 24
Grambling 68	Mississippi Vocational 0
Jackson State 20	Grambling 14
Grambling 20	Texas Southern 14
Grambling 39	Arkansas AM&N 13
Grambling 70	Wiley College 12
Grambling 27	Southern University 20

Starting Lineups
The Orange Blossom Classic
December 2, 1967 ▶

FLORIDA A&M RATTLERS

Offense

SE John Eason
LT Charles Henderson
LG Sharon Stallworth
C Jimmy McCaskill
RG Walter Spicer
RT Horace Lovett
TE Herman Jackson
QB Ken Riley
RB Hubert Ginn
FB Robert Lampkin
FL Eugene Milton

Defense

LE Alvin Logan
LT Richard Ford
RT Rudolph Sims
RE Roger Finnie
LLB Leroy Jackson
MLB Raymond Wilcox
RLB Melvin Rogers
LCB Otis Collier
LS Major Hazelton
RS Eddie Cooper
RCB Nathaniel James

GRAMBLING TIGERS

Offense

SE Charlie Joiner
LT John Lee
LG Henry Davis
C Thomas Ross
RG Walter Hughes
RT Robert Jones
TE Billy Ray Newsome
QB James Harris
RB Willie Armstrong
FB Henry Jones
WB Essex Johnson

Defense

LE Clarence Powell
LT Ernest Sterling
LG Clifford Gasper Jr.
RG Walter Breaux
RT Robert Smith
RE Edward Watson
MLB George Muse
LCB Hilton Crawford
LS Joseph Carter
RS Robert Atkins
RCB Delles Howell

Source: Official program, Orange Blossom Classic

Notes ▶

Prologue: Behind God's Back

Page

3   "*It is the race-conscious*": *Crisis,* January 1934, p. 20.

3   *fashion their own cleats:* Hurd, *Black College Football,* pp. 27–29.

4   "*the chitlin' circuit*": Hurd, *Collie J,* p. 72.

4   "*behind God's back*": The phrase is widely attributed to John Merritt, the coach of
Tennessee State, though the term was part of southern black parlance outside of
sports as well—for instance, in referring to the geographical isolation of the Gullah
people on the South Carolina and Georgia coastal islands.

I: Draw Water Where You Can

Page

8   "*Could I have*": Gaither oral history, Florida State Archives, M77-164, Box 2.

9   "*This is your last warning*": Howard, *Vigilante Justice and National Reaction.*

9   "*As lynchings go*": "An Unfortunate Incident in City's Record," *Tallahassee Daily
Democrat,* July 20, 1937.

10   "*golddusters*"; "*Blacks in Tallahassee*": Howard, *Vigilante Justice,* and Glenda Alice
Rabby, *The Pain and the Promise: The Struggle for Civil Rights in Tallahassee, Florida,*
pp. 2, 3.

10   *Gaither spotting the Carnegie Library:* Gaither oral history.

11   *Lee's dealings with legislators and Governor Cone:* Gaither oral history; author inter-

view with Garth Reeves, April 11, 2009; and Neyland and Riley, *History of FAMU,* p. 172. The governor's quote is sometimes rendered in a sanitized form with the word "Negro."

11 *"never missed a game":* Eason dissertation, p. 26.

12 *"I know that the laws of the state":* Gaither oral history.

12 *"The same instincts":* Leroy Davis, *A Clashing of the Soul.*

13 *Description of Robinson's neighborhood in Baton Rouge:* Hendry, *Old South Baton Rouge,* pp. 13, 23, 44, 56, 75.

14 *City sewer route:* Ibid., pp. 44, 54.

14 *Suspected of stealing watch:* Robinson and Lapchick, *Never Before, Never Again,* pp. 42–43.

14 *Beaten with a belt:* Ibid., p. 17.

14 *"We had come up with segregation":* Ibid., p. 41.

15 *"We were infected with the idea":* Author interview, Rev. Gardner C. Taylor, November 4, 2009.

16 *most lynchings of any county:* Adam Fairclough, *Race & Democracy,* p. 9.

17 *Description of Williams's lynching:* Gelpi, "Strange Fruit," *Louisiana History;* Fairclough, *Race & Democracy,* pp. 29–30.

17 *Favorable treatment of German POWs:* Gelpi, "Piney Hills Stalag," *Louisiana History.*

17 *Student band doing minstrel shows:* Gallot, *A History of Grambling State University,* p. 28.

17 *"College of Common Sense":* Hurd, *Collie J,* pp. 92–93.

18 *Robinson's various duties:* "This coach was the epitome of what's best in America," Jerry Izenberg, *Newark Star-Ledger,* April 5, 2007.

18 *"Maybe we better go back":* "He's Tracking the Bear," Rick Telander, *Sports Illustrated,* September 1, 1983.

19 *"You have to put down your bucket":* Phil Elderkin, "Bucket Parade," *Christian Science Monitor,* November 26, 1971.

19 *"I'm starting a program":* Author interview, Curtis Armand, February 11, 2010.

19 *"just a little old shanty-looking thing":* Ibid.

20 *"Football teaches the lesson":* Eddie Robinson Papers, Louisiana State Archives, Box 106.

20 *"Coach this may sound funny":* Ibid., Box 8.

20 *"Don't bring that nigger bus in here":* Robinson and Lapchick, *Never Before, Never Again,* pp. 124–25.

21 The Negro player insulted by the coach was a UCLA running back named Jackie Robinson, later to become famous in a different sport.

21 *"monkeys":* Letter to the editor by Thomas Hilton, *Monroe Morning World,* May 29,

1955; "Grand Canyon of Socialism," L. D. Napper quoted in *Ruston Daily Leader*, May 31, 1955.

21 *"When you get your opportunities"*: Author interview, Douglas Porter, January 23, 2008.

21 *"This is a great country"*: Lee, *Quotable Eddie Robinson*, p. 100.

21 *"If you've never been a minority"*: Ibid., p. 103.

22 *"Here is what I want you to do"*: Gaither Papers, Florida A&M Black Archives, box 4, file 11.

23 *"I don't mean hungry"*: Wilson, *A-gile, Mo-bile, and Hos-tile*, p. XV: 3.

24 *"[W]e go to make the world safe"*: Publication and date unknown. Photocopy of the original provided to author by Francina King, Gaither's niece.

25 *"I want to talk to you"*: Gaither Papers, Florida A&M Black Archives, box 4, file 18.

25 *"I'll tell you what"*: Wilson, *A-gile, Mo-bile, and Hos-tile*, p. IX: 3. Also recounted in Jackson, *Coaching Against the Wind*.

26 *Recruiting of blacks by only a few southern schools*: Martin, *Benching Jim Crow*, pp. 180–82, 256–58.

26 *"For a black boy"*: Curry, *Jack Gaither*, p. 82.

2: The Laboratory for Manhood

Page

29 *"Dear God of the Rattlers"*: Several variations of Gaither's standard prayer exist. This one draws upon the text in Roosevelt Wilson's biography *A-gile, Mo-bile, and Hos-tile* as well as the author's e-mail exchange with Eddie Jackson, the former sports information director.

30 *"laboratory for manhood"*: "Jake Gaither, 90, Successful and Influential Football Coach," *New York Times*, February 19, 1994.

31 *"You trying to make a fool"*: Author interview, Bobby Lang, July 12, 2006.

34 *"It slides, slithers, swivels"*: Foster, *The Man Behind the Baton*.

34 *The aspirants who couldn't*: The hazing tradition that began in Foster's time led decades later to abuse, scandal, and tragedy. In November 2011, after a game against Bethune-Cookman, drum major Robert Champion died after collapsing in a band bus during a hazing ritual. Ultimately fourteen other band members were charged with crimes related to the incident. Band director Julian White retired under pressure and FAMU president James Ammons resigned.

35 *denying his own imminent departure*: "Marion Jackson Views Sports of the World," *Atlanta Daily World*, March 1, 1967.

36   *"I'll tell you what":* Jackson, *Coaching Against the Wind,* p. 36.

40   *"The Nation's Ghettos Speak!":* Pittsburgh Courier, August 5, 1967.

41   *"the new breed":* "Concessions—and Lies," *Sports Illustrated,* September 8, 1969.

41   *Picketing the Florida Theater:* Rabby, *The Pain and the Promise.*

41   *"There are no Benedict Arnolds in our race":* Jake Gaither Papers, Florida A&M Black Archives, box 4, file 18.

41   *"I can't tell you what to do":* Author interview, Bobby Lang, January 11, 2007.

41   *Black girl pulled out of church by her hair:* Alton White oral history, Florida Civil Rights Oral History Project.

42   *Incident at the diner in Ohio:* Curry, *Jake Gaither,* pp. 167–68.

42   *"We must throw our shoulders back":* Gaither Papers, Florida A&M Black Archives, box 4, file 18.

43   *"The 'middle class' Negro":* Thaddeus T. Stokes, "Victim of His Own Insecurity," *Atlanta Daily World,* August 24, 1967.

44   *"Always in the back of your mind":* Author interview, Eddie Jackson, April 26, 2011.

44   *"There were a lot of different messages":* Author interview, John Eason, December 6, 2010.

3: Spared for Something

Page

51   *Description of auto accident and conversation afterward:* Author interviews: James Harris, October 22, 2008, and March 25, 2011; Delles Howell, September 9, 2011; Leamon Gray, December 21, 2009.

53   *"He's big as a bear"* continuing through *"or I'll blind you":* James Harris, eulogy at Eddie Robinson's funeral, April 11, 2007.

54   *"the black pope":* Dressman, *Eddie Robinson,* p. 172.

55   *"We existed in this environment":* Robert Atkins, e-mail to author, March 2010.

57   *Members of NAACP resign:* Ammons, *From Voter Registration to Political Representation: The "Long Civil Rights Movement" in Ruston, Louisiana, 1940s–1970s,* p. 25.

58   *"The resurgent ghost":* Hurd, *Collie J,* p. 121.

58   *"I got me a plane ticket":* Jerry Izenberg, "A Whistle-Stop School for Big-Time Talent," *True,* September 1967.

58   *NFL had only a single black player:* As of the 1948 and 1949 seasons, there also were two black players in a rival league, the All-America Football Conference.

58   *"You have to make it":* Eddie Robinson, speech at SWAC Hall of Fame induction ceremony, May 27, 1994.

59   *"Gambling College? Grumbling College?":* Dressman, *Eddie Robinson,* p. 179.

59   *"They'll know . . . They will know":* Willie Davis, eulogy at Eddie Robinson funeral, April 11, 2007.

59   *Robinson and Jones exchanging tips:* Author interview, W. A. "Dub" Jones, March 15, 2011.

60   *"You know, you got a lot of dry wood":* Author interview, Jerry Izenberg, December 12, 2011.

61   *Izenberg telling Cosell about Grambling:* Author interview, Jerry Izenberg, September 22, 2011.

61   *Poll tax in the South:* To this day, seven southern states, including Louisiana, have not ratified the amendment.

62   *Cosell and Robinson radio interview:* A full recording of the original broadcast does not survive. This account comes from an interview Robinson gave in 1994 to Tim Price of the *San Antonio Express News*. The undated article is in Box 64 of the Eddie Robinson Papers in the Louisiana State Archives.

64   *Harris family watching King's "I Have a Dream" speech:* Author interviews, Lucille Richards, December 2, 2008, and James Harris, October 22, 2008.

64   *"I had no chance":* Author interview, James Harris, November 27, 2007.

65   *"Get your education":* Author interview, Lucille Richards, December 2, 2008.

66   *Lula Harris finding out about football scholarship:* Author interviews, Lucille Richards, December 2, 2008, and James Harris, November 30, 2010.

68   *"What kind of arm":* Transcript of Harris interview with ESPN Classic, 2008.

70   *"I never met a man":* Author interview, James Harris, November 27, 2007.

70   *"There's none playing now":* Ibid.

71   *"Glum Eddie will embark":* Collie J. Nicholson, "Tigers Eyeing Repeat," *Pittsburgh Courier,* August 26, 1967.

72   *"Looking over your shoulder":* Author interview, Doug Porter, June 4, 2008.

73   *"It's a position":* Author interview, Eddie Robinson Jr., June 3, 2008.

76   *"Interviews 101":* Hurd, *Collie J,* p. 135.

76   *"Don't ever let them see you angry":* Author interview, Ophelia Nicholson, July 19, 2009.

77   *"The civil rights movement was helping to change laws":* Cited in a display at Eddie G. Robinson Museum, Grambling, LA.

78   *Deacons for Defense firearms:* Hill, *The Deacons for Defense,* pp. 116, 146; the description of the derringer hidden in the Bible is on p. 104.

79   *"We watched . . . with fear, hatred, and sorrow":* Atkins, e-mail to author, March 2010.

79   *Nicholson during and after Liuzzo's murder:* Author interview, Ophelia Nicholson, July 19, 2009.

79   *White Citizens Council in Ruston:* Ammons, *From Voter Registration to Political Representation,* pp. 25–26.

79   *dubious allegation of theft:* Steward, *The Desegregation of Louisiana Tech, 1965– 1970,* pp. 12, 44–45.

79   *"Someday we're not gonna":* Author interview, Ophelia Nicholson, July 19, 2009.

80   *"If you waste your time being bitter":* Author interview, Doug Porter, June 4, 2008.

80   *"Coach really waves":* Author interview, James Harris, March 25, 2011.

80   *"Coach thought we had to exist":* Author interview, James Harris, October 14, 2011.

4: Somebody Has Got to Pay

Page

84   *"Florida A&M can be stopped":* "Florida A&M Can Be Stopped," *Orangeburg (SC) Times and Democrat,* September 21, 1966.

84   *"the Bulldogs are kings":* Bill Nunn, "Change of Pace," *Pittsburgh Courier,* October 8, 1966.

85   *"It's like beating your father":* Author interview, Oree Banks, July 13, 2010.

85   *"You don't make excuses":* Author interview, Eddie Jackson, April 26, 2011.

85   *"There's a mighty poor dog":* Author interview, Bobby Lang, June 6, 2011.

86   *"Like being called":* Author interview, John Eason, December 6, 2010.

86   *"Excuse me, gentlemen":* Author interview, Bobby Lang, July 12, 2006.

86   *"so quiet you could hear":* Ibid.

87   *"Somebody's got to pay!":* Wilson, *A-gile, Mo-bile, and Hos-tile,* chapter XV, pp. 19–21.

87   *Fence between Claflin and SC State:* Nelson and Bass, *The Orangeburg Massacre,* p. 6.

88   *"It wasn't easy for me":* Author interview, Oree Banks, October 17, 2011.

89   *Campus activism by The Cause:* "'The Cause': A Summary," *Collegian,* May 1967; Nelson and Bass, *The Orangeburg Massacre,* p. 5.

90   *"consciousness-raising":* Author interview, Cleveland Sellers, October 28, 2011.

90   *"You're making history":* Author interview, Johnny Jones, October 12, 2010.

90   *"There's an expression":* Author interview, Willis Ham, September 15, 2010.

92   *"Vicious" anecdote:* David Daniels in "Great Floridians" film documentary about Gaither. Numerous former teammates, during interviews with the author, spoke about Sims's sexual orientation.

93   *"Florida can be stopped":* "Rattlers Await S.C. State Team," *Orangeburg (SC) Times and Democrat,* September 22, 1967.

95   *Bartow's black schools shut down:* Brown, *None Can Have Richer Memories,* pp. 8, 41.

95   *Crosses planted on school lawn:* Dorina Garrard, *African-American History in Polk County, 1881–1960,* vol. 13, p. 84.

97   *Shooting at integrated beach:* Ibid., vol. 6, p. 10.

100   *Gaither and his quarterbacks in the car:* Author interview, Ken Riley, January 19, 2008.

100   *"Two things don't live long":* Author interview, Elroy Morand, December 1, 2010.

102   *"You supposed to be my coach":* Author interview, Ken Riley, January 19, 2008.

102   *"Let them know what it's like":* Author interview, John Eason, December 6, 2010.

103   *"Oh, Big Red":* Author interview, Johnny Jones, September 15, 2010.

103   *"Don't make it close":* Author interview, Ken Riley, November 1, 2010.

104   *"Coach, I don't know":* Author interview, R. C. Gamble, November 22, 2010.

104   *"They're not that much better":* Author interview, Oree Banks, October 19, 2011.

5: The Best Quarterback Tonight

Page

112   *"A boy who lives on a dirt floor":* "Small Colleges," *Sports Illustrated,* November 2, 1970.

112   *two of Merritt's regulars with OVC logos:* Author interview, Doug Porter, January 22, 2008.

112   *Merritt coming into Grambling locker room:* Author interview, Robert Atkins, April 6, 2010.

113   *"Dickey can definitely make it":* Dave Wolf, "Eldridge Dickey's Special Mission," *Sport,* December 1966.

113   *"If they won't give me a real chance":* "Tennessee A&I's Eldridge Dickey to be 1st Pro Quarterback, Says Houston General Manager," *Philadelphia Tribune,* November 22, 1966.

114   *"This was truly the only time":* Author interview, James Harris, November 27, 2007.

115   *"We've got to get someone":* Author interview, James Harris, October 22, 2008.

117   *Pimp outside Grambling locker room:* Author interview, Delles Howell, November 2, 2011. Several other Grambling players confirmed the incident.

117   *Merritt with his players at Friday practice:* Gary Ronberg, "Finally, Tennessee State Didn't Have a Prayer," *Sports Illustrated,* September 25, 1967; Jay Searcy, "Tennessee State: 17 in a Row on a Shoestring," *New York Times,* November 20, 1973; author interview, Joe Gilliam Sr., December 16, 2008.

118   *"You can't handle Gilliam":* Author interview, Joe Gilliam Sr., December 16, 2008.

119   *"Tell your daddy":* Ibid.

119   *"We will be an offensive defense":* Author interview, Craig Gilliam, October 5, 2009.

120 *Merritt's roll of dollar bills:* Author interview, Jeff Hanna, October 13, 2009.

120 *"Not a belly on this team":* Searcy, "Tennessee State: 17 Years on a Shoestring."

120 *"All you guys":* Author interview, Joe Gilliam Sr., December 6, 2008.

120 *specialized in "clotheslining":* The clothesline was later outlawed in both college and pro football.

121 *Tennessee State's comeback against Southern:* Brad Pye Jr., "In Southern's Homecoming, Dickey Excites the Pros as QB," *Los Angeles Sentinel,* November 4, 1965; author interview, Joe Gilliam Sr., December 6, 2008.

122 *Tennessee State players trying not to get hurt:* Author interviews, Joe Gilliam Sr., December 6, 2008, and Craig Gilliam, October 5, 2009.

123 *Lloyd Wells's nicknames and personality:* Joe Posnanski, "Wells' Substance Found in His Style," *Kansas City Star,* September 15, 2005.

123 *"You got to go out today":* Author interviews, James Harris, July 19, 2010, and November 1, 2011.

130 *The account of Sonia Gilliam's illness and death:* Author interviews, Joe Gilliam Sr., December 6, 2008, and Craig Gilliam, October 5, 2009, and November 14, 2011; "6-Story Plunge at Dormitory Kills Student," *Nashville Tennesseean,* October 6, 1967; "Hold Final Rites for Coed Killed in Six-Story Fall," *Atlanta Daily World,* October 1967.

130 *"Coach Gilliam is the only man":* "A&I Hoping to Win Over Grambling," *Nashville Tennesseean,* October 7, 1967.

130 *"We felt sorry":* Author interview, Claude Humphrey, October 31, 2011.

130 *Description of the game is based upon these sources*: Film shot by Grambling University and maintained in the Louisiana State Archives; commentary on the film by James Harris, Delles Howell, Doug Porter, Robert Atkins, Melvin Lee, Eddie Robinson Jr., Joe Gilliam Sr., and Craig Gilliam; and articles about the game in the *Pittsburgh Courier, Atlanta Daily World,* and *Nashville Tennesseean.*

6: Diplomacy with Downtown

Page 137 *Governor Kirk's visit to FAMU practice:* "Rattlers Await Morris Brown," *Tallahassee Democrat,* October 13, 1967; *Atlanta Daily World,* October 26, 1967, and November 14, 1967; "Florida: I, Claudius," *Time,* December 15, 1967.

139 *Kirk cursing at FAMU player and Gaither's reaction:* Author interview, Bobby Lang, January 11, 2007.

139 *"He'll always let you know":* George Curry, *Jake Gaither,* p. 172.

140 *"We will have segregation":* Colburn, *From Yellow Dog Democrats to Red State Republicans: Florida and Its Politics Since 1940,* p. 43.

140 *"the fact that the Negro does not now"*: Wagy, *LeRoy Collins of Florida: Spokesman of the New South,* p. 80.

140 *"little short of rebellion and anarchy"*: Colburn, *From Yellow Dog Democrats to Red State Republicans,* p. 43.

140 *"battle to protect our state's customs"*: Wagy, *LeRoy Collins of Florida,* p. 69.

140 *desegregated exactly one school district*: Colburn, *Racial Change and Community Crisis: St. Augustine, Florida, 1877–1980,* p. 26.

140 *"maintain segregation by every honorable"*: Colburn and Scher, *Florida's Gubernatorial Politics in the Twentieth Century,* p. 78.

141 *"candidate of the NAACP"*: Bartley, *The Rise of Massive Resistance,* p. 342.

141 *"I won't even admit"*: Colburn and Scher, *Florida's Gubernatorial Politics in the Twentieth Century,* p. 228.

141 *Tuskegee baseball team mistaken for militants*: Eason, dissertation, p. 103.

141 *"I am frankly worried"*: Rabby, *The Pain and the Promise,* p. 39.

142 *"your kind consideration"* continuing through *"sound, practical, and progressive"*: Governors' papers, Florida State Archives, carton 139, file 14; carton 146, files 16, 17.

142 *"Jefferson Davis negotiators"*: Rabby, *The Pain and the Promise,* p. 27.

142 *"You start the day happy"*: Gaither oral history.

143 *"It might be interpreted"*: Ibid.

143 *"When I look around me"*: Curry, *Jake Gaither,* p. 162.

144 *"I favor integration on buses"*: Wally G. Vaughan and Richard W. Wills, eds., *Reflections on Our Pastor Dr. Martin Luther King Jr. at Dexter Avenue Baptist Church, 1954–60,* p. 129.

145 *Board of Regents' powers*: Colburn and Scher, *Florida's Gubernatorial Politics in the Twentieth Century,* pp. 238–57.

146 *FAMU losing faculty members*: Florida Board of Regents, *Minutes,* September 1, 1966.

147 *FAMU received one-quarter of its request for research grants*: Ibid., July 19, 1965.

147 *State meetings held in buildings without facilities for blacks*: Rabby, *The Pain and the Promise,* p. 38.

147 *"I would like to build a university"*: Eason dissertation, p. 21.

147 *"a very smooth lobbyist"*: Author interview, Dr. Louis Murray, October 22, 2009.

147 *"He would ingratiate himself"*: Author interview, Burke Kibler III, October 8, 2009.

148 *Gaither and Dyson*: "Former Regent Dies in Collision," *Palm Beach Times,* February 21, 1972.

149 *"They were being cautious"*: Curry, *Jake Gaither,* p. 158.

149 *"nothing would go wrong"*: Author interviews, Burke Kibler, October 8, 2009, and Louis Murray, October 22, 2009.

149 *Gaither's joke about a bigot in hell:* Curry, *Jake Gaither,* p. 162.

150 *The description of Gaither's illness draws on accounts in*: Curry, *Jake Gaither,* pp. 19, 21–23; Gaither oral history; and Wilson, *A-gile, Mo-bile and Hos-tile,* chapter II, pp. 7–8, and chapter III, pp. 1–14. All direct quotations are from Wilson.

152 *"the Nashville Way":* Houston, "The Nashville Way: A Southern City Confronts Racial Change, 1945–1975," PhD diss., p. 21.

152 *Bias against black customers and loan applicants:* Ibid., p. 19.

152 *Black postal worker made to wait in a closet:* Summerville, *Educating Black Doctors: A History of Meharry Medical College,* p. 122.

152 *"at soul an artist and humanitarian":* John H. Dewitt Jr., quoted in transcript of memorial service, Vanderbilt University, October 7, 1949.

152 *sought the challenge of "massive brain tumors":* Riley and Meacham, "Cobb Pilcher, MD: A Remarkable Neurological Surgeon," *Southern Medical Journal* 84, no. 1 (January 1991): 82–83.

154 *"How can I hate white people":* Author interview, Eddie Jackson, January 9, 2007.

154 *Regents do not keep formal record of decision that FAMU can play against a white team: Minutes,* Florida Board of Regents, October 30, 1967; author interviews, Burke Kibler, October 8, 2009, and Louis Murray, October 22, 2009.

7: That's My Blood

Page

157 *Students coming to President Jones's home:* Ralph Waldo Emerson Jones, deposition in *Zanders* case, p. 50. National Archives, Fort Worth, Texas.

158 *"When we are playing football":* Gallot, *A History of Grambling State University,* p. 83.

159 *Students serenading Jones:* Jones deposition, p. 50.

160 *"We've got to take it to the people":* Author interview, Ophelia Nicholson, July 19, 2009.

161 *"If Collie told me there's cheese":* Author interview, Jimmy Nicholson, February 9, 2011.

162 *"We had cheered them on":* Zanders, *Reflections: 67 Days in '67,* page not numbered in original.

163 *"I never saw Prez as more":* Author interview, Kenneth Armand, March 14, 2011.

163 *Near confrontation between players and protesters:* Zanders, *Reflections,* page not numbered in original.

164 *"What do you think"* continuing through *"too nice, son": 100 Yards to Glory.*

165 *"We had seen the inequality":* Author interview, James Harris, March 25, 2011.

166 *"You had a feeling":* Author interview, Doris Robinson, March 10, 2010.

166 *"Grambling is feeding you":* Author interview, James Harris, March 25, 2011.

166 *Robinson referred to as an Uncle Tom:* Author interview, Doris Robinson, March 10, 2010.

167 *Protesters and Jones on the morning of October 25:* Jones deposition, p. 53; Zanders, *Reflections,* page not numbered in original; author interviews, Willie Zanders, July 30, 2008, and December 22, 2011.

168 *"Is it true":* A copy of the "We Wonder" flyer was introduced into the record of the Zanders case. It is in the case file at the National Archives, Fort Worth, Texas.

168 *Nicholson blaming Black Power advocates:* Conley, *Prez Lives!,* p. 151.

168 *"I suggest you come and get him":* Testimony of Paul King, college security officer, Louisiana State Department of Education hearing, December 5, 1967. National Archives, Fort Worth, Texas.

169 *Izenberg and his crew arrive:* Michael Hurd, *Collie J,* p. 153. Author interview, Jerry Izenberg, December 12, 2011.

169 *"These kids never lived it":* Author interview, Jerry Izenberg, December 12, 2011. Author interview, Jimmy Nicholson, February 9, 2011.

169 *"Those are not your children":* Conley, *Prez Lives!,* p. 155.

170 *"a little out-of-the-way place . . . piney woods":* Ibid., p. 97; author interview, Wilbert Ellis, March 16, 2011.

171 *"The day is done":* "Unite and Liberate," unsigned editorial, *FAMUAN,* November 1967.

171 *"are striving"* contining through *"'field nigger' stakes":* Nathan Hare, "Behind the Black College Student Revolt," *Ebony,* August 1967.

171 *Scores of black students on standardized tests:* Jencks and Riesman, "The American Negro College," *Harvard Educational Review,* Winter 1967, p. 25.

172 *"academic disaster areas":* Ibid., p. 26.

172 *"[I]nstead of trying to promote":* Ibid., p. 21.

172 *"These men are in an impossible":* James Baldwin, "They Can't Turn Back," *Mademoiselle,* August 1960. (Later included in the anthology *The Price of the Ticket.*)

173 *Text of The Mandates:* Original from the private collection of Willie Zanders.

174 *"Students have protested at Grambling before":* Jones deposition, p. 61.

174 *"And don't come back":* Zanders, *Reflections.*

175 *"I ain't got no problem":* Ibid.

175 *"We had pretty much lived":* Author interview, Delles Howell, December 1, 2008.

176 *Encounter between Kenneth Armand and Harold Jones:* Author interview, Kenneth Armand, March 14, 2011.

176 *The freshman and assumed beating by protesters:* Author interview, Delles Howell, December 1, 2008.

177 *Conversation between Jones and McKeithen:* Jones testimony, *Zanders et al. v. Louisiana State Board of Education,* January 2–3, 1968.

178 *"And this thing falls back"* continuing through *"intelligent to play our kind of football": 100 Yards to Glory.*

178 *"On the very first play":* Ibid.

179 *"You got to understand this":* Ibid.

179 *"It isn't sour grapes":* Jerry Izenberg, "Grambling Coach Pursues Greatness," *New York Post,* November 12, 1985.

180 *"Yeah, I wonder": 100 Yards to Glory.*

180 *Zanders's conversation with governor:* Zanders, *Reflections,* p. 72.

180 *Zanders allowing King to retrieve game tickets:* Paul King testimony, Louisiana State Board of Education hearing, December 5, 1967; author interviews, Willie Zanders, July 30, 2008, and December 22, 2011.

181 *Protesters voting with their feet:* Zanders, *Reflections,* p. 77.

183 *"Hell, they're not blocking": 100 Yards to Glory.*

184 *"Playing Grambling . . . was like":* Author interview, Ken Burrough, February 9, 2011.

185 *"We told you before you went"* continuing through *"let's get after them": 100 Yards to Glory.*

186 *"Sometimes people didn't understand":* Author interview, James Harris, March 25, 2011.

187 *"You have satisfied yourself": 100 Yards to Glory.*

189 *"It should be clear":* Louisiana State Department of Education hearing, December 5, 1967, p. 103 of transcript. National Archives, Fort Worth, Texas.

8: Borrowed Time

Page

193 *"We'll need our best": Miami Times,* November 10, 1967.

195 *"Why didn't you jump":* Author interview, Hollis Jones, December 14, 2010.

195 All game descriptions based on game film provided by Black Archives at Florida A&M, screened for and analyzed by Ken Riley, John Eason, Elroy Morand, Bobby Lang, Eddie Jackson, Otis Collier, Hollis Jones, Carlmon Jones, Herman Jackson, and Zeke Sims. Also articles about the game in the *Baton Rouge Advocate, Tallahassee Democrat, Atlanta Daily World, Pittsburgh Courier,* and *Southern University Digest.*

196 *Gaither awakening in pain and being taken to hospital:* Marion Jackson, "FAMU Coach Has Broken Leg," *Atlanta Daily World,* November 17, 1967.

196 *Bob Hayes's visit to Gaither:* Bob Hayes with Robert Pack, *Run, Bullet, Run,* p. 66.

197 *"I plan to get out of here":* "A&M Coach in Hospital with Injury," *Tallahassee Democrat,* November 13, 1967.

197 *"We're an earthly people":* Author interview, George Thompson, September 15, 2009.

197 *Gaither's questions for his assistant coaches:* Author interview, Bobby Lang, March 19, 2008.

198 *Gaither asking for Sadie:* Author interview, Lillian Hagins, September 16, 2009.

198 *Gaither speaking with Griffin:* Author interview, George Thompson, September 15, 2009.

198 *Riley and Morand observations about Gaither's injury:* Author interviews, Ken Riley, February 18, 2010, and Elroy Morand, December 1, 2010.

199 *"My team needs me":* Author interview, Lillian Hagins, September 16, 2009.

199 *"Blacks helped to literally":* Pete Griffin, "Black Physical Fitness," n.d., from personal collection of Charlotte Griffin.

199 *Griffin training Hayes:* Hayes, *Run, Bullet, Run,* pp. 69–70.

201 *"You get it done":* Author interview, Hansel Tookes, November 9, 2006.

202 *"Everybody was concerned":* Author interview, Otis Collier, January 10, 2011.

202 *"You look at going":* Author interview, John Eason, June 24, 2008.

203 *"It was all . . . about":* Author interview, Ken Riley, February 18, 2010.

9: Juneteenth in December

Page

205 *Description of FAMU disrupting Grambling practice and of Robinson's response:* Author interviews, James Harris, Robert Atkins, Delles Howell, Eddie Robinson Jr., Ken Riley, John Eason, Bobby Lang, Otis Collier, and Zeke Sims.

207 *"Coach, I can't eat this":* Author interview, Robert Atkins, April 6, 2010.

209 *"We have one big problem"* continuing through *"with a jackass":* Tommy Fitzgerald, "Grambling, A&M: Battle of PR Men," *Miami News,* December 1, 1967.

210 *"When we played Florida A&M":* Author interview, James Harris, November 27, 2007.

210 *"They are trying to make":* Bill McGrotha, "Injured Gaither to Miss Classic: 'They Tricked Me,'" *Miami Herald,* December 1, 1967.

212 *"Stay at home":* Author interview, Doug Porter, June 4, 2008.

214 *"Grambling College was completely ignored":* "Pros Keep Their Eyes on Grambling," *Miami News,* November 29, 1967.

214 *"The boys they pick":* Tommy Fitzgerald, "Pros Eye Orange Blossom Classic," *Miami News,* December 2, 1967.

214 *"a little frothy":* Ibid.

214 *"If a Negro athlete can come on":* Neil Amdur, "Rattlers Poised for Grambling," *Miami Herald,* December 2, 1967.

215 *History of Coconut Festival:* Dunn, *Black Miami in the Twentieth Century,* pp. 151–52.

216 *Origin of Orange Blossom Classic:* Hurd, *Collie J,* pp. 147–49.

217 *"crowded like the state fair":* Author interview, Castell Bryant, January 12, 2011.

217 *Soul music shows and fashion specials:* Various advertisements, *Miami Times,* December 1, 1967.

217 *"The selection of Grambling":* Leon Armbrister, "Looking the Sports World Over," *Miami Times,* December 1, 1967.

219 Game details from films in Wolfson collection and Louisiana State Archives: film was screened for and analyzed by James Harris, Delles Howell, Doug Porter, Melvin Lee, Eddie Robinson Jr., Ken Riley, John Eason, Elroy Morand, Zeke Sims, Otis Collier, Herman Jackson, Bobby Lang, and Eddie Jackson.

220 *"Duty, honor, country":* Foster, *Band Pageantry,* pp. 123–24.

221 *Band's objections to patriotic halftime show:* Author interview, Adam Richardson, November 20, 2010.

221 *Crimes committed after band parade:* Jon Nordheimer, "Looting Follows Parade," *Miami Herald,* December 2, 1967.

229 *"Your offense must dare":* Eddie Robinson Papers, Louisiana State Archives, Box 89.

233 *"intimidation of the offense":* Ibid., Box 106.

240 *"Guys, you let 'em kill me":* Author interview, Castell Bryant, January 12, 2011.

240 *greatest game in series history:* Some longtime FAMU fans did dissent, saying the greatest Classic was the Rattlers' 41–39 loss to Tennessee State in 1956.

240 *"Times have changed":* John A. Diaz, "News Commentary," *Miami Times,* December 8, 1967.

10: History in the Air

Page

244 *"This is historic":* Author interview, Jim Gardner, March 13, 2012.

245 *Bellamy's experiences as first black player at Miami:* Alexander Wolff, "Breaking Down Barriers: How Two People Helped Change the Face of College Football," http://www.sportsillustrated.cnn.com/2005/writers/alexander_wolff/11/02/wolff.1102/index.html.

245 *"I had those feelings":* Author interview, Fran Curci, December 20, 2011.

246 *Exchange between Curci and Gaither:* Author interview, Fran Curci, October 22, 2009.

247 *Racial disparities in Tampa: Report of the National Advisory Commission on Civil Disorders,* pp. 42–46.

250 *"This game is going to make"* continuing through decal on McQuay's helmet: Bob Smith,"Tampa Preps for Rattlers," *Tampa Tribune,* November 26, 1969.

250 *"He turned me down":* Jackson, *Coaching Against the Wind,* pp. 57–58.

251 *"An invisible asterisk":* Eddie Jackson, "Historic Game Sealed Jake Gaither's Legacy," *Tallahassee Democrat,* November 3, 2001.

251 *Gaither's physical weakness during 1969 season:* Wilson, *A-gile, Mo-bile, and Hos-tile,* chapter XX, p. 2.

252 *"Although neither coach wants":* Fred Girard, "FAMU-Tampa Isn't 'Just Another Game,'" *St. Petersburg Times,* November 28, 1969.

253 Game details from the following sources: Curry, *Jake Gaither,* pp. 108–15; Jackson, *Coaching Against the Wind,* pp. 57–61; Wilson, *A-gile, Mo-bile, and Hos-tile,* chapter XIV, pp. 6–9; Bob Smith, "Rattlers Win Wild Scoring Tampa Duel," *Tampa Tribune,* November 30, 1969.

255 *Reaction on team bus to Gaither's offer of day off:* Curry, *Jake Gaither,* p. 117.

256 *This apparent mob:* Mike Barber, "Game Helped Break Down Racial Barriers," *Tampa Tribune,* November 24, 1994.

256 *"They carried Jake Gaither off":* Fred Girard, *St. Petersburg Times,* November 30, 1969.

256 *"That game has to be":* Jack Hairston, "Gaither Remembers Tampa and Not Just as a Win," *Gainesville Sun,* July 30, 1972.

256 *"We're at the place":* Frank Klein, "Robinson Lauds Classic," *Tampa Tribune,* November 30, 1969.

Epilogue: Their Lives, Their Legacy

Page

258 *"The decision is yours":* Author interview, James Harris, September 12, 2012.

261 *Death threats against Harris:* Rhoden, *Third and a Mile,* p. 123.

261 *"The thing that I regret":* Author interview, James Harris, September 12, 2012.

262 *"I just pull for them":* Ibid.

263 *"For all intents and purposes":* http://bleacherreport.com/articles/932780-50-most -glaring-pro-football-hall-of-fame-omissions/page/23.

264 *Robinson's ranking in career wins:* After Robinson retired, he was surpassed for total wins by Joe Gagliardi of St. John's University in Minnesota, who had 443 at the Division III school, and Joe Paterno of Penn State, who totaled 409. Paterno's win

total was later reduced by 111 as part of the NCAA's penalties against Penn State for the Jerry Sandusky sexual-abuse scandal.

267 *"[T]here was no play as vicious":* Oral history, Harold Riley, Orangeburg Massacre Oral History Project, South Carolina State University.

269 *Graduation rates for black athletes:* "Keeping Score When It Counts," Richard Lapchick, Institute for Diversity and Ethics in Sport, Orlando, FL, 2012.

Bibliography ▶

BOOKS AND SCHOLARLY PAPERS

Ammons, Jaclyn. *"From Voter Registration to Political Representation: The 'Long Civil Rights Movement' in Ruston, Louisiana, 1940s–1970s."* MA thesis, Louisiana Tech University, 2005.

Brown, Canter, Jr. *None Can Have Richer Memories: Polk County, Florida, 1940–2000.* Tampa: University of Tampa Press, 2005.

Capparell, Stephanie. *The Real Pepsi Challenge: The Inspirational Story of Breaking the Color Barrier in American Business.* New York: *Wall Street Journal* Books, 2007.

Colburn, David R. *From Yellow Dog Democrats to Red State Republicans: Florida and Its Politics since 1940.* Gainesville: University Press of Florida, 2007.

———. *Racial Change and Community Crisis: St. Augustine, Florida, 1877–1980.* New York: Columbia University Press, 1985.

Colburn, David R., and Richard K. Scher. *Florida's Gubernatorial Politics in the Twentieth Century.* Tallahassee: University Presses of Florida, 1980.

Commission on Higher Educational Opportunity in the South. *The Negro & Higher Education.* August 1967.

Conley, Frances Swayzer. *Prez Lives!: Remembering Grambling's Ralph Waldo Emerson Jones.* Victoria, BC: Trafford Publishing, 2006.

Curry, George E. *Jake Gaither: America's Most Famous Black Coach.* New York: Dodd, Mead, 1977.

Davis, Leroy. *A Clashing of the Soul: John Hope and the Dilemma of African American Leadership and Black Higher Education in the Early Twentieth Century.* Athens: University of Georgia Press, 1998.

Dressman, Denny. *Eddie Robinson: "He was the Martin Luther King of football."* Denver: ComServ Books, 2010.

Due, Tanarive, and Patricia Stephens Due. *Freedom in the Family: A Mother-Daughter Memoir of the Fight for Civil Rights*. New York: One World/Ballantine, 2003.

Dunn, Marvin. *Black Miami in the Twentieth Century*. Gainesville: University Press of Florida, 1997.

Eason, Arcenouis John. "The Philosophy, Impact, and Contributions of Alonzo Smith 'Jake' Gaither to Black Athletes, Football, and Florida Agricultural and Mechanical University." PhD diss., Florida State University, 1987.

Fairclough, Adam. *Race & Democracy: The Civil Rights Struggle in Louisiana, 1915–1972*. Athens: University of Georgia Press, 1995.

Foster, William P. *Band Pageantry: A Guide for the Marching Band*. Winona, MN: Hal Leonard, 1968. PhD diss., University of Florida, 2006.

———. *The Man Behind the Baton*. Tallahassee: William P. Foster Foundation, 2001.

Gaither, A. S. "Jake." *The Split-Line T Offense*. Englewood Cliffs, NJ: Prentice-Hall, 1963.

Gallot, Mildred B. G. *A History of Grambling State University*. Lanham, MD: University Press of America, 1985.

Gasman, Marybeth. "Salvaging 'Academic Disaster Areas': The Black College Response to Christopher Jencks and David Riesman's 1967 *Harvard Educational Review* Article." *Journal of Higher Education* 77, no. 2 (March/April 2006).

Gelpi, Paul D., Jr. "Piney Hills Stalag: The Internment of Axis Prisoners of War in Camp Ruston, Louisiana." *Louisiana History* L, no. 3 (Summer 2009).

———. "Strange Fruit: Race and Murder in Small Town Louisiana." *Louisiana History* LII, no. 52 (Winter 2011).

Hayes, Bob, with Robert Pack. *Run, Bullet, Run: The Rise, Fall, and Recovery of Bob Hayes*. New York: Harper & Row, 1990.

Hendry, Petra Munro, and Jay D. Edwards. *Old South Baton Rouge: The Roots of Hope*. Lafayette: University of Louisiana at Lafayette Press, 2009.

Hill, Lance. *The Deacons for Defense: Armed Resistance and the Civil Rights Movement*. Chapel Hill: University of North Carolina Press, 2004.

Houston, Benjamin. "The Nashville Way: A Southern City Confronts Racial Change, 1945–1975." PhD diss., University of Florida, 2006.

Howard, Walter T. "Vigilante Justice and National Reaction: The 1937 Tallahassee Double Lynching." *Florida Historical Quarterly* 67:1 (1988).

Hurd, Michael. *Black College Football, 1892–1992. One Hundred Years of History, Education, and Pride*. Virginia Beach, VA: Downing, 1993.

———. *"Collie J": Grambling's Man with the Golden Pen*. Haworth, NJ: St. Johann Press, 2007.

Jackson, Eddie. *Coaching Against the Wind: National Championship Seasons of the Florida A&M University Rattlers*. Tallahassee: self-published, 2009.

Jencks, Christopher, and David Riesman. "The American Negro College." *Harvard Educational Review* (Winter 1967).

Lapchick, Richard. "Keeping Score When It Counts: Assessing the 2012–13 Bowl-bound College Football Teams' Graduation Rates." Institute for Diversity and Ethics in Sport, Central Florida University, Orlando, FL, 2012.

Lee, Aaron S. *Quotable Eddie Robinson.* Nashville: TowleHouse, 2003.

Malone, Jacqui. "The FAMU Marching 100." *Black Perspective in Music* 18, nos. 1–2 (1990).

Martin, Charles H. *Benching Jim Crow: The Rise and Fall of the Color Line in Southern College Sports, 1890–1980.* Urbana: University of Illinois Press, 2010.

Mohl, Raymond A. *South of the South: Jewish Activists and the Civil Rights Movement in Miami, 1945–1960.* Gainesville: University Press of Florida, 2004.

Nelson, Jack, and Jack Bass. *The Orangeburg Massacre.* New York: World, 1970.

Neyland, Leedell, and John W. Riley. *The History of Florida Agricultural and Mechanical University.* Gainesville: University Press of Florida, 1963.

Rabby, Glenda Alice. *The Pain and the Promise: The Struggle for Civil Rights in Tallahassee, Florida.* Athens: University of Georgia Press, 1999.

Rhoden, William C. *Forty Million Dollar Slaves: The Rise, Fall, and Redemption of the Black Athlete.* New York: Crown, 2006.

———. *Third and a Mile: The Trials and Triumphs of the Black Quarterback.* New York: ESPN Books, 2007.

Riley, Harris D., Jr., MD, and William F. Meacham, MD. "Cobb Pilcher, MD: A Remarkable Neurological Surgeon." *Southern Medical Journal* 84, no. 1 (January 1991).

Robinson, Eddie, with Richard Lapchick. *Never Before, Never Again: The Stirring Autobiography of Eddie Robinson, the Winningest Coach in the History of College Football.* New York: St. Martin's Press, 1999.

Smith, Charles U., ed. *The Civil Rights Movement in Florida and the United States: Historical and Contemporary Perspectives.* Tallahassee: Father and Son, 1989.

Steward, Jenna Elayne. "The Desegregation of Louisiana Tech, 1965–1970." MA thesis, Louisiana Tech University, 2010.

Summerville, James. *Educating Black Doctors: A History of Meharry Medical College.* Tuscaloosa: University Press of Alabama, 1983.

US National Advisory Commission on Civil Disorders. *Report of the National Advisory Commission on Civil Disorders.* Washington, DC: US Government Printing Office, 1968.

Vaughan, Wally G., and Richard W. Wills, eds. *Reflections on Our Pastor Dr. Martin Luther King Jr. at Dexter Avenue Baptist Church, 1954–60.* Dover, MA: Majority Press, 1999.

Wagy, Tom. *LeRoy Collins of Florida: Spokesman of the New South.* Tuscaloosa: University Press of Alabama, 1985.

Wilson, Roosevelt. *A-Gile, Mo-Bile, and Hos-Tile: The Jake Gaither Story.* Tallahassee: self-published, 1976.

Zanders, Willie. "Reflections: 67 Days in '67." Unpublished manuscript, 1986.

MAGAZINE ARTICLES

Baldwin, James. "They Can't Turn Back." *Mademoiselle,* August 1960.

Frazier, George, IV. "100 Yards and 60 Minutes of Black Power." *Esquire,* October 1967.

Izenberg, Jerry. "A Whistle-Stop School with Big-Time Talent." *True,* September 1967.

Ronberg, Gary. "Finally, Tennessee State Didn't Have a Prayer," *Sports Illustrated,* September 25, 1967.

Telander, Rick. "He's Tracking the Bear." *Sports Illustrated,* September 1, 1983.

Underwood, John. "Concessions—and Lies." *Sports Illustrated,* September 8, 1969.

Wolf, Dave. "Eldridge Dickey's Special Mission." *Sport,* December 1966.

Wolff, Alexander. "Breaking Down Barriers: How Two People Helped Change the Face of College Football," http://www.sportsillustrated.cnn.com/2005/writers/alexander _wolff/11/02/wolff.1102/index.html.

ARCHIVAL MATERIALS

Davis, Robert Lee, Jr. Oral History. Orangeburg Massacre Oral History Project, South Carolina State University, Orangeburg, SC.

Eason, John. Collected Papers. Black Archives Research Center and Museum, Florida A&M University, Tallahassee.

Gaither, Jake. Collected Papers. Black Archives Research Center and Museum, Florida A&M University, Tallahassee.

———. Oral History. State Library and Archives of Florida, Tallahassee.

Garrard, Dorina. *African-American History in Polk County, 1881–1960.* Polk County Historical and Genealogical Library, Bartow, FL.

Louisiana State Department of Education, hearing into Grambling student protests, December 5, 1967. Transcript archived at National Archives, Fort Worth, TX.

Riley, Harold. Oral History. Orangeburg Massacre Oral History Project, South Carolina State University, Orangeburg, SC.

Robinson, Eddie. Collected Papers. Louisiana State Archives, Baton Rouge, LA.

White, Alton. Oral History. Florida Civil Rights Oral History Project, University of South Florida, Tampa.

Zanders et al. v. Louisiana State Board of Education. Civil action 13427. US District Court, Western District of Louisiana, Monroe Division, March 8, 1968. Case file archived at National Archives, Fort Worth, TX.

VIDEO AND AUDIO MATERIALS

100 Yards to Glory, originally broadcast on ABC.

Florida A&M vs. Allen, North Carolina A&T, and Southern Universities, original game films, Black Archives, Tallahassee.

Grambling vs. Alcorn State, Jackson State, Tennessee State, and Texas Southern Universities, original game films, private collection of Ron Pennington.

"Great Floridians" film series, documentary of Jake Gaither, Florida Department of State.

Harris, James. Interview transcript, ESPN Classic, 2008.

Orange Blossom Classic, practice sessions and first-half highlights, Lynn and Louis Wolfson II Florida Moving Image Archives, Miami.

Orange Blossom Classic, second-half highlights, Louisiana State Archives, Baton Rouge, LA.

Robinson, Doris, KGRM-FM, Grambling, LA.

SELECTED NEWSPAPERS

Atlanta Daily World

Collegian (South Carolina State University, Orangeburg, SC)

Daily Democrat (Tallahassee)

FAMUAN (Tallahassee)

Florida Star (Jacksonville)

Gramblinite (Grambling, LA)

Jackson (Miss.) Clarion-Ledger

Miami Herald

Miami News

Miami Times

Monroe (LA) Morning World

Monroe (LA) News Star

Nashville Banner

Nashville Tennesseean

Newark (NJ) Star-Ledger

New Orleans Times-Picayune

New York Times

Orangeburg (SC) Times and Democrat

Pittsburgh Courier

Ruston (LA) Daily Leader

St. Petersburg (FL) Times

Shreveport (LA) Times

Southern University Digest (Baton Rouge, LA)

Tampa (FL) Tribune

LIST OF INTERVIEWEES

Anthony, Ralph
Armand, Curtis
Armand, Kenneth
Atkins, Robert
Aubespin, Jacob
Banks, Oree
Bashful, Emmett
Bentley, Robert
Blade, Dorth
Brown, Willie
Bryant, Castell
Burns, Jerry
Burrough, Ken
Cheffin, Ralph
Climer, David
Collier, Otis
Corbett, J. J.
Coto, Jefferson
Curci, Fran
Daniels, Willie
Davis, Willie
Due, Patricia
Eason, John
Ellis, Wilbert
Gallot, Mildred
Gamble, R. C.
Gardner, Jim
Gelpi, Paul

Gilliam, Craig
Gilliam, Joe, Sr.
Gray, Leamon
Griffin, Charlotte
Hagins, Lillian
Ham, Willis
Hanna, Jeff
Harris, James
Harvey, Doc
Howell, Delles
Humphrey, Claude
Jackson, Eddie
Jackson, Herman
James, Nathaniel
Johnson, Essex
Joiner, Charlie
Jones, Dub
Jones, Johnny
Kibler, Burke
King, Francina
Kittles, Costina
Lang, Bobby
Lapchick, Richard
Lee, Melvin
Morand, Elroy
Moss, Mildred
Murray, Louis
Newsom, Jackie

Neyland, Leedell
Nicholson, Jimmy
Nicholson, Ophelia
Niles, Nathaniel
Nunn, Bill
Paige, Rod
Pennington, Ron
Porter, Doug
Reeves, Garth
Richards, Lucille
Richardson, Adam
Riley, Barbara
Riley, Ken
Robinson, Doris
Robinson, Eddie, Jr.
Rosen, Bernie
Sellers, Cleveland
Sims, Zeke
Smith, Charles
Smith, Delores
Taylor, Rev. Dr. Gardner C.
Thompson, George
Tookes, Darryl
Tookes, Hansel
White, Julian
Williams, Doug
Wilson, Roosevelt
Zanders, Willie

Photo Credits ▶

Index ▶

About the Author ▶

amuel G. Freedman is an award-winning author, columnist, and professor. A columnist for the *New York Times* and a professor of journalism at Columbia University, he is the author of six acclaimed books, most recently *Who She Was: My Search for My Mother's Life* (2005) and *Letters to a Young Journalist* (2006). His previous books are *Small Victories: The Real World of a Teacher, Her Students, and Their High School* (1990); *Upon This Rock: The Miracles of a Black Church* (1993); *The Inheritance: How Three Families and America Moved from Roosevelt to Reagan and Beyond* (1996); and *Jew vs. Jew: The Struggle for the Soul of American Jewry* (2000).

    Small Victories was a finalist for the 1990 National Book Award and *The Inheritance* was a finalist for the 1997 Pulitzer Prize. *Upon This Rock* won the 1993 Helen Bernstein Book Award for Excellence in Journalism. *Jew vs. Jew* won the National Jewish Book Award for Non-Fiction in 2001. Four of Freedman's books have been listed among the *New York Times'* Notable Books of the Year.

Freedman was a staff reporter for the *Times* from 1981 through 1987 and currently writes the column On Religion. From 2004 through 2008, he wrote the On Education column, which won first prize in the Education Writers Association's annual competition. He was also a regular columnist on American Jewish issues for the *Jerusalem Post* from 2005 through 2009. He has contributed to numerous other publications and websites, including *USA Today, New York, Rolling Stone, Salon, Tablet, Forward,* and *BeliefNet.*

A tenured professor at the Columbia University Graduate School of Journalism, Freedman was named the nation's outstanding journalism educator in 1997 by the Society of Professional Journalists. In 2012, he received Columbia University's coveted Presidential Award for Outstanding Teaching. Freedman's class in book-writing has developed more than sixty-five authors, editors, and agents.

Freedman holds a bachelor's degree in journalism and history from the University of Wisconsin–Madison, which he received in May 1977.

Freedman lives in Manhattan with his wife, Christia Chana Blomquist, and his children, Aaron and Sarah.